ADVANCE PRAISE FOR

Jesus of Nazareth Among the Nations

This book is about Jesus of Nazareth, his compassion and hope, and the demand he makes on us to follow him. When this collection was first published as a Special Issue of *Theological Studies*, I believe it did some real good. Certainly, that was true for me.

I am delighted that it is being republished by Crossroads Publishing/Herder & Herder as *Jesus of Nazareth Among the Nations: One Gospel, Many Peoples*. My hope is that it continues to do good, spreading the message that, just as Ellacuria said, "With Monsignor Romero, God visited El Salvador," so we might learn to say with greater conviction that, "with Jesus of Nazareth, God visits our entire world!"

Jon Sobrino, S.J.
Universidad Centroamericana, San Salvador, El Salvador

Jesus of Nazareth is one, and the Evangelists narrate how their communities experienced him, not "a dead man whom Paul alleged to be alive" (Acts 25:19), but as one who is with us "always until the end of time" (Matt 28:20).

In this book, contemporary scholars describe encounters with Jesus in their diverse parts of the world. Through its title and content, this book has the potential to stimulate global readers to personally encounter Jesus as he lives among them, and to enjoy life together (John 15:11) in their inclusive faith-based communities: as God's liberating, barriers-transcending and life-promoting gift to humanity (John 3:16; 4:42; 10:10).

Teresa Okure, SHCJ
Port Harcourt, Nigeria

This book invites the reader to dream, in the here and now, the dreams of the Kingdom of God revealed and expressed by the Galilean Jesus. 21st century scholars and disciples from around the world, including the U.S., Asia, Latin America, and Africa, ask, "Where is Galilee, and who is Jesus today?" Readers will enjoy the strikingly different cultural tunes and rhythms of their responses, while recognizing the unifying melody of the life-giving Gospel and a God spell of Hope grounded in the historical reality of the world today.

Sophia Park, snjm
Holy Names University, Oakland, CA

The Easter command of the gospels is clear: go back to Galilee and there you will see the risen Jesus. This marvelous volume illuminates that journey for our times. From marginal spaces and borderlands, with intercultural and interdisciplinary acumen, the essays collected here are a guide for discovering the Galilean Jesus with intellect and rigor. More importantly, however, they are an invitation to take up Jesus' mission as one's own by confronting the suffering in our world today with solidarity and compassion.

Michael E. Lee
Fordham University, The Bronx, New York

Jesus of Nazareth
Among the Nations

JESUS OF NAZARETH AMONG THE NATIONS

One Gospel, Many Peoples

ROBERT LASSALLE-KLEIN

A Herder & Herder Book
The Crossroad Publishing Company
New York

A Herder & Herder Book
The Crossroad Publishing Company
www.crossroadpublishing.com

© 2020 by Robert Lassalle-Klein

Crossroad, Herder & Herder, and the crossed C logo/colophon are registered trademarks of The Crossroad Publishing Company.

All rights reserved. No part of this book may be copied, scanned, reproduced in any way, or stored in a retrieval system, or transmitted, in any form or by any means, electronic, mechanical, photocopying, recording, or otherwise, without the written permission of The Crossroad Publishing Company. For permission please write to rights@crossroadpublishing.com.

In continuation of our 200-year tradition of independent publishing, The Crossroad Publishing Company proudly offers a variety of books with strong, original voices and diverse perspectives. The viewpoints expressed in our books are not necessarily those of The Crossroad Publishing Company, any of its imprints or of its employees, executives, owners. Although the author and publisher have made every effort to ensure that the information in this book was correct at press time, the author and publisher do not assume and hereby disclaim any liability to any party for any loss, damage, or disruption caused by errors or omissions, whether such errors or omissions result from negligence, accident, or any other cause. No claims are made or responsibility assumed for any health or other benefits.

The text of this book is set in 10/14 Meridien

Composition by Carey Nershi for Integrated Books International
Cover design by Teresa Lagrange
Cover image GREAT CATCH © 1993 by John August Swanson

Library of Congress Cataloging-in-Publication Data
available upon request from the Library of Congress.

ISBN 978-0-8245-9700-9 paperback
ISBN 978-0-8245-0292-8 cloth
ISBN 978-0-8245-0293-5 ePub
ISBN 978-0-8245-0294-2 mobi

Books published by The Crossroad Publishing Company may be purchased at special quantity discount rates for classes and institutional use. For information, please e-mail sales@crossroadpublishing.com.

*With love for Lynn, Kate, Rosie, Peter, and Martina,
who has joined our family to hers in
Todos Santos Cuchumatán, Guatemala,
and in gratitude to the Oakland Catholic Worker*

Contents

New Introduction: Jesus of Nazareth Among the Nations:
One Gospel, Many Peoples
xi

Robert Lassalle-Klein, *Guest Editorial/Introduction*
xiii

Virgilio Elizondo, *Jesus the Galilean Jew in Mestizo Theology*
1

Sean Freyne, *The Galilean Jesus and a Contemporary Christology*
23

Daniel G. Groody, C.S.C., *Jesus and the Undocumented Immigrant:
A Spiritual Geography of a Crucified People*
43

Gustavo Gutiérrez, *The Option for the Poor Arises from Faith in Christ*
65

Elizabeth A. Johnson, *Galilee: A Critical Matrix for Marian Studies*
77

Robert Lassalle-Klein, *Jesus of Galilee and the Crucified People:
The Contextual Christology of Jon Sobrino and Ignacio Ellacuría*
101

Michael E. Lee, Galilean Journey *Revisited: Mestizaje,
Anti-Judaism, and the Dynamics of Exclusion*
137

Teresa Okure, S.H.C.J., *Jesus and the Samaritan Woman
(Jn 4:1–42) in Africa*
165

Sophia Park, S.N.J.M., *The Galilean Jesus: Creating a Borderland
at the Foot of the Cross (Jn 19:23–30)*
187

Jon Sobrino, S.J., *Jesus of Galilee from the Salvadoran Context:
Compassion, Hope, and Following the Light of the Cross*
209

New Introduction

Jesus of Nazareth Among the Nations: One Gospel, Many Peoples

During four decades with migrant families at the Oakland Catholic Worker, I have discovered three simple truths. First, God has chosen to save the world through the invitation to love and solidarity with those who suffer, many due to the sins of others. Second, embracing the frustrated hopes and aspirations of others means sharing their pain and allowing it to disrupt our lives. Third, when we choose love and solidarity, God comes to meet us with unexpected gifts of joy, friendship, love, and forgiveness for not doing enough.

This volume is a collection of reflections by leading scholars from around the world on "experiments with the gospel." Each writer recounts how God came to meet a community of faith who accepted the invitation to love, kindness, and solidarity with those who are hungry, thirsty, naked, sick, in prison, or a stranger. We hear one gospel interpreted by many peoples using different languages in dissimilar cultural contexts. Yet all turn to the historical reality of Jesus of Nazareth as the criterion for discipleship. For this reason, I have chosen the title, *Jesus of Nazareth among the Nations: One Gospel, Many Peoples*, to draw attention to the dizzying diversity and unpretentious unity of the Gospel that makes us a truly world church.

Christians, Muslims, and Jews speak reverently of Holy Mystery as a personal reality who comes to meet us in the poor and rejected of our planet. But what happens when we reject God's invitation to mercy and kindness? Does the Holy Mystery turn away? When we leave Lazarus the beggar to his fate (Luke 16:19-31), does this mean that we have rejected God's self-offer (Matthew 25: 31-46)?

There can be no doubt that the innocence of humanity's poor and rejected majorities exposes the guilt of neighbors who snatch away their lives for personal gain. And we love to extol the sometimes-stunning beauty, resilience, and creativity of their struggle to protect and nurture their children. Yet so many of us habitually turn away from the *mysterium tremendum et fascinans* of evil and grace with which their suffering confronts us.

I am so grateful that *Herder and Herder/Crossroads Publishing* has chosen to republish this 2009 special issue of *Theological Studies*, the leading English language theological journal in the world, so that it can reach a larger audience. On behalf of Virgilio Elizondo (presente!) and Gustavo Gutierrez, who inspired many of the authors to participate, may this harvest from global Christianity inspire others to dedicate their lives to love, kindness, and solidarity with the hopes and aspirations of all who struggle for life.

Robert Lassalle-Klein
May 2020

Guest Editorial/Introduction

Robert Lassalle-Klein

Pope Benedict XVI recently invited Christian believers and theologians to interrogate research on the historical Jesus with the question, "What has Jesus really brought . . . if he has not brought world peace, universal prosperity, and a better world?"¹ The "great question" driving Benedict's study *Jesus of Nazareth* (2007) emerges from his confrontation with the charge that Jesus "can hardly be the true Messiah," since the kingdom of God that biblical exegetes tell us he claimed to inaugurate has "not brought world peace" or "conquered the world's misery."² This query places the Gospel accounts of the life, death, and resurrection of Jesus Christ in a hermeneutical circle with the hopes and the tragedies of humankind at the dawn of a new millennium. What does Jesus offer to the half of humanity who struggles for life in the face of grinding poverty?³ to those whose very culture and human dignity are under assault by predatory forms of globalization? to the innocent who yearn for peace amidst endless wars "of choice" like the recent conflagration in Iraq?⁴ and to billions living in the shadow of looming planetary environmental crisis?⁵

In this special issue of *Theological Studies* Catholic theologians from Africa, Asia, Central America, Europe, South America, and the United States respond to the pope's invitation, focusing on the significance for Christian churches and communities of faith around the globe of what we have learned about Jesus of Galilee. This project emerged from events leading up to the 40th anniversary of the option for the poor embraced by the bishops of Latin America at Medellín (1968), and the 30th anniversary of Virgilio Elizondo's groundbreaking dissertation (1978) on the Galilean Jesus in Mexican American Catholicism. Widely considered the heralds or "fathers" of two important post-Vatican II contextual theologies, U.S. Hispanic/Latino/a theology and Latin American liberation theology, Virgilio Elizondo and Gustavo Gutiérrez served as co-editors of this volume, which would not have been possible without their friendship, leadership, guidance, and support. Their latest work has emphasized, respectively, the option for the poor and intercultural theology. Thus, it is appropriate that, while the locations, methods, and substance of the articles are diverse, they articulate and serve the universal faith of the church as it is lived by local Catholic Christian communities with whom the writers live out an active option for the poor and ongoing engagement in intercultural dialogue.

For historical perspective, it is worth noting that Benedict's call echoes that of Pope John XXIII when he convoked Vatican II on December 15, 1961. Speaking in the aftermath of two world wars and two U.S. nuclear attacks against civilian populations, Pope John reminded us that, while "distrustful souls see only darkness burdening the face of the earth," the church must insist that God "has not left the world which he redeemed." Recognizing the urgent need to discern anew what Jesus Christ actually brings to the hopes and aspirations of a suffering planet, John urged the coming council to heed "the recommendation of Jesus" to learn "how to distinguish 'the signs of the times' (Mt 16:4)" in order to better discern how to cooperate with historical developments that "augur well for the fate of the Church and of humanity."[6] John's call was adopted and expanded in *Gaudium et spes,* which sent the bishops home with the mandate "of reading the signs of the times and of interpreting them in light of the Gospel" (GS no. 4) on every continent. The postconciliar contextual theologies represented here are but a small sample of the fruits of this process, a process that places the Gospel witness about Jesus in a hermeneutical circle with the life of local churches around the world. Neither the editors nor *Theological Studies* claims that this collection is representative or complete—and we especially regret that a leading African American theologian had to drop out too close to the publication deadline to be replaced.[7]

The contributions treat a number of interconnecting themes and issues from a variety of locations, perspectives, approaches, and theological subdisciplines. *Gustavo Gutiérrez* articulates an important evolution in his thinking on the priority of the option for the poor as the driving insight of his groundbreaking work in Latin American liberation theology. He describes this commitment as an essential aspect of following Jesus and Christian discipleship, which gives believers "reason to hope" and lends ultimate meaning to human existence. This position reflects Gutiérrez's view of faith as a hermeneutics of hope enacted in the lives of individual believers and communities of faith through the option for the poor. It seems likely that this statement approximates his final position on this important matter.

Virgilio Elizondo reprises and defends his own pioneering work on the Galilean Jesus with the claim that Galilee "must have had salvific meaning for early Jewish Christians, since it clearly plays an important role in the post-Easter memory of his followers and is part of the earliest kerygma" (Acts 10:37–41). This contribution represents an evolution of Elizondo's position in light of recent critiques that his early work on the importance of the "Galilean Jesus" for Mexican American Catholicism may have unintentionally incorporated anti-Semitic aspects of German scholarship on the historical Jesus and early Christianity. His article stresses the Jewish identity of Jesus much more than any of Elizondo's previous writings, while adding a new dimension and potentially reframing aspects of his widely read work on the relevance of the cultural context of Galilee for marginated peoples and culturally contextualized theologies.

Michael Lee acknowledges the validity of these and certain other critiques of Elizondo's *Galilean Journey* while arguing that the book nonetheless legitimately highlights the significance of New Testament portrayals of Jesus as Galilean, and that Elizondo enumerates principles that guard against anti-Jewish, supersessionist readings of the Gospels. Lee asserts that his position on this aspect of Elizondo's work relies on and in some sense parallels the argument that Jesus' prophetic ministry enacts faithful dissent against forces of marginalization and exclusion that impacted first-century Jewish culture. Lee's article can be understood as a critical reframing and repristination of Elizondo's visionary effort to draw a hermeneutical circle between the Galilean identity of Jesus and the faith of culturally marginalized Christians the world over.

Sean Freyne examines three sociocultural aspects of the Galilean career of Jesus, which, he argues, shape the early Christian kerygma about Jesus. First, he asserts (a) that by establishing the Twelve, Jesus assumes the mantle of Elijah (Sir 48:10) and the Davidic messiah (Ps of Sol 17:25), symbolically gathering Israel's dispersed tribes in preparation for final unification and restoration; and (b) that his many journeys in the northern region enact a symbolic "map of restoration. Second, he suggests that Jesus' frequent encounters in Galilee with the (culturally, religiously, politically, etc.) "other" likely influence his injunction to "love your enemy" and to be open to Gentiles as implications of his total trust in the creator God whom he knew as Father. Third, he believes that Jesus' Galilean experience of oppression and marginalization led him to unite his messiahship with openness to Gentiles, and to universalize both in his role as prophet and seer of the wisdom of God. It is fair to suggest that Freyne's work on what I would call the intercultural aspects of the Galilean career of Jesus has been influential in Elizondo's rethinking on the Jewishness of Jesus.

Elizabeth Johnson's article on Mary of Galilee as a critical matrix for Marian studies integrates a commitment to an option for the poor and the empowerment of women with an appreciation for the sociocultural context of Jesus' ministry. Employing current research on the region to provoke the reader's historical imagination about the Mary of Nazareth described in the Gospels, and situating her vis-à-vis the quest for justice today, Johnson notes that in the Gospels Galilee serves as shorthand for the scandal of God's preference for the lowly of the earth. The article summarizes and explores the potential contribution of recent archeological, economic, political, and religious research on Galilee to Marian interpretation, noting consequential theological ramifications.

Jon Sobrino, perhaps the foremost writer on Jesus in Latin America today, focuses on the methodological and hermeneutical presuppositions that have informed his work in El Salvador. Some readers will find his article a valuable summary of material from his two-volume Christology (1991, 1999); others will see it as his most sustained response to recent criticisms by the Congregation for the Doctrine of the Faith of unstated "methodological presuppositions" in his works, including the accusation that "the 'Church of the poor' assumes the fundamental position which properly belongs to the faith of the Church."[8] Without mentioning these criticisms Sobrino insists that his method is to create a hermeneutical circle between the normative faith of the church about Jesus Christ and the contemporary situation of the church in El Salvador. He enumerates three isomorphisms: between the historical realities of Galilee and El Salvador, between the historical Jesus and the Salvadoran martyrs, and between the paschal mystery lived by Jesus and what Ignacio Ellacuría calls the crucified people, understood as the Suffering Servant of Yahweh who brings salvation.

My article (*Robert Lassalle-Klein*) places Sobrino's project in a larger historical context, arguing that Ellacuría's fundamental theology and Sobrino's systematic theology constitute a unique and powerful collaboration, one of the most complete Catholic contextual theologies developed since Vatican II. The article examines how Ellacuría's Christian historical realism shapes and informs what I call (following Rahner) the "saving history" character of Sobrino's two-volume Christology. I argue that the two projects are unified by a pair of claims: the historical reality of Jesus is the real sign of the Word made flesh, and the *analogatum princeps* of the life, death, and resurrection of Jesus of Nazareth is to be found among the "crucified peoples" of today. I also situate Sobrino and Ellacuría as important interpreters of Rahner, Ignatius Loyola, Augustine, Medellín, and key figures from Continental phenomenology.

Daniel Groody uses the metaphor of the crucified people and the spirituality of the desert fathers in a timely and original exploration of the spirituality of undocumented immigrants crossing the dangerous U.S./Mexico border. The article incorporates firsthand interviews on, and original research into, the faith of migrants, exploring connections between the physical geography of their perilous trek and the inner landscape of their spiritual journey. The article examines how these modern-day sojourners turn to Gospel accounts of the life, death, and resurrection of Jesus for the strength to face death and sustain hope for themselves and their families, and suggests what this spirituality offers to the universal church.

Teresa Okure's article develops a new contextualized approach to a familiar Johannine story of intercultural contact between Jesus and an outsider (Jn 4:1–42).[9] Creating her own version of the hermeneutical circle described above, she asks, "What do Jesus of Nazareth in Galilee and the Samaritan woman share in common from their own contexts with those they would likely meet in a . . . visit to Africa?" She argues that John highlights the common experience of rejection, prejudice, and isolation shared by the two main characters, and examines how their encounter brings Jesus, the woman, the Samaritans, and the disciples into a communion fellowship of faith. Noting the complex variety of sociocultural, gender, and religious barriers overcome in John's narrative, Okure examines what this story offers to those concerned about the social and cultural ills affecting African society today.

Finally, *Sophia Park* uses postcolonial theory to explore the crucifixion scene in John 19:23–30. She argues that the Gospel creates a "borderland" at the foot of the cross, where the displaced—Jesus' followers, including women—are offered acceptance as members of a family/community of fragmented and dislocated disciples. Reading from the dual perspective of a native-born Korean and recent immigrant, she argues that John's narrative is constructed to allow dislocated persons to achieve a hybrid identity by joining this community. Her analysis complements and expands Okure's in that she examines the language of exclusivism and inclusivism that runs throughout the Gospel, showing how it supports the drive of John's narrative toward the creation of a borderland community at the foot of the cross.

In formulating his portrait of the life, death, and resurrection of Jesus of Nazareth, Benedict declares, "I trust the Gospels."[10] On behalf of Virgilio Elizondo, Gustavo Gutiérrez, and all the authors, I wish to thank *Theological Studies* for this opportunity to explore the impact of what we have learned since Vatican II about Jesus and his Galilean context on how local churches read the Gospels and theologize about Jesus Christ.

Notes

1. Pope Benedict XVI, *Jesus of Nazareth: From the Baptism in the Jordan to the Transfiguration* (New York: Doubleday, 2007) 44.
2. Pope Benedict XVI, *Jesus of Nazareth* 116.
3. *Human Development Report 2005: International Cooperation at a Crossroads* (New York: United Nations, 2005) 3.
4. Ten weeks before the U.S. invasion of Iraq, Pope John Paul II said it would be "a defeat for humanity," arguing that "the Charter of the United Nations Organization and international law itself remind us, war cannot be decided upon, even when it is a matter of ensuring the common good, except as the very last option and in accordance with very strict conditions" (Address of His Holiness Pope John Paul II to the Diplomatic Corps, [January 13, 2003], http://www.vatican.va/holy_father/john_paul_ii/speeches/2003/january

/documents/hf_jp-ii_spe_20030113_diplomatic-corps_en.html [accessed April 6, 2009]).
5. Intergovernmental Panel on Climate Change, *Climate Change 2007: Synthesis Report* (New York: United Nations, November 17, 2007).
6. Giuseppe Alberigo and Joseph A. Komonchak, eds., *History of Vatican II*, vol. 1, *Announcing and Preparing Vatican Council II: Toward a New Era in Catholicism* (Maryknoll, N.Y.: Orbis, 1995) 168.
7. This also impacted the gender balance of the list.
8. Congregation for the Doctrine of the Faith, Notification on the Works of Father Jon Sobrino, S.J., in *Hope and Solidarity: Sobrino's Challenge to Christian Theology*, ed. Stephen J. Pope (Maryknoll, N.Y.: Orbis, 2008) 255–66, at 256.
9. See her earlier study, *The Johannine Approach to Mission: A Contextual Study of John 4:1–42*, Wissenschaftliche Untersuchungen zum Neuen Testament, series 2, 31 (Tübingen: Mohr, 1988).
10. Pope Benedict XVI, *Jesus of Nazareth* xxi–xxii.

Jesus the Galilean Jew in Mestizo Theology

Virgilio Elizondo

Galilee must have had special salvific signification for the first Christians, as it played an important role in the post-Easter memory of the followers of Jesus and was part of the earliest kerygma (Acts 10:37–1). This article narrates a Mexican-American pastor's journey that led to a theological exploration of Galilee. It examines why this ethnic reference was so important to bring out the beauty and originality of the liberating way of Jesus, beginning with his very particular identity as a Jewish Galilean from Nazareth.

AT SOME POINT in my life, Galilee and the Jewish Galilean identity of Jesus came to be fundamental reference points for my theological and pastoral endeavors. To understand the Galilean insight at the core of my work, it must be linked to my journey as a Mexican American priest seeking to probe deeply into the gospel as good news to the poor, as freedom to those imprisoned by structures of exclusion, and as sight to those deprived of seeing and appreciating their own dignity and self-worth.

My theology is driven by pastoral concerns grounded in a pastoral praxis, which it signifies, nurtures, enriches, illuminates, and motivates. Several starting points in this pastoral circle led me to see the theological importance of Galilee. After 30 years I am still fascinated by the Galilee of Jesus, and continue to investigate and develop its significance as new evidence emerges, and the responses of so many people, especially the poor, excluded, and marginalized, encourage me with new insights. Drawing from the experience of victimization, the poor sometimes have insights into Scripture that even the best of scholars might miss. This pattern, which has come to be known as the hermeneutical or epistemological privilege of the poor and excluded, is proclaimed by Jesus in the earliest collections of his sayings: "I give praise to you, Father, Lord of heaven and earth, for although you have hidden these things from the wise and the learned you have revealed them to the childlike. Yes, Father, such has been your gracious will" (Mt 11:25–26; Lk 10:21–22).[1] In the end, a variety of personal, pastoral, and theological concerns has nurtured my appreciation of the manner in which the incarnation and the life of Jesus of Galilee unveils the true meaning and mission of our lives today.

The Quest for Theological Meaning

Jesús Nazareno is one of the basic icons of my Latino Mestizo spirituality.[2] Since childhood I have related to Jesus as a close friend and fellow sojourner, and have always been fascinated with his humanity. While I never doubted his divinity, I became intrigued with how the divine had become so human. The more I probed into his humanity, the more I appreciated his divinity, for it was precisely through his humanity that followers of Jesus discovered his divinity. I knew he was the Son of God, Second Person of the Trinity, Lord, Savior, and Redeemer, but wondered what that meant for Latinos/as in our daily lives, especially in our struggles for identity and belonging in a society that questions our very humanity.

As a Mexican American priest ordained in the 1960s in San Antonio, Texas, I faced issues of social justice irrupting with great force among my people, especially in relation to questions of racial/ethnic identity and belonging. The Southwest of the United States was the great *"frontera"* between the worlds of Catholic Mestizo Latin America and Protestant White Nordic America, between Mexico and the United States, and the Mexican American people lived in this great "in-between." The same region had been home to great native populations; then it had become New Spain, then Mexico, and is now the United States. Our people were considered too Mexican by mainline U.S. society, and too *"gringo"* by our families and friends in Mexico. We celebrated all our Catholic and civic feasts and had great loyalty to the shrine of Our Lady of Guadalupe in Mexico, yet on our pilgrimages there we were often ridiculed by our Mexican friends and family.

Whether we liked it or not, consciously or unconsciously, through tensions, conflicts, associates in the workplace, and friendships, we felt we were becoming part of mainline U.S. culture without losing our Mexican soul. U.S. priests and vowed religious would tell us our religious practices were too pagan and superstitious, while those from Mexico said we were losing the true Catholicism and becoming too Protestant. The U.S. Catholic Church of the 1950s and early 1960s, balancing remnants of the Counter-Reformation with a desire for acceptance in a predominantly Protestant culture, offered religious expressions that seemed foreign to our sensibilities. True, we shared the same creed and sacraments, but our everyday expressions of what it meant to be a good Catholic were notably different.

The 1960s was a time of great turmoil, optimism, and expectations. The civil rights movement awakened expectations for racial and ethnic equality, while the Second Vatican Council aroused hopes for a more authentic sense of Christian unity, emphasizing not uniformity but unity in diversity. Church leaders proclaimed the rights of peoples to maintain their unique cultures and spiritual traditions as they were brought into the communion of the faithful. Church documents counseled that cultural differences should not be seen as a threat to unity, but rather as an enrichment of Catholicity.

Conciliar constitutions and decrees affirmed that the sacred liturgy should be adorned with music, arts, and customs that reflect "the genius and talents of the various races and peoples," and that churches should incorporate and ennoble "whatever good lies latent in the religious practices and cultures of diverse peoples" around the world. Missioners were reminded that they, like the Apostles "following the footsteps of Christ," were to preach the word of truth that would beget churches, so that "the kingdom of God [would] be proclaimed and established throughout the world." "Thus from the seed which is the word of God, particular autochthonous churches should be sufficiently established and should grow up all over the world, endowed with their own maturity and vital forces."[3]

Vatican II also emphasized that the word of God is the seed that sprouts new life in the land that has received it. We realized that, having been born from the evangelization of Mexico, we were one of those young churches. And we felt that the Decree on the Church's Missionary Activity provided the following mandate for our pastoral work:

> The young churches . . . borrow from the customs and traditions of their people, from their wisdom and their learning, from their arts and

disciplines, all those things which can contribute to the glory of their Creator, or enhance the grace of their Savior, or dispose Christian life the way it should be.

To achieve this goal, it is necessary that in each major socio-cultural area, such theological speculation should be encouraged, in the light of the universal Church's tradition, and may submit to a new scrutiny the words and deeds which God has revealed, and which have been set down in Sacred Scripture and explained by the Fathers and by the magisterium.

Thus it will be more clearly seen in what ways faith may seek for understanding, with due regard for the philosophy and wisdom of these peoples; it will be seen in what ways their customs, views on life, and social order can be reconciled with the manner of living taught by divine revelation. From here the way will be opened to a more profound adaptation in the whole area of Christian life.[4]

Thus, guided and motivated by this and similar ecclesial exhortations, we studied the great *mestizaje* that began with the 15th-century European conquest of the Amerindians along with the fascinating evangelization that accompanied and sometimes clashed with the colonizing enterprise. This encounter gave birth to a new human group and the new church of Latin America.[5] For us today, the decree *Ad gentes* still serves as a guide for understanding the development of such new churches, as it reminds us to stay in communion with the universal church while at the same time developing an ecclesial life in accordance with local culture, music, art, traditions, and religious expressions. For this development to occur, however, it soon became clear that serious theological reflection would be required to help the younger churches grow into maturity and assume their rightful place in the communion of churches.

This type of theological reflection became evident to me while attending the Medellín Conference in 1968.[6] The Church in Latin America was on fire with a zeal for interpreting and applying Vatican II to the Latin American context. The pope, bishops, theologians, priests, religious, and laity came together to probe the meaning and challenges of faith on the Continent. The theological reflection was critical, dynamic, and creative in responding to the question, What does it mean to be church in the context of Latin America—with its long history of conquest, colonization, exploitation, sexism, and racism, and its increasing plague of poverty and misery? Great insights emerged, but by far the most provocative and illuminating were the preferential option for the poor/excluded, and the realization that sin is embedded in unjust social structures of institutionalized violence.[7] Pope John Paul II would later refer to the latter as structural or social sin.[8] Structural sin distorts and perverts the priorities, values, perceptions, understandings, and even conceptualizations of God of those born and raised in social settings under its influence, leading them to do evil, all the while thinking it good and noble. Such distorted thinking has justified collective and individual crimes of conquest, extermination, segregation, and enslavement throughout history, and unfortunately continues to do so today.

While Medellín was fascinating, we Mexican Americans faced not just poverty but also lingering issues of segregation, exclusion, and marginalization. And, as we soon discovered, we were equally distanced from both our U.S. brothers and sisters and our Latin American brothers and sisters by being from the United States. We were and certainly continue to be deeply inspired and edified by our Latin American brethren, but we had to pick up on their spirit and probe the meaning of faith in our own reality within the United States. Our Latin American friends challenged us: "You are living an entirely new situation. You must do the theological and catechetical reflection that the church needs in your region; we cannot do it for you."

Living in the great *"frontera,"* the great border "in-between" the United States and Mexico, some of us, though descendants of the cultural and ecclesial *mestizaje* of Latin America, began to see our reality as a "second *mestizaje*"[9] with contemporary mainline U.S., Anglo-Saxon, Protestant culture. Thus, in the late 1960s a small group of Mexican American priests and religious men and women, inspired by the civil rights movements and the directives of Vatican II, formed a group to examine our cultural and religious identity and belonging. There were few of us, since Mexican Americans had been prevented from entering many seminaries and religious orders, but we were determined to make a difference and to bring positive recognition by the church to the religious treasures of our people. At that time, our religious traditions were regarded by many as backward and even pagan, but today Pope Benedict XVI refers to them as the great spiritual heritage, soul, and treasure of the Latin American people.

We formed associations to pray and reflect together. We experienced tremendous enthusiasm as we began to study the documents of Vatican II, our history, the evangelization that brought us Christian faith, the socioeconomic conditions of our people, and the religious practices that had sustained our faith through the frequent absence of priests or sacraments. But enthusiasm was not enough. We needed academic tools to probe more critically and creatively into the reality of our people, and to formulate a theological understanding of our faith as lived and practiced. Other cultural contexts had produced ground-breaking theologies, and we had much to learn from them, but they only motivated us to seek to understand ourselves from within the theological meaning of our own reality and life. As pastors and religious leaders, we had an obligation to our people and to our Church.[10]

In 1968, I was challenged by friends and colleagues to lead the way and was offered the opportunity to spend a year at the East Asian Pastoral Institute in Manila, where I lived with Indian, Asian, and African students studying forms of evangelization and inculturation. We were blessed with great scholars who, inspired by the way of the Incarnation, explored Christianity not just theologically but also anthropologically, bringing out the human signification of God's salvific process.

At the East Asian Pastoral Institute I learned that culture is not simply folklore, but the common soul and defining spirit of a people, the colored lens through which we see and interpret reality. I realized that authentic evangelization and the development of local churches are impossible without a deep anthropological appreciation of the people's heritage and culture, and without a sound anthropological translation and interpretation of Scripture and church teaching. I was also fascinated to discover the need for critical biblical exegesis as a condition for authentic evangelization.[11] The life of the local church draws new and deeper insights and meaning from scripture, which requires not only exegesis but also cultural hermeneutics to explain what their faith, experience, and cultural life contribute to their (and our) understanding of the meaning of the text.

Several years later while studying in Paris, I would realize that the Fathers of the Church were quite practiced in cultural hermeneutics.[12] Mexican American activists together with the bishops of Texas founded the Mexican American Cultural Center (MACC) in San Antonio in 1972 to promote this type of reflection for our people. MACC was to be a place of research and formation with a small resident international faculty, working in close collaboration with friends and colleagues in

Latin America, Asia, India, and Europe.[13] We had not yet started to make friends in Africa, but later, enriching relationships were to come.

Later, because of my work at MACC, I was invited to do doctoral studies at the Institut Catholique de Paris, where I had the good fortune to study historical theology with Marie Dominique Chenu, O.P., ecclesiology with Yves Congar, O.P., sociology and theology with Jacques Audinet, *nouvelle théologie* with Claude Gefre, O.P., and René Marlé, S.J., and patristic theology and methods for actualizing the word of God with Charles Kannengiesser, S.J. In Paris I learned that all theological reflection, consciously or not, is socially and culturally situated.[14] Our social situation gives us a unique perspective, and when we come together in communion and dialogue, the perspectives of each enriches the entire church. It is not a question of placing one theology against the other, but of bringing them together as various beautiful pieces of one mosaic.

Against this background, I formulated my theological frame of reference: (1) study and present the historical, social, and religious situation of the people as the arena for the work of both sin and grace; (2) read the gospel matrix from our sociocultural situation; (3) read the culture in light of the gospel in order to discern the meaning of the word of God today.[15] This approach would bring out aspects of the gospel we had not anticipated and uncover aspects of the historical-cultural situation we ourselves had missed. The idea was to "submit to a new scrutiny the deeds and words which God has revealed" so that the faith of the people might develop a more complete self-understanding.[16]

The Galilean Insight

In writing my doctoral thesis in Paris (1976–1978), it was not difficult to put together the historical, cultural, and religious sections. I had been gathering material and developing the key concepts with our inter-disciplinary and inter-ethnic team at the Mexican American Cultural Center for several years. The historical context would be the twofold conquest and colonization: first Spain's conquest of today's Latin America, and then the U.S. conquest of the northern region of Mexico. This historical process had produced our *mestizaje* with deep contemporary problems of identity and belonging rooted in marginalization—and sometimes total exclusion—from both parent groups. It was from within this perspective that I began to search the Gospels for the Christian meaning of our quest.

The great theologies I studied and loved were fascinating but still distant, and they offered no theological understanding of the Mestizo reality of our living faith. What did the gospel have to offer our people? Could the gospel help us understand the deeper meaning of our historical process and culture? In what ways did the gospel bring healing and empowerment to Mexican-American people in the context of an Anglo-American culture that marginalized and excluded us? Some scriptural concepts started to emerge as programmatic: the rejected "suffering servant," and the "new heaven and new earth" of Isaiah's universalism; Philippians' total self-emptying of the Son; the kingdom of God wherein all are welcomed; the positive dealings of Jesus with the "impure" and "excluded"; and the declaration that "the stone rejected by the builders has become the cornerstone" (Mt 21:42, Mk 12:10, Lk 20:17, Acts 4:11, 1 Pt 2:7). Since the New Testament asserts that Jesus brings about a new creation, I wondered if the "stone rejected" becoming the cornerstone of the new creation might not be a critical allusion to the builders of unjust and arrogant societies harkening back to the Tower of Babel (Gen 11)—the very ones rejected by them would become the foundation stones of the new!

In praying over Scripture and reading through various theological and biblical journals in light of the fascination of our people with the earthly (carnal) *Jesús Nazareno*, a question emerged, a curiosity at first, as to why the constant mention of Galilee in the Gospel narratives was not, as far as I could see, a contemporary theological point of reference? More than 60 times the Gospels mention "Galilee," "Galileans," and places in Galilee. Luke places the Annunciation (1:26–38) and the beginning of the public ministry of Jesus in Galilee (4:14–21). Mark places "the beginning of the good news of Jesus Christ" there (1:1, 9), along with the majority of his ministry. In three Gospels the risen Lord sends the disciples to Galilee where they will see him (Mt 28:7; Mk 16:7; Jn 21:1) Luke does not send them back to Galilee, but at Pentecost the speakers are identified as Galileans (Acts 2:7).

In Galilee Peter is commissioned to be the leader of the new flock (Jn 21:15–17), and from Galilee the disciples are sent to all nations and to the ends of the earth (Mt 28:16–20). Given the importance of Jerusalem to Jewish restoration thinking at the time, I wondered why Galilee had become such an important point of reference in the Gospels. Galilee seemed of little or no importance in the Hebrew Bible and had apparently negative connotations for some of the people at the time of Jesus (Mt 21:10–11; Jn 1:46, 49; 7:52). It seemed to me that Galilee must have been of special salvific signification to the first Christians, since it plays an important role in the post-Easter memory of the followers of Jesus and becomes part of the earliest kerygma (Acts 10:37–41).[17] The question pressed itself: why is Jesus' ethnic identity as a Jewish Galilean from Nazareth an important dimension of the incarnation, and what does it disclose about the beauty and originality of Jesus' liberating life and message?

In one of the few references found in the Hebrew Bible the Prophet Isaiah (9:1–2) refers to "Galilee of the Gentiles."[18] Isaiah also speaks of universal salvation for all the nations, of a new era of peace and harmony, and even of a new heaven and a new earth. The influence of Isaiah's perspective in the New Testament seemed to suggest a unique and unsuspected role for Galilee in God's salvific plan for the restoration of unity among the human family, a unity and harmony that had been destroyed by sin since the very beginning of creation (Gen 3–11).[19] The relative unimportance of Galilee seemed to fit with the idea that the gospel is absurd to many, that the ways of God appear as foolishness to the wise of this world, and that the redemptive grace of God is an unexpected gift.[20]

As I read the available literature, I began to identify more and more with Galilee as the land of various invasions and multiple ethnic encounters.[21] Occupied by many nations, centuries of rebuilding on previously occupied layers had left its mark on the land and its people. It appeared to have been a frontier region of Israel surrounded by foreign nations, a land of multiple borders! Being surrounded and even partially populated by cities of various ethnicities, cultural encounters, tensions, and exchanges would have taken place in various degrees.[22] Rural Galilean Jews spoke with a regional accent (Lk 22:73) apparently regarded as laughable, and were ridiculed by people in Jerusalem.[23] They may have gone for work or even been conscripted as forced labor in the great building projects of the area, as poor people go wherever work is available.

While the culture, politics, and Judaism of Galilee were closely related to that of Judea, the various implications of what it meant to be

"Galilean" were ambiguous, ranging from simple regional identification to very derogatory connotations. The inhabitants were mostly poor rural peasants exploited by distant landowners and even the Temple officials, some of whom considered them backward, impure, rebellious, and ignorant. Many negative stereotypes about the Galilean Jews abounded, and despite their love and loyalty to Jerusalem and the Temple, they were despised among some elites who lived there.[24] While Jewish by population, Galilee was a land of regular, often tense cultural encounters and exchange of locals with occupying foreigners and/or non-Jewish neighbors, a kind of *"frontera"* where relatively homogeneous Jewish villagers met and interacted with diverse others under difficult circumstances.

Jesus lived and moved along the fringes of Galilee, making his home base in Capernaum, a crossroads between local peasantry and some international trade routes.[25] He also apparently made various visits into the regions of the Decapolis—"These 'crossings over' in the Gospels refer at a literal level to the lake, but reflect also the crossing over of a cultural barrier."[26] All this would have put him into contact with people of other ethnicities and religions. As Sean Freyne has stated, "Jesus' movements in these 'outer' border regions of an essentially Jewish Galilee pointed to his greater sense of freedom with regard to contact with non-Jews than that displayed by some at least of his Galilean co-religionists."[27]

Historical, literary, and archeological investigation continues to produce new evidence and historical insights into the cultural, political, and religious realities of Galilee.[28] These findings are important for New Testament interpretation and certainly for my work. On the other hand, while such studies provide a rich understanding of the stage setting for Jesus' life and ministry, they can never replace the New Testament as the inspired memory of Jesus. As Pope Benedict XVI writes in his *Jesus of Nazareth*, "I trust the Gospels."[29] Various theologians have engaged the aforementioned studies to profound effect, such as Elizabeth Johnson, whose *Truly Our Sister* examines the lives of Galilean women and Mary.[30] Pablo Alonso, S.J., in *The Woman Who Changed Jesus: Crossing Boundaries* examines the effect of foreigners on Jesus.[31] Sean Freyne's article in this issue is a marvelous example of how historical, geographical, and archeological studies yield a deeper understanding of the life of Jesus as it appears in the Gospel narratives.

For me, however, the point of departure has been the question described above: what was the theological significance of Jewish Galilee and its Gentile surroundings for the Gospel writers and early Christians? In view of the emphasis in the Gospels on the identity and mission of Jesus to uplift the downtrodden and to bring the kingdom of God to everyone beginning with Israel, how did the reputation of Galilee shape the writing and reception of the canonical Gospels and their salvific message? The question is not so much about historical or archeological knowledge of the social world of Galilee, as important and helpful as that is, but about the possible symbolic-theological meaning of Galilee for the first Christian communities and their writings about Jesus.

Given that the New Testament is to be read within the totality of Scripture, and since the redemption brought by Jesus Christ was nothing less than a new creation, I have come to the realization that it is important to situate Jesus both within the context of the Jewish heritage of his time and within the larger biblical notion of creation and sin. Jesus goes to the very depths of the tradition to bring out its farthest-reaching implications. Sin divides individuals and nations, transforming them into enemies. It creates, legitimizes, and imposes marginalization, exclusion, and exploitation, robbing people of knowledge about their God-given dignity as human beings. Jesus came to break the many divisive, deep-rooted, and even sacralized barriers that thwart the unity of the human family and consign certain individuals and entire groups to unworthiness and inferiority.[32]

When God became human, healing humanity through his experience as a person who was wounded and hurt in many ways, God did not become a generic human being, a Roman, a Greek, or even an elite Judean Jew. He became a marginal, Galilean Jew, a small village craftsman living with his family and neighbors in a village situated on the periphery of the political, intellectual, and religious powers of the world.[33] From his childhood visits to the Temple to his death on the cross, it is evident that Jesus loved his Jewish religion with its unwavering hope in the God who saves. He dies as a pious Jew reciting the evening prayer of his people, placing hope and confidence in the God who saves (Lk 24:46). It is equally true, however, that he does not seem to have been limited by an overly strict religious interpretation of the *Sabbat*, and the codes of purity/impurity and exclusion that seemed to have been common in his times. God's love is greater than any human tradition that tends to limit or even hide it (Mk 2:27-28).

Jesus became a man at once distant from all power centers of domination and at the crossroads where various peoples encounter one another. Since grace builds upon nature, I wondered if his Galilean experience could have been a cultural preparation for the new humanity inaugurated by Jesus and promoted by the New Testament, one that would not be limited by blood or ethnicity. In the end, I started to see the vision of Jesus as rooted in, yet transcending, his experiences in Galilee; a vision that could serve as a prototype of the *"fronteras"* of the world—whether they be nations or neighborhoods—where diverse peoples encounter one another not to fight, humiliate, or exclude one another, but to form new friendships and families in a space where the "impure" and excluded can find new possibilities and inaugurate new beginnings. Jesus the Galilean Jew who interprets his context in light of God's way thus appears as the doorway—the sheep gate—through which all peoples are invited into the new flock, the new humanity.

In becoming a Galilean Jew, a craftsman in an insignificant village, and son of Mary, Jesus becomes one of the rejects and marginalized of society, along with the millions who suffer exclusion, segregation, and rejection simply because of ethnicity or origin. He suffers in his flesh the multiple effects of the victims of the sin of the world. Yet, in his baptism, he comes out of this oppressive and dehumanizing situation of rejection as the beloved Son of God (Mk 1:11; Mt 3:17; Lk 3:22), leaving behind the dehumanizing scars of rejection, while still knowing the pain. From here he sets out on his mission to proclaim the kingdom of God wherein all who believe in him will be welcomed, especially those excluded and humiliated by society. He takes a most common, beautiful, and emotional symbol of his people, the "kingdom of God," and proposes an earth-shaking new interpretation—everyone will be welcomed, beginning with the very despised and impure of his society (Mt 21:31). The "rejected one" rejects rejection by living and proclaiming a universal welcome and love for all. He invites all to repent of their feelings and attitudes of inferiority or superiority, of impurity or purity, of belonging or rejection, and to recognize that we are all children of God called to share in the common table, the table of the new family that goes beyond blood or social status. It is in this experience of radical acceptance that new life begins.

One of the unquestioned constants in the life of Jesus was his association with the socially despised outsiders and untouchables. Through contact with him, the lowliest of society recover their sense of God-given dignity, and the excluded experience a new sense of belonging. Jesus was not afraid to touch and associate with the impure, and with public sinners, even dining with them. Jesus loved people and was not afraid to share in their joys and sorrows, regardless of what society thought of them. I suspect that in this he scandalized everyone because he refused to be scandalized by anyone. He did not merely proclaim a new understanding of the kingdom, but he lived it out in his practice of joyful table fellowship with everyone. It was this experience of table fellowship, especially with tax collectors and public sinners, that was most meaningful to the followers of Jesus and most offensive and scandalous to his followers.[34]

The response of Jesus to his Galilean context is a key to the salvific understanding of the identity and mission of Jesus. In choosing the rejected of our sinful world, God reveals the lie of the world; and in welcoming everyone into the reign of God, beginning with the rejected, God demolishes the power of this world's segregating structures and reveals the truth of God's creation. Creation is for everyone, and not exclusively for any one person or human group. No wonder the Temple veil rips apart upon Jesus' death! This rejection of rejection is good news to the downtrodden but threatening to those in control of status and belonging, whose laws and traditions often exclude and disgrace others (Lk 11:46, Mt 23:4).

As a man, Jesus was certainly conditioned and prepared for his mission by the historical-cultural and geographical setting of his upbringing, yet in his intimate contact with Abba, the Creator God, he brings insights that transcend his particular historical-cultural location. The divine initiative works through the culturally conditioned humanity of Jesus. He comes out of the restorationist hopes of his Jewish people, but he interprets them in a freeing, loving, creative, and universal way that is quickly demonized by many of the scholars and hierarchs of his religion. His detractors called him a blasphemer and a troublemaker; questioned by his family, he was eventually "handed over" to the Romans who condemned him to crucifixion. Thus Jesus must confront the structures that legitimize the unjust ways of his sinful world that hide and pervert the truth of God. He must go to Jerusalem where the

Jewish aristocratic elite collaborated with the Roman authorities in the domination and exploitation of their own people.[35] He goes to confront, not with violence, military might, or armed revolution, but as the suffering servant who confronts only with the power of truth in the service of love. He came to break the spiral of violence, and even if the cost was the cross, he would triumph through the power of unlimited love. While it is never easy, Jesus shows us that we must confront the sin structured so deeply within our own ways of life that we often take it as natural, sometimes even sacred, truth!

When we see through the seeming tragedy of Golgotha and discover that sin, both structural and personal, was the real cause of this drama, we realize that blaming the Jewish people or even their first century elites can lead us to ignore the role of our own sinfulness today, which crucify not one, but many people.[36] Only when we can see that it was the twisted logic of power and unjust social structures that demanded the crucifixion of Jesus (Jn 11:50; Mk 14:1b; Lk 26:4; 22:2) will we begin to unveil the same absurdities that continue to demand the crucifixions of prophets and the innocent victims of every type. Blaming the Jewish people or even their leaders is an easy way to mask our own unjust social arrangements (our idols) and to ignore their consequences.[37]

Misuse of Scripture is not uncommon. Many in Europe marginalized and persecuted our Jewish brothers and sisters out of a warped reading of the gospel. Many in the Americas used Scripture to justify the enslavement of Africans, the exploitation of the Amerindians through the *encomienda* system as an aspect of evangelization, and the elimination of the natives as God's will. Some in the United States today justify persecuting and imprisoning poor, defenseless, undocumented immigrants through a superficial reading of Romans 13 on obedience to civil authority. This perversion of the gospel must be denounced. Jesus is the prophet who remains faithful to the poor and confronts injustice with the power of love in the service of truth He witnesses to the truth that love unites all in a new humanity; knowing it would cost him his life, he did not remain silent.[38]

In rejecting Jesus, those invested in the sinful structures he sought to change decided he must be eliminated; they even stirred up the people to demand his crucifixion. The one who rejects rejection is violently rejected by the leaders and people of a disordered world. With his death on the cross, it remains to be seen whose way is true. Yet in raising him from the dead, God identifies the way of Jesus as his own; confirming his announcement of God's kingdom of love, reconciliation, and compassion will always be a challenge to the unjust persons and structures of the world. The power of God's loving truth will triumph over the powers of death and the forces of evil, no matter how righteous and sacred they might appear to be.

Luke-Acts tells us that on the morning of Pentecost, the Apostles received the Holy Spirit and were empowered to proclaim this new way of love to all humanity. The nations that were scattered and became enemies at Babel, now begin to be reunited as one people. The great miracle of Pentecost is not only that each one hears in his or her own tongue, but that it is the new Galileans, the very ones whose speech was difficult to understand and often ridiculed, that are now understood by all. Those who had nothing to offer—"Can anything good come from Nazareth " (Jn 1:46); "no prophet arises in Galilee" (Jn 7:52)—now have the best thing to offer, and thus begins the Christian movement.

All these considerations led me to formulate what I have called the "Galilean principle": out of the rejects and ridiculed of society a new society of universal welcome and love is possible. From the margins Jesus does not initiate a new center, but rather a new movement of the Spirit that enables people to cross segregating boundaries and form a new human family based on love of God and love of neighbor. Thus, in going to Jerusalem, Jesus not only confronts unjust structures that sacralize exclusion and legitimize exploitation, but through his loving passion and sacrifice on the cross, he crosses the ultimate boundary of death into new life, beckoning us to follow in his saving footsteps. After his resurrection, he sends his followers back to Galilee, where they would see him and continue to expand his border-crossing movement. Galilee would never become the center, but it was the point of departure for the beginning of a new creation, as the Galilees today continue to be points of departure for new humanities to emerge.

Jesus reflects the restorationist aspirations of first-century Judaism common to Judea and Galilee, but his religious imagination, illuminated by prayer, creates new alternatives that surpass anyone's expectations. From the peripheries of power and closed belonging, which tend to become "idols" confusing their own ways with God's, God raises followers of Jesus in each generation to be visionaries and prophets of new humanities shaped by his vision. The early Christian movement is a powerful witness to this ongoing border-crossing that enables diverse people to continue being who they are, but in a radically new way that defies the power of any border to prevent the love of God and neighbor. Enemies could become friends, foreigners could now become neighbors, and strangers could become family.

These insights into the life of Jesus in Galilee enabled me to see our situation of border-crossings and *mestizaje* in South Texas not as deficient but as pregnant with multiple possibilities for a broader, more generous future for humanity. Looking through the eyes of Jesus as I knew him, I came to see our protests and social movements as our way of following him into Jerusalem. I began to see our fiestas, especially the massive celebrations of Our Lady of Guadalupe, as expressions of his resurrection, celebrations of the new life begun in us, not yet complete.

A Galilean Interpretation for Today

Galilee led me to reflect on traditional theological themes in a way that unveiled unexpected theological dimensions of Mestizo identity. Through numerous Bible-reading community groups[39] throughout the Southwest and many other parts of the United States, we started to see our situation through the eyes of Jesus the Galilean Jew who reveals the truth of life. We started to see our rejection and marginalization as Mestizos as an element of our election by God to start something new.[40] God chooses and calls individuals and groups. What was our call? We started to see our ambiguous "in-between" identity as the basis for a new, more universal identity, a new source of belonging, and a call to service. We started to investigate parallels between our Mestizo experience of living in the "in-between," and crossing borders on a daily basis, with the constant border-crossings of Jesus in Galilee. This has given us useful insights, addressing the rich potential of the multiple and massive border crossings that characterize the emerging global village. While we cannot live without borders of various kinds, they do not have to be divisive and destructive. Mestizo peoples inhabit the "in-between" of nations and cultures, playing a painful but creative mediating role in processes of intercultural encounter that foster a gradual movement from closed particularities to a more open universality. As in Galilee, in our Mexican-American fiestas, the joy of inclusive table fellowship serves as a living sign of the universal reign of God begun by Jesus, full of promise, though not yet complete.

I believe that we have been called to work, as Jesus did, so that others will not have to suffer the pains of exclusion, marginalization, and segregation that we have suffered. The simplicity of our devotions and the festive spirit of our religious traditions, when considered in light of the prayer life of Jesus and his participation in festive rituals, are revealed not as underdeveloped, superstitious, or pagan vestiges of earlier practices, but as beautiful expressions of a Mestizo people living joyfully in communion with God. Beyond any human suffering, there is the joy of living in communion with God and with one another.

The journey of Jesus to Jerusalem and the cross is likewise a call to be involved in the issues and movements of social justice. This is what I have called the Jerusalem principle. It is not sufficient merely to do good and avoid evil, rather we must do good and struggle against evil. The journey embodies the gradual but necessary tearing down of deeply rooted traditions of segregation, exclusion, and degradation, as symbolized by the tearing asunder of the Temple veil. The path is never easy—there is no escape from the violence of the cross—and human experience is full of violence and injustice. But Jesus shows us that we should not allow these negative experiences to deter us from the work of building the reign of God. We must pass through violence in order to follow Jesus in cooperating with God's efforts to bring forth new forms of life.

Movements like the United Farm Workers of César Chávez and Dolores Huerta; the Southwest Voter Registration League of Willie Velazquez; grass-roots community organizing; the efforts of the National Council of La Raza, and Mexicans and Americans Thinking Together (MATT) to promote humanitarian immigration reform; pro-life groups; and many other such efforts can be seen as actions of the Spirit as we confront injustices that have become ingrained in the structures of our society.

As a resurrected people, even in the midst of our suffering and our struggles, we do not lose the joy of our new life, which we know through our faith is already beginning within us. Just as the Galileans had something of value to offer at the time of Jesus, what we offer society is not just for ourselves, but for the good of humanity. Nowhere is this better captured than in our all-inclusive religious fiestas—affirmations of the triumph of the spirit of love despite forces that oppose it. As a resurrected people following the way of Jesus, we are constantly on the move, going beyond the limits of our borders toward a broader and more inclusive humanity, helping to bring about not just the redemption of individuals but the progressive redemption of humanity.

Through the optic of the path tread by the Galilean Jesus, our own Mexican-American Mestizo life takes on a new and beautiful meaning: shame is transformed into honor, resentment into gratitude, exclusion into mission, and sadness into joy. Involvement in movements for social justice is our way to Jerusalem, while our festive celebrations are an affirmation of the Lord who has risen for and in us. In Christ crucified and resurrected, the sufferings of the moment are the birth pains of a new existence. In Jesus the Galilean Jew, our people's love and devotion to *Jesús Nazareno* is a dynamic, living source of life, affirmation, mission, strength, encouragement, and joy.

VIRGILIO ELIZONDO earned Ph.D. and S.T.D. degrees from the Institut Catholique in Paris and is currently Notre Dame Professor of Pastoral and Hispanic Theology at the University of Notre Dame. Specializing in the study of Our Lady of Guadalupe, pastoral and Hispanic theology, and inculturation, his recent publications include, besides numerous articles, *A God of Incredible Surprises: Jesus of Galilee* (2003). Forthcoming from Orbis is a monograph entitled *Charity* (2009).

Notes

1. For a further clarification of the hermeneutical privilege of the poor, consult Daniel G. Groody, *Globalization, Spirituality, and Justice: Navigating the Path to Peace* (Maryknoll, N.Y.: Orbis, 2007) 32; and Andrés Torres Queiruga, "Jesus: Genuinely Human," in *Jesus as Christ*, Concilium 2008/3, ed. Andrés Torres Queriuga et al. (London: SCM, 2008) 33–43.
2. "*Mestizo*" is the Latin American expression for the English "mixed race." In Latin America it started with the European-Amerindian encounter of the 15th century when race-mixture became the regular practice throughout the land. It comes through the conjugal and spiritual encounter between persons of different ethnic groups. The process is called *"mestizaje."* In the Carribean and in some parts of Latin America the mixture with Africans has been referred to as *"mulatez."* The Mestizo/mulatto tends to be rejected as "impure" by both parent groups. This process of racial/ethnic mixing

had been prohibited in the United States, and even now is feared and abhorred by many. Mexican Mestizos in the United States were considered undesirable mongrels and inferior in every way. Mixed race marriages were prohibited in the United States and only in 2000 did the last state (Alabama) abolish its law against this. For a good introduction to "Mestizo Theology" consult Jacques Audinet, "A Mestizo Theology," in *Beyond Borders: Writings of Virgilio Elizondo and Friends*, ed. Timothy Matovina (Maryknoll, N.Y.: Orbis, 2000); and Audinet, *The Human Face of Globalization: From Multiculturalism to Mestizaje*, trans. Frances Dal Chele (Lanham, Md.: Rowman & Littlefield, 2004).
3. *Sacrosanctum concilium* no. 37; *Lumen gentium* no. 17; *Ad gentes* nos. 1 and *gentes* no. 6. All quotations from Vatican II documents are taken from the official translation on the Vatican Web site.
4. *Ad gentes* no. 22.
5. For an excellent and comprehensive investigation of the evangelization of Mexico, consult Jaime Lara, *City, Temple, Stage: Eschatological Architecture and Liturgical Theatrics in New Spain* (Notre Dame, Ind.: University of Notre Dame, 2004); and Lara, *Christian Texts for Aztecs: Art and Liturgy in Colonial Mexico* (Notre Dame, Ind.: University of Notre Dame, 2008). The core thesis of these two books is that the indigenous religious ethos was not destroyed; it was recycled. This recycling is what I call the religious *mestizaje* of Latin American Catholicism.
6. The General Conferences of Latin American Bishops are fascinating gatherings of the pope, members of the Roman Curia, bishops, clergy, religious, laity, and experts from various fields in theology, catechetics, economics, sociology, etc. to pray, critically discuss, and elaborate a theology and pastoral plan for Latin America. The later conferences have included the bishops of the Caribbean. The first conference was held in Rio de Janeiro; the second met in Medellín, Colombia (1968); and the last one met in Aparecida, Brazil (2007). It is a good example of a regional church doing theology collaboratively.
7. Second General Conference of Latin American Bishops, *The Church in the Present-Day Transformation of Latin America in the Light of the Council* (Washington: Secretariat for Latin America, NCCB, 1979). For a critical development of the basic notions of this document, see the works of Gustavo Gutiérrez, especially "A Theology of Liberation" (Maryknoll, N.Y.: Orbis, 1973).
8. John Paul II, *Solicitudo rei socialis* (December 30, 1987) no. 30; *Reconciliatio et paenitentia* (December 2, 1984) no. 16; *Catechism of the Catholic Church* no. 408 (Washington: USCC, 1994).
9. For a more complete explanation of this concept in my work, see Virgilio Elizondo, *Galilean Journey: The Mexican-American Promise* (Maryknoll, N.Y.: Orbis, 1983, 2000, 2002) 13–16; *The Future Is Mestizo: Life Where Cultures Meet* (Boulder: University of Colorado, 2000); and for a more expansive

application within the United States, see Roberto Goizueta, *Caminemos con Jesús: Toward a Hispanic/Latino Theology of Accompaniment* (Maryknoll, N.Y.: Orbis, 1995)

10. A few years ago John P. Meier affirmed this obligation in his *A Marginal Jew: Rethinking the Historical Jesus*, 3 vols. (New York: Doubleday, 1991: "We learn from past quests, to be sure, but we cannot substitute the lessons of others for our own personal wrestling with the central problems of life, problems that affect each person must face squarely alone.... It is also true of every educated Christian's need to search for answers about the reality and the meaning of the man named Jesus" (1:4).
11. This is precisely what I understand Benedict XVI to be referring to in his introduction to *Jesus of Nazareth* (New York: Doubleday, 2007) esp. xvi–xxii.
12. Charles Kannengiesser, "Avenir des traditions fundatrices: La Christologie comme tâche au champ des études patristiques," *Recherches de science religieuse* 65 (1977) 139–68. The subject of this particular issue was: "Visages du Christ: Les tâches présentes de la christologie." This article along with many conversations with the author were very influential in clarifying the vision of my task.
13. Using the pedagogical approach of Paulo Freire's *The Pedagogy of the Oppressed*, trans. Myra Bergman Ramos (New York: Herder & Herder, 1970), MACC brought in Mexican Americans from throughout the country to reflect on our reality and our aspirations; our team also traveled throughout the Southwest, to many parts of the country, and even overseas to consult with our people stationed there, listening to the people's narratives and gradually developing a historical, social, and religious self-study of our reality and our collective aspirations.
14. I would like to see theologians and biblical scholars start with a brief biographical statement of their sociocultural conditioning. It would help the reader to appreciate both the richness and limitations of their work.
15. I am grateful to Michael Lee for his analysis of my pastoral/theological method in this issue of *Theological Studies* in terms of the traditional categories of *ver, juzgar, actuar* (to see, to judge, and to act), which he says means (1) to do a critical analysis of reality, (2) to scrutinize the inspired word and tradition for guidance, and (3) to discern a Christian response. This is the method used by the Church of Latin America, which has become basic to the work of MACC, and which I have used in hundreds of grassroots Bible reading sessions throughout the Southwest. It has become so ingrained that I did not even think of identifying it.
16. *Ad gentes* no. 22.
17. Sean Freyne, *Jesus, a Jewish Galilean: A New Reading of the Jesus Story* (New York: T. & T. Clark, 2005) 171–74.
18. Whether this was the case or not, as argued by contemporary scholars, this certainly seems to be the way it was perceived by Isaiah and later on framed in Matthew's Gospel.

19. *Catechism of the Catholic Church* nos. 386–409.
20. See 1 Corinthians 1:18–25 where the theme of wisdom and foolishness is brought out not only in the cross but also in the annunciation to Mary in the Galilean town of Nazareth. See also *Catechism of the Catholic Church* nos. 486, 498.
21. For a further development of this point, see Virgilio Elizondo, *A God of Incredible Surprises: Jesus of Galilee* (Lanham, Md.: Rowman & Littlefield, 2003).
22. For a clear, precise presentation of the Jewish and Gentile presence in Galilee and its surrounding regions, see Mark A. Chancey, *The Myth of A Gentile Galilee* (New York: Cambridge University, 2002) 120–66.
23. Meier, *A Marginal Jew* 3:631.
24. It seems from the Gospel narratives as though Jesus never spent a night in Jerusalem. Could this be because Galileans were not welcome in Jerusalem at night because they were regarded as troublemakers, or simply because of who they were?
25. Paul Hertig, "The Multi-ethnic Journeys of Jesus in Matthew: Margin-Center Dynamics," *Missiology: An International Review* 26 (1998) 23–36, at 25. There were more important international trade routes elsewhere but some did pass through Galilee, allowing for some encounters with foreigners.
26. Jonathan Reed, *Archaeology and the Galilean Jesus: A re-examination of the Evidence* (Philadelphia: Trinity Press International, 2002) 216.
27. Freyne, *Jesus, A Jewish Galilean* 109–10.
28. Sean Freyne, "Jesus the Jew," *Concilium* (2008/3) 24–32.
29. Benedict XVI, *Jesus of Nazareth* xxi.
30. Elizabeth A. Johnson, *Truly Our Sister: A Theology of Mary in the Communion of Saints* (New York: Continuum, 2003).
31. Pablo Alonso Vicente, "The Woman Who Changed Jesus: Crossing Boundaries in Mk 7,24–30" (Ph.D. diss., Katholieke Universiteit Leuven, 2006).
32. The great tragedy of this type of mentality is that it has helped produce and continues to inflame not only the exclusion, but even the genocide, of millions of people.
33. For an excellent and very concise summary description of the identity of a marginal Galilean Jew, see Meier, *A Marginal Jew* 1:6–9.
34. For a beautiful and profound elaboration of this point, see Norman Perrin, *Rediscovering the Teaching of Jesus* (San Francisco: Harper & Row, 1967).
35. Note the confrontations of Jesus with the Temple authorities in all four Gospel accounts: Matthew 21:12–27; Mark 11:11–33; Luke 19:45–20:8; John 2:1–22.
36. Consult the various works of Ignacio Ellacuría, Jon Sobrino, and Robert Lassalle-Klein on the crucified peoples; see esp. Ignacio Ellacuría, "The Crucified People," in *Mysterium Liberationis: Fundamental Concepts of Liberation Theology*, ed. Ignacio Ellacuría and Jon Sobrino (Maryknoll, N.Y.: Orbis, 1993) 580–604; Jon Sobrino, *Jesus the Liberator: A Historical-Theological Reading of*

Jesus of Nazareth, trans. Paul Burns and Francis McDonagh (Maryknoll, N.Y.: Orbis, 1993) and *Christ the Liberator: A View from the Victims*, trans. Paul Burns (Maryknoll, N.Y.: Orbis, 2001); and Robert Lassalle-Klein, "Jesus of Galilee and the Crucified People: Jon Sobrino, S.J., Ignacio Ellacuría, S.J., and the Future of Contextual Christology," in this issue of *Theological Studies*; and Lassalle-Klein, "A Postcolonial Christ," in *Thinking of Christ: Proclamation, Explanation, Meaning*, ed. Tatha Wiley (New York: Continuum, 2003) 135–53; also Daniel G. Groody, C.S.C., ed., *The Option for the Poor in Christian Theology* (Notre Dame, Ind.: University of Notre Dame, 2007); Groody's award-winning documentary *Dying to Live* (2006); and his article in this issue of *Theological Studies*. See also Leonardo Boff and Virgil Elizondo, eds., *1492–1992: The Voice of the Victims, Concilium* 1990/6 (Philadelphia: Trinity Press International, 1990); and Virgil Elizondo, ed., *Way of the Cross: The Passion of Christ in the Americas* (New York: Orbis, 1992).

37. Virgilio Elizondo, "Unmasking the Idols," and "Evil and the Experience of God," in *Beyond Borders: The Writings of Virgilio Elizondo and Friends*, ed. Timothy Matovina (Maryknoll, N.Y.: Orbis, 2000) 217–24; 225–32.

38. Examples of those in our own times who did not remain silent are Archbishop Oscar Romero and the Jesuit martyrs of the University of Central American in El Salvador; also in El Salvador were Maryknoll Sisters Mora Clarke and Ita Ford, Ursuline Sister Dorothy Kazel, and Jean Donovan; in Guatemala, Bishop Juan José Gerardi, Father Stanley Rother, and the many other catechists and *ministros de la palabra* who were killed because of their proclamation of the truth of the Scriptures.

39. Using the approach of Brazilian biblical scholar Carlos Mesters, MACC organized hundreds of Bible reading groups that would discuss the participants' life situation before reading and discussing the Gospel text. The main interest is not to interpret the text's historical-literal meaning (although this can be brought out by the leader), but to interpret the life of the participants through the Bible. This method is a communitarian adaption of the *lectio divina*. Some of the insights of my own work came from these Bible study groups. For an explanation of this method, see Carlos Mesters, *Defenseless Flower: A New Reading of the Bible*, trans. Francis McDonagh (Maryknoll, N.Y.: Orbis, 1989).

40. Divine election is not a privilege to lord it over others, but a responsibility to be of service in the construction of a new humanity. See Jon Sobrino, "El reino de dios y Jesús, compassion, justicia, mesa compartida," *Concilium* 326 (Junio 2008) 403–4.

The Galilean Jesus and a Contemporary Christology

Sean Freyne

Current interest in the Galilean Jesus as a historical figure has obscured the christological claims of the New Testament with regard to his person and ministry. This article seeks to build bridges between Jesus and the proclamation about him by exploring three themes arising from accounts of his ministry (messiahship, openness to gentiles, and the role of wisdom teacher), by examining each theme within the context of Galilean life in the Herodian period, and by demonstrating how these aspects of Jesus' Galilean career are carried forward and developed into the early Christian proclamation.

IN THIS ARTICLE I seek to integrate three different aspects of Jesus' career in Galilee with the early Christian proclamation about him: Jesus as messianic claimant, the openness of Jesus to Gentiles, and Jesus as wisdom teacher. I suggest that these aspects take on richer and deeper significance when they are interpreted in the context of the everyday experiences of Galilean life and landscape in the Herodian period. My contention is that only such a historico-theological approach can illustrate the universal meaning that is disclosed in and through the particularity of Jesus' life. God did not become human as a universal, but in the particularity of the life and praxis of Jesus.

Methodological Reductionism

In an oft-repeated introductory statement to his *Theology of the New Testament*, Rudolph Bultmann declared that "*the message of Jesus* is the presupposition for the theology of the New Testament rather than a part of that theology itself."[1] This statement may well arise from Bultmann's belief, expressed elsewhere, that we should only be interested in the *daß* (the "that") of Jesus, not the *was* (the "what"), since the sources are both legendary and mythological. Yet his skepticism seems to have carried over to the Synoptic gospels also, since the theologies of Jesus according to Matthew, Mark, and Luke play no part in Bultmann's synthesis, which is based on the pillars of Paul and John. Recent scholarship has reversed this trend by relying heavily on the Synoptics, not in terms of constructing a New Testament theology—an enterprise that has virtually collapsed—but rather as sources from which data for constructing a life of Jesus could be mined.

Unlike the 19th century liberal quest for the historical Jesus, the target of Bultmann's skeptical reaction, the present so-called third quest is often conducted in ways that seek to retrieve the historical figure of Jesus independently of his relationship with the movement that emerged in his name. Thus the historical skepticism of Bultmann has, it would seem, been replaced by late 20th century historicism. Yet neither can be said to do justice to the remembered Jesus of early Christian witness, which affirms his continued and unique significance for Christian belief and identity. Both are seriously reductionist: the Bultmannian position ignores the importance of Jesus' life for an adequate theology of the New Testament, and the more recent trends seek to discover a Jesus without Christianity.

Exploring a Via Media

In this article I explore a *via media* by highlighting the importance of the life of Jesus, that is, what he said and did, within the theologies of the Synoptic Gospels. While redaction criticism has taught us to recognize the different portrayals of Jesus in these three writings, they share a common *gestalt* of Jesus as a Galilean teacher/prophet/healer, whose life and ministry continued to have significance in different contexts for different early Christian congregations. To be sure, other portrayals of Jesus' life were also current, most notably John's, but this situation of diverse accounts did not give rise to an ethos of anomie in early Christianity. It is surely noteworthy that the emerging great church of the second century, even when confronted with pagan taunts about contradictions between the various accounts, opted for the fourfold gospel witness, rather than a single version of Jesus' life, such as Tatian attempted. While an adequate New Testament theology has to take full cognizance of this diversity and avoid reducing it to an imposed unity, it should equally be remembered that this creedal and myth-making diversity within early Christianity was based on the memory of the actual Jesus. Christian gnostic writings did indeed minimize the importance of the pre-Easter Jesus, but even then there is some connection with the received story of Jesus, such as the reliance on the sayings tradition in the Gospel of Thomas, or encounters of known members of Jesus' inner circle with the Risen One in the Gospels of Mary and Judas, and the Apocalypses of Peter and James. It is only in works such as the Gospel of the Egyptians, or the Gospel of Truth, where the full-blown gnostic redeemer myth has taken over, that reference to the historical figure of Jesus disappears completely.

A Historical-Theological Approach

In a thought-provoking introduction to a recent collection of essays on New Testament theology, Rowan Williams distinguishes the two different approaches to the New Testament today—the theological and the historical—with reference to the Barth-Bultmann debates of the early 20th century.[2] He suggests that their different perspectives represent two different reading strategies—one a reading *with* the text in order to enter its world and experience the challenge that this otherness presents, and the other a reading *of* the text to determine what the text *does not know* in order to correct or supplement it, thereby aiding our understanding of its genre, its represented world, and its intentions. I suggest that these two strategies are not mutually exclusive, even if the first seems more straightforward in that it is the text rather than the interpreter that sets the agenda. Yet the second approach has a legitimate and highly significant role as well, one that goes beyond merely pointing out errors or omissions in the text, but has a more positive function of aiding the reader by showing what aspects of the past of Jesus were important for the choices of the gospel writers and their audiences, and why this might be the case.

Jesus, Judaism, and Galilee

One aspect of the life of Jesus on which all three Synoptics agree is that the public ministry of Jesus was primarily located in Galilee. Indeed, each in their different way wants to underline the singular importance of that fact. They also agree that it was only after the arrest of John that Jesus moves to Galilee, thus associating his ministry with that of the Baptist who is described as the Elijah who was to come. Matthew is particularly emphatic applying two of his Scripture fulfillment texts to this fact. As a child, Jesus is brought by his parents to Nazareth in Galilee to avoid Archelaus's tyrannical rule in Judea, and the name of his village immediately evokes for Matthew the Isaian prophecy of the shoot (*nazir*) of Jesse, David's father (Is 11:1; 53: 2). When the adult Jesus settles in Capernaum after his baptism, the Matthean author again senses divine providence at work, and applies to Jesus' ministry the Isaian prophecy for the northern tribes of restoration after the eighth-century Assyrian devastation and deportations (Is 8:23; Mt 4:14–16). Mark emphasizes that Jesus' coming into Galilee to proclaim the arrival of the eschatological kingly rule of God is linked with "the fulfillment of time" (*kairos*, Mk 1:14–15), that is, God's appointed and appropriate moment. Luke uses the equally pregnant term *arche* to highlight the beginning in Galilee of Jesus' ministry that will eventually take him to Jerusalem (Lk 4:44; 23:3; Acts 10:37). Entering into the spirit of the texts, it is clear that, for the Evangelists, the fact that Jesus' ministry takes place in Galilee is no accident. The Evangelists present the Galilean ministry of Jesus as (a) the divinely foretold theater for (b) the manifestation of the eschatological event of God's saving act, which could (c) also be seen as a new beginning for humanity, and thus likened to the new creation.

Further, a second, more critical reading of the texts will show that much can be added to fill out the highly selective representation of Galilee that the different Evangelists present.[3] All three are looking back to the originating Galilean moment through resurrection-tinted glasses, yet all agree that Galilee was the place of beginnings. That fact could not be glossed over, even if apologetic concerns of a later time might have suggested that it would have been better had this not been the case. Galilee would forever be an integral part of the Christian proclamation of the good news by and about Jesus Christ. Such a second reading engages in what I have elsewhere described as an intertextual exercise, borrowing Ernst Renan's much-used description of the Galilean landscape as "a fifth gospel, torn but still legible."[4] As is well known, the Galilean landscape is today *torn* in ways that Renan could scarcely have dreamed of, through scientific surveys and excavations of various sites. The data gathered from this work, as well as the critical readings of other literary sources concerning Galilee, provide a more comprehensive view from below of life in the region that can greatly assist in our understanding of various aspects of Jesus' life and ministry, aspects left hanging or indeterminate in the Gospel narratives. By bringing these Gospel narratives into a critical dialogue with our knowledge of Galilee, it is possible to suggest new and challenging readings of various sayings, episodes, and incidents, thereby sharpening the focus on the actual Jesus of the Gospel texts, and his ways of confronting the social and religious life of his own time. Such an exercise of critical retrieval is not to engage in the historicist approaches of recent studies of the historical Jesus. These studies often discard the so-called framework statements of the Gospels as secondary and generalized, replacing them with a narrative framework within which the isolated scraps of information deemed authentic can be rearranged, and which present a modernized and often liberal account of Jesus that bears little resemblance to what the original was likely to have been.

In what follows I propose to focus on three separate aspects of Jesus' ministry as represented in the kerygmatic Gospel accounts. I seek to illustrate the theological implications of these aspects by placing them in the larger political and social, but also religious, setting of first-century Galilee, as this can be critically reconstructed from available sources. In this respect it is important to remind ourselves that Jesus was not a freestanding and isolated figure, waiting to be clothed suitably by his followers in images arising from Jewish hopes and expectations. As a Galilean Jewish figure, he must have participated in and been affected by the everyday experiences of life as lived in the region. He would have been inspired and challenged by the stories of Israel's life in the north, been keenly aware of the ways his fellow Galileans in the past had responded to threats from within and without to their identity, and been acutely conscious of the dangers confronting him and his community in the immediate present. In other words, we must allow Jesus a fully human history as a Galilean, but one that is also steeped in his own Jewish religious traditions and the hopes emanating from them, something that his sojourn with John the Baptist must have both clarified and deepened. In seeking to build bridges between Jesus and his followers, it is often forgotten that they shared many of the same memories and hopes, and that both could draw on this rich repertoire of Jewish beliefs in order to understand and interpret their own experiences and feelings.

Galilean Roots of New Testament Themes in the Kerygma about Jesus

Jesus, the Messiah of Israel

This awareness of Jewish expectations is certainly true in the case of the messiahship of Jesus, a topic that has returned to the scholarly agenda in the wake of some important discussions on the variety of messianic hopes in the literature of Second Temple Judaism.[5] Certainly the Synoptic authors invested the Galilean career of Jesus with messianic status. The fact that a term previously used to describe a role was transformed at quite an early (pre-Pauline) stage into a personal name, Jesus *Christ*, raises the question as to whether it might already have been associated with the pre-Easter Jesus. In that event the New Testament texts bear witness to the transformation of Jewish messianism into early Christology.

There is, however, a significant difference in the various Synoptic presentations of Jesus' career as messianic.[6] The so-called messianic secret, which features Jesus' desire not to have his true identity disclosed, dominates the Markan narrative. Nowhere does Jesus declare himself to be the messiah until the final trial scene. When others recognize him as such, he silences them as in the case of the demons (Mk 1:25; 3:11–12; 5:8–9), or changes the terms of discussion as after Peter's confession (Mk 8:31). Even in Mark's trial before the high priest when Jesus replies "I am" to the question, "Are you the *Christos*, the son of the Blessed One?" He immediately elaborates on his answer by declaring that his claim will be authenticated in the future by his enthronement as the Son of Man at God's right hand, and his coming on the clouds of heaven (Mk 15:61–62).

By contrast, both Matthew and Luke remove the secrecy in their redaction of the Markan account. Both extend messianic status to the birth of Jesus, where his true identity and purpose are already made known by heavenly signs and voices. For Matthew, Jesus' messianic status is plain to see, since his life is the fulfillment of scriptural expectations at every step of the way, most especially in his words and healings, which are described as "the works (*erga*) of the Christ" (Mt 11:2). Throughout, Matthew is at pains to show that Jesus is the Son of David, and on each occasion the declaration gives rise to a heated discussion with the Jewish authorities. Yet, significantly, as we shall see, Jesus' actions and demeanor do not correspond with popular expectations of the Son of David, as these are expressed in the contemporary Jewish literature. Clearly, by the time of the writing of Matthew's Gospel the messianic status of Jesus has become a major bone of contention with the synagogue, as was also true in the case of the Fourth Gospel (Jn 7:25–44; 10:24–25; 12:34–35).

Luke invests the career of Jesus with a messianic aura from the outset as well. Thus the hopes of Israel are repeatedly to be found on the lips of various characters in the infancy stories (Lk 1:32–33; 1:68–79; 2:11; 2:25). The programmatic scene in the synagogue at Nazareth (Lk 4:16–22) is particularly important for Luke's presentation of Jesus' career, when he applies to himself the Isaian passage (Is 61:1–2) dealing with the prophet *anointed* (*chrio*) by the Lord to bring good news to the poor (Lk 4:18). At his trial the Lukan Jesus is accused of stirring up revolt throughout the country from Galilee to Jerusalem (Lk 23:2,5), thus underlining the social aspects of Jesus' teaching as Luke presents it in the narrative. The theme of Israel's liberation is continued in the post-Resurrection encounters when the two disciples on the road to Emmaus declare that they had hoped that Jesus would be the redeemer of Israel (Lk 24:21). By the time of Luke's writing such a purely political hope lay in ruins, together with Jerusalem. But, for Luke, the messianic hope is not frustrated by Jesus' death as a prophet of justice, a true martyr/witness. Contrary to Jewish ideas about a glorious triumphant messiah figure, the risen Jesus reassures the eleven and those gathered with them that the death of the messiah was foretold in the Law, the Prophets and the Psalms, and that he would eventually triumph (Lk 24:26, 46). The way has been opened up for them to continue the witness about this alternative messianic community "from Jerusalem to the end of the earth," as Luke will report in Acts.

From this brief survey it is clear that the early Christian claims about messianic status of Jesus were highly contentious, and we can see signs of later polemics influencing the Gospel accounts of the life and ministry of Jesus in Galilee. Yet, especially in view of the early emergence of

Christos as a name for Jesus, we are entitled to inquire whether or not such claims might plausibly reflect his earthly career, and, if so, which aspects were most likely to resonate with distinctively Galilean hopes? Clearly, his ministry was not going to satisfy the dominant Jewish expectation of a Davidic king who would liberate Israel from her enemies, purify Jerusalem of the impious, and establish a kingdom of justice and peace. Jesus' career could not match war-like profiles like that of the Psalms of Solomon, where such hopes found their fullest expression, especially Psalm 17. Jesus did indeed proclaim peace—"blessed are the peace-makers"—but unlike the imposed peace of Roman imperial rule and their Herodian retainers, the peace of Jesus came from the heart and called for openness, trust, and respect for the other. In this view, true peace can occur only when true justice reigns.

Other aspects of Jesus' activity in Galilee were highly compatible with a messianic profile, especially his healings and exorcisms. While he himself makes an explicit link between these actions and the presence of the kingdom of God (Mt 12:28; Lk 11:20), they also point to his own person as the one through whom that kingdom was both proclaimed and realized now.[7] This connection between the deeds of Jesus and his person is most clearly expressed in the Fourth Gospel, where the crowds proclaim him as prophet and want to take him by force to make him king, but he escapes their overtures (Jn 6:14–15). Here it would seem that claiming the title of Messiah was of no great interest to Jesus. Indeed, Mark says it is a sign of a false messiah to proclaim oneself in such a way (Mk 13:6, 21). For Jesus, the challenge seems to have been to live out the messianic values as he understood them, and to leave the future to his heavenly Father.

The establishment of the Twelve as the symbolic core of his new family could well have been understood as making a strong messianic claim. Indeed, there is evidence that some of his own closest disciples thought along these lines (Mk 10:35–37; Acts 1:6). One of the roles of Elijah was to gather the tribes that had been dispersed in preparation for the end time restoration (Sir 48:10), and the Davidic messiah was expected to do a similar task according to the Psalm of Solomon 17:25. This recurring hope was based on the legend of the northern tribes still existing across the Euphrates. This legend had a long "shelf life," clearly indicating just how devastating the Assyrian conquest of the north had been in Israelite memory. As mentioned previously, an Isaian oracle of redemption to come was addressed to *Galilee of the nations*, which once had been occupied by four northern tribes: the Land of Zebulon and the land of Naphtali (the two major tribes), the way of the Sea (i.e., the coastal plain, which the tribe of Asher had once inhabited), and beyond the Jordan (to where the tribe of Dan migrated, Isa 8:23).[8] While Matthew uses this Isaian text to link the coming of Jesus into Galilee to the theme of fulfillment, there is no reason why it would not also have played a role in Jesus' own sense of mission and that of his contemporaries. As I have argued elsewhere, the journeys of Jesus in the northern region can be seen as enacting this "map of restoration," which recurs at several places in the Jewish literature.[9]

In selecting the Twelve, Jesus clearly draws on this tradition and its implications for the north. But it is important to note how he redeploys the symbol for his own particular vision of what restoration means. When the idea of the twelve tribes (or its territorial equivalent in the north) is mentioned in Jewish literature there is a clear sense of boundaries. Detailed lists of places are given (Ezek 47:13–23; Josh 13:2–7; Num 34:7–9), or alternatively, the right to occupy the territory in question is affirmed in terms of ancestral lands (1 Macc 15:33). On the other hand, for the Jesus of the Gospels and his movements, the establishment of the Twelve has no such territorial implications. We are told instead that the Twelve will sit at his table in his kingdom (Luke) or sit on thrones judging the twelve tribes of Israel (Matthew). Both images—meal and judgment seat—have a clear eschatological dimension. They symbolize the restored and renewed Israel of Jewish expectations, which involves a partnership, not a hierarchical model of community solidarity.

Thus, while other Galileans, both immediately before and after his time, engaged in violent reaction to the exploitation they were encountering, Jesus chose to challenge the status quo in a more subtle but in the end more effective and long-lasting, manner, namely, through the power of symbolic actions and choices. This way was more effective because it did not continue the spiral of violence that was endemic in that society, but rather it sought to challenge both the oppressors and his overly enthusiastic followers to see the world differently and to prioritize their value system accordingly.[10] The second-century Christian apologist, Justin Martyr, has Trypho, his Jewish interlocutor, declare: "You Christians have shaped for yourselves a Christ for whom you are blindly giving up your lives" (*Dialogue with Trypho* 8:4). In fact, however, it was Jesus who long beforehand in Galilee had begun this process of reinterpreting the idea of the messiah in the light of his understanding of God's kingdom.

Jesus and the Nations

The links between this theme of restoration and the messianic significance in the Synoptics of the Galilean career of Jesus bring us to the attitude of Jesus toward the Gentiles, and their place in the Galilean ministry. In his ground-breaking study, E. P. Sanders writes: "Jesus started a movement which came to see the Gentile mission as the logical extension of itself."[11] Yet, after some discussion of the evidence, Sanders is not able to identify any plausibly authentic saying of Jesus that might give some clues as to his views regarding the admission of Gentiles into his movement, either in the present or at the eschatological *denouement*, as Joachim Jeremias had suggested.[12] Thus, we shall have to infer what Jesus' attitude might have been on the basis of the more securely established aspects of his ministry.

One could point to the Isaian citation about the Temple as "the house of prayer for all the nations" (Isa 56:7), which Mark puts on the lips of Jesus during the Temple incident (Mk 11:15–19). But, given the symbolic nature of this whole episode, one would like to be able to show that such sentiments reflected a more general attitude of Jesus toward Israel's relationship with the Gentiles, especially in view of his regathering of the tribes of the restored Israel at the end-time, which seems to have been central to his project, as was argued above. There is need, therefore, to search more widely to see how Israel's restoration and the inclusion of the Gentiles can form a single vision.

Sanders points out conflicting points of view on this topic, ranging from God's annihilation of the Gentiles as idolaters and serial sinners to the belief that the nations would come streaming to Zion in search of the wisdom of the restored Israel, a view particularly favored by Isaiah. As regards individual conversions and the question of daily contacts, the evidence is equally ambiguous. Attitudes obviously varied at different times and between the Diaspora and the homeland. Every shade of opinion seems to have been represented: from full-blown conversion (proselytes), to adherence to Israel's God while retaining one's former allegiances (God fearers), to the recognition by some rabbis that some Gentiles could be righteous.[13]

Early Christian practice might be our best witness to the more general situation, recognizing that it only represents how one group of Christ-believing Jews dealt with the matter. Paul, but also James, the brother of the Lord, can give us some insight into the issues at stake and perhaps also point us in the right direction for understanding Jesus' views. Recent studies have moved away from the history of religions view of Paul as the founder of a Hellenistic Christ-cult association toward views that favor Paul the Jew, deeply concerned with his own people from the outset of his mission.[14] In this revised, and surely correct, view of Paul's overall concerns, he and Jesus can be seen to share a similar Isaian model of the relationship of Israel and the nations, as I have argued elsewhere.[15]

At this point James's view must also be taken into account with regard to how Jesus' vision and praxis could best find expression. The point at issue between Paul and James was not whether Gentiles could or should be admitted to the new movement, but rather the conditions under which that should be allowed. Cultural as much as religious differences come into play between the Galilean Jewish perspective of James—a perspective that caused him to be centered in Jerusalem, as the logical outcome of his (belated) acceptance of Jesus as Messiah[16]—and that of Paul, the Diaspora Jew, with a more tolerant approach to Gentiles and their cultural affiliations. In Acts, Luke, writing for a later generation, sought to smooth out the differences between James and Paul, while acknowledging the latter's importance by giving him the right to decide on the matter in the account of the so-called Council of Jerusalem (Acts 15:13–21). Reading between the lines of the various Pauline epistles, Galatians, Philippians, and 2 Corinthians in particular, one gets the impression that the different backgrounds gave rise to deeper theological fissures in which the Christ of faith of the Pauline school encountered the Jesus of history, as he was remembered and preached by Jerusalem/Galilean followers of Jesus.

The fact that no direct appeal to Jesus could be made to resolve the debate points us back to the initial question, namely, the attitude of Jesus toward Gentiles during his Galilean ministry. As is well known, the Isaian epithet *galil ha-goyim/ Galilee of the Nations* has sometimes been used to describe the actual world of Jesus' ministry, supporting the claim that he was only marginally Jewish, or, in its most extreme form, not Jewish at all. However, this view of Galilee can be exposed for what it was, and still is today, namely, the product of a 19th-century overemphasis on the Hellenized and therefore enlightened, it is claimed, ethos of the region, and the devaluing of Galilee's Jewishness as sterile and outmoded.[17] It has been one of the major achievements of the archeological investigation of the region to show how one-sided and biased the older view was. The largely village culture within which Jesus' ministry was conducted, it can now be safely asserted, was thoroughly Jewish in ethos, affiliation, and practice.[18]

However, balance is needed in assessing this finding with regard to Jesus. For one thing, the Gospels, especially Mark, stress that Jesus moved in the periphery of Roman Galilee: Tyre and Sidon, Caesarea Philippi/Banias and the Decapolis. The very name *Galilee*, meaning *the circle*, may well have resurfaced from earlier times with the rise in the Hellenistic and Roman period of the Greek cities in the wake of Alexander's conquest, in order to express the same feeling of being encircled by a non-Israelite culture. Even within the Galilee of Jesus' day there were tangible signs of Romanization at the Herodian centers of Sepphoris and Tiberias. In other words, Jesus may have been concerned with the largely Jewish population of the region, but it was not a Gentile-free zone. In terms of day-to-day contacts, the purity laws, especially as developed by the Pharisaic party, functioned to separate Jew from Greek (and Syrian). There is evidence that some of the more observant elements had developed their own boundary between areas where Jewish observance (with regard to the food and agricultural laws, e.g.) could be assured, and places (mainly close to the pagan cities) where it was less certain. [19]

The journeys of Jesus as described by Mark took him to those very regions of doubtful observance according to Pharisaic standards. But that did not make him or the inhabitants of the region any less Jewish in terms of their loyalties and worldview. The story of his encounter with the Syro-Phoenician woman whom he met in the region of Tyre (Mk 7:24–30) illustrates this point. Mark gives her a double identification: she was culturally Greek but Syro-Phoenician by birth.[20] That is, she was a thoroughly Hellenized inhabitant from one of the mixed, non-Jewish ethnic minorities of the area. Now relations between the Galilean Jews and the coastal cities varied considerably. And there is evidence of trading exchanges: Tyrian coins and pottery on the one hand, and Galilean agricultural produce (wheat, olives, and wine) on the other. Nonetheless, at certain moments the deep-seated religious and ethnic suspicions and animosities that were endemic to the ancient spiral of violence in the region would flare up, leading to bloodshed, destruction, and enslavement.

Thus, from the viewpoint of a Galilean Jew, Jesus' willingness to engage with this representative of an alien culture, and a woman besides, shows that he was not bound by the rigid purity and other markers of difference inscribed in that setting. Yet, his initial reaction to the woman's request for healing—likening her and her people to dogs—was disparaging, despite the best efforts of exegetes to soften its impact. Not deterred, the woman's response had the effect of opening Jesus' eyes to recognize the dark side of what he had said. It unmasked the potentially racist dimensions of his inherited tradition and revealed the ethnocentric leanings of his own vision of restoration.[21]

It is difficult to imagine a story such as this with its implications of Jesus' narrowed vision being the creation of Mark. Actual or not, the story illustrates the real world of everyday interaction, its plot moving between the poles of suspicion and openness, human need and plenty, within which the Galilean ministry of Jesus was conducted. We are entitled to enquire what might have been the impact of such an encounter on Jesus' own understanding. For Mark the episode is the prelude for Jesus' journey in the outer rim of Galilee that takes him via Sidon to the midst of the Decapolis (Mk 7:31). [22] How might this encounter have helped him clarify the values he had inherited and how best to sharpen them in order to reflect and express the graciousness of God's kingly rule that he proclaimed, as well as the gift of the land that he and his people had received? On the one hand, there is evidence in contemporary Jewish literature that one should forgive one's enemy (Sir 28:6–7), not refuse bread to the needy (Prov 25:21–22), not return evil for evil (Joseph and Asenath 28:14), and do good (Test of Joseph 18:2). On the other hand, nowhere except in the sayings of Jesus do we hear the injunction, "love your enemy," precisely because God's universal and individual care is for the whole human family, irrespective of their moral probity (Mt 5:24–25).[23] Thus, one might indeed wonder whether Jesus' seeming casual encounter with this *other*—other by culture, race, and gender—helped him see more clearly the ethnic, yet universal, implications of his total trust in the creator God, whom he could call Father.

Jesus, Wisdom, and Creation

Thus far I have attempted to show how the theological themes found in the Gospels of the messiahship of Jesus and his attitude toward the Nations might have emerged from the historical context of his life and ministry as a Galilean Jew. In this section I will suggest how those narratives were deepened and universalized by a theme that appears in one of the earliest postresurrection reflections on the identity of Jesus, the putative Q document, which Matthew and Luke used independently. I will also explore the possible historical roots of this Gospel theme in the ministry of the Galilean Jesus and what those roots can suggest for its significance in contemporary Christology.

Twice in the Q document Jesus is identified with personified wisdom, *Sophia*. For Matthew this identification is based on his works, whereas Luke probably retains the more likely original children of wisdom (Mt 11:19; Lk 7:35). Later, we hear that *Sophia* has sent various emissaries to Israel (Mt 23:34: "prophets, wise men and scribes"; Lk 11:49: "prophets and apostles"), but they have all been rejected. Both evangelists clearly endorse this early designation of Jesus as Wisdom, but Mark also mentions wisdom as a suitable category for understanding Jesus (Mk 6:2). Furthermore, Mark's account of the Passion has strong echoes of the persecution of the just wise one who is vindicated by God, as described in the Wisdom of Solomon (2:10–20). Paul is also aware of this identification of Jesus when he speaks of him as "Christ, the power of God and the wisdom of God" (1 Cor 1:24). The opening *Logos* hymn in the Fourth Gospel is a further development of this early christological trajectory, highlighting a role in creation, even if the term *Sophia* does not occur. Thus the Johannine Jesus can later declare: "My father is working until now and I am working," alluding to the creation story of Genesis as his justification of healing on the Sabbath (Jn 5:17).

How might this identification with Wisdom, then, have its roots in Jesus' own career, and what light might a consideration of its implication have for our contemporary christological reflections based on the memory of the Galilean Jesus?[24] A first step toward an adequate answer is to recall the contrast between Jesus as a wisdom teacher and his Jerusalem namesake, Jesus ben Sirach. The latter places the ideal scribe among the elite: only those who have leisure can acquire wisdom. The work of others is important for "maintaining the fabric of the world," but for Jesus ben Sirach, only the scribe can acquire true insight (Sir 38:24–39:11, at 38:34).

As a craftsman, Jesus of Nazareth does not fit into that category. Indeed we hear of scribes from Jerusalem coming to Galilee to discredit him (Mk 3:22; 7:1). The Jerusalem scribes sneer dismissively in John's account, "These people who do not know the law are accursed. . . . Are you too a Galilean?" because Nicodemus had asked for a fair hearing for Jesus (Jn 7:49.51–52). The tenor and range of images in Jesus' teaching—parabolic, pithy, and proverbial—clearly reflects the gnomic wisdom of the peasant based in their experience of coping with life's struggles.[25] Yet while clearly tapping into this rich source of human insight, Jesus develops his own distinctive voice. His wisdom, though proverbial in style, is subversive in content, as the strange outcomes of the plots in his parables demonstrate. These innocent-sounding simple stories are packed with surprise and irony, thus challenging addressees to hear and see the world differently from their everyday expectations, fears, and hopes. Hence, as employed by Jesus, the wisdom orientation of his teaching presupposed a deeper knowledge of God and God's ways in the world. This suggests that Jesus was no ordinary scribe, but rather a seer to whom the deeper, hidden mystery of things had been given. "To you has been given the mystery of the kingdom of God, but for those outside everything happens in riddles" (Mk 4:10).

According to the Book of Proverbs, Lady Wisdom gained the insight that she shares with humanity through her presence with God in the creation of the world (Prov 8:21–31). Little wonder that Jesus, as the wisdom teacher who claimed such knowledge of the mystery of the kingdom, could declare it to be "good news" for all. He thus showed a deep understanding of God as creator and sustainer of all. "I thank you, Father, Lord of heaven and earth," he declares, clearly echoing the opening verse of Genesis, before going on to invite "the little ones," that is, the poor and the marginalized, to come to him, just as Lady Wisdom had done (Mt 11:25–30; Proverbs 9:1–6). Jesus' understanding of God as creator underpins his whole life's work and his ethical teaching, so much so in fact that it seems to universalize his distinctively Jewish experience of God as the Yahweh of the Exodus. Thus, he can contemplate many people coming from the four cardinal points of the compass to join Abraham, Isaac, and Jacob at the great eschatological banquet foretold by Isaiah, while the children are excluded, painful as such a conclusion must have been for him (Mt 8:11–12; Lk 13:28–29).

The care of this creator God transcends ethnic boundaries: "He makes his sun to shine on the bad and the good and rains on the just and the unjust alike," (Mt 5:45; Lk 6:35). Hence there is no need for anxious concerns about the necessities of life (Mt 6:25–34; Lk 12:22–34). The fertile land of lower Galilee, where most of the ministry of Jesus was conducted, presents a sharp contrast to the desert experience with John, not to speak of the Egyptian experiences of his forebears. One can imagine that his own exodus from the desert of John to the land of Galilee gave Jesus a new appreciation of the divinely blessed reality of this "land of hills and valleys which drinks in water from heaven, a land which the Lord God cares for, since the eyes of the Lord God are upon it from the beginning of the year to the end" (Deut 11:10–11).[26] The land also provided Jesus with a rich repertoire of metaphors for God's ongoing creative presence. Thus, the experience of the farmer awaiting patiently for the harvest as "the earth of itself, he knows not how, brings forth the ripe grain" (Mk 4:30–32), is a yearly reenactment of the miracle of the first creation: "Let the earth bring forth . . ." (Gen 1:11). The creator God is always engaged in the act of creation, and Wisdom can reveal that active presence for those who have ears to hear and eyes to see, as it did for Jesus himself.

Unfortunately, the resources of this land were unevenly distributed. A new ruling elite had entered the scene when Jesus was a young adult growing up in lower Galilee. These were the Herodians of the Gospels and the two centers of Sepphoris and Tiberias, one refurbished and the other a new foundation, were not only home to Herod and his collaborators but also symbols for their neighbors of an oppressive imperial regime in their midst. Natural and human resources were now being exploited for the benefit of these centers. The surrounding villages were likely to be denuded not just of the necessities of life—water and food, but their way of life and the values associated with it were also being eroded. Jesus distanced himself from those centers, and declared the poor and the deprived blessed rather than the rich and powerful. He visited their villages and homes, reassuring them of God's paternal care and acting as the agent of that care through his mighty deeds of healing and sharing.

Those first theologians had recognized that Jesus was not merely another wisdom teacher, but Wisdom herself who had penetrated deeply into the secret of this world, so deeply, in fact, that they came to recognize the presence of Jesus as the new creation already unfolding in their midst. They saw his words and deeds as important because they were the words and deeds of Wisdom, fashioned by his experience of God's presence in those hills and valleys of Galilee, just as others of his contemporaries surely believed that it was in Jerusalem alone that this God could be encountered. Jesus did not abandon this central belief of his tradition, that Yahweh resided among his people in the Jerusalem Temple. Yet his emphasis on the creator God's presence in the everyday lives of the Galilean peasants meant that access to Israel's God no longer had to be mediated by an official representative of the people. God was accessible to all, because his creation was meant to be shared alike and equally by all. Thus, on the one hand, it is historically likely that the one recorded visit of Jesus as an adult to the Temple became a direct challenge to the priestly aristocracy and their way of life because the very class of priests who so jealously guarded their privileged access to God had become collaborators with the Roman occupiers who denied the peasants their share of the fruits of the land as gifts of the creator God. On the other hand, it is equally true that in Jesus' theological view the Temple as sole symbol of God's presence to Israel was already under judgment as a result of his Galilean ministry that offered God's forgiveness to the just and unjust alike. The historical action in the Temple merely confirmed that theological reality.

Conclusion

In this article I have tried to suggest how Jesus' career in Galilee helped to shape the early Christian proclamation about him, and how this may aid contemporary readers to understand that proclamation more fully. I have argued that Jesus begins his reinterpretation of the idea of messiahship in Galilee, where the Synoptics tell us he formulated his understanding of the kingdom of God and his role in its arrival. I have suggested that his encounters with the *other* in Galilee and the surrounding provinces helped him to formulate his injunction to "love your enemy," and to be open to Gentiles, as implications of his total trust in the creator God whom he knew as Father. And I have argued that Jesus' experience of the oppression and marginalization of God's people in Galilee deepened and universalized the themes of messiahship and openness to Gentiles by uniting them in his self-understanding as the prophet and seer of the creative wisdom of God.

Thus, I have sought to demonstrate how each theme takes on a richer and deeper theological significance when it is set back into the concrete, everyday experiences of Galilean life and landscape in the Herodian period. My intent was to show how a historico-theological approach can illustrate the universal meaning disclosed in and through the particularity of Jesus' life. God did not become human as a universal, but in the particularity of Jesus' life and praxis, which began in Galilee. From a Christian theological perspective, therefore, every particular human life can become a Galilean experience of divine disclosure within the world of actual things.

The final injunction of Mark's Gospel declares: "Go back to Galilee; there you will see him as he told you" (Mk 16:7). Yet Mark never tells us whether that meeting took place. Instead, the disciples in Mark must remember that he had said, "I will *go before* you to Galilee" (Mk 14:28, emphasis added). Their challenge was to discover the risen Jesus as leader by following in his way. Theirs was a journey to discover how, in the light of his earthly activities and words, everyday encounters with a variety of *others*—especially the weak and the marginalized—could ultimately lead to a disclosure of the ultimate *Other*, God.

SEAN FREYNE received his S.T.D. from St. Thomas University, Rome, and his L.SS. from the Pontifical Biblical Institute, Rome. He is currently professor of theology (emeritus) at Trinity College, Dublin, and visiting professor of early Christian history and literature at Harvard Divinity School. Specializing in the Synoptic Gospels, the Jewish world of early Christianity, and the history and archeology of the Roman period Galilee, he has recently published: *Jesus, a Jewish Galilean: A New Reading of the Jesus Story* (2005) and "Galilee as Laboratory: Experiments for New Testament Historians and Theologians," *New Testament Studies* 53 (2007) 147–64.

Notes

1. Rudolf Bultmann, *Theology of the New Testament*, 2 vols., trans. Kendrick Grobel (London: SCM) 1:3, emphasis original.
2. Rowen Williams, "Foreword," in *The Nature of New Testament Theology: Essays in Honour of Robert Morgan*, ed. Christopher Rowland and Christopher Tuckett (Malden, Mass.: Blackwell, 2006) xiii–xix.
3. For a detailed discussion see Sean Freyne, *Galilee, Jesus, and the Gospels: Literary Approaches and Historical Investigations* (Minneapolis: Fortress, 1988) 33–115,
4. Ernst Renan, *The Life of Jesus* (1863; Buffalo, N.Y.: Prometheus, 1935, 1991) 23.
5. John J. Collins, *The Scepter and the Star: The Messiahs of the Dead Sea Scrolls and Other Ancient Literature* (New York: Doubleday, 1995).
6. Graham Stanton, "Messianism and Christology: Mark, Matthew, Luke and Acts," in *Redemption and Resistance: The Messianic Hopes of Jews and Christians in Antiquity*, ed. Marcus Bockmuehl and James Carlton Paget (New York: T. & T. Clark International, 2007) 78–96.
7. Lidija Novakovic, *Messiah, the Healer of the Sick*, Wissenschaftliche Untersuchungen zum Neuen Testament (hereafter WUNT) 170 (Tübingen: Mohr Siebeck, 2003).
8. The precise geography of this prose introduction to the poetic oracle is ambiguous, but it probably refers to the territories of the three Assyrian provinces in the region, Dura (Dor), Maggidu (Megiddo), and Galidu (Gilead). Thus the whole extent of the promised land as described by Ezekiel 47:15–19 and Joshua 13:2–7 are included in the redemption to come. The territory in question also covers the regions traversed by Jesus as described in Mark 7:31.
9. Sean Freyne, "Messiah and Galilee," in Freyne, *Galilee and Gospel: Collected Essays* WUNT 125 (Tübingen: Mohr Siebeck, 2000) 230–70, esp. 253–56; and Freyne, *Jesus, a Jewish Galilean: A New Reading of the Jesus Story* (New York: T. & T. Clark, 2005) 74–91.
10. Gerd Theissen, "Die Jesusbewegung als charismatische Werterevolution," *New Testament Studies* 35 (1989) 343–60.
11. E. P. Sanders, *Jesus and Judaism* (London: SCM, 1985) 220.
12. Joachim Jeremias, *Jesus' Promise to the Nations* (London: SCM, 1958).
13. Paula Fredrickson, "Judaism, the Circumcision of Gentiles, and Apocalytic Hope: Another Look at Galatians 1 and 2," *Journal of Theological Studies*, n.s. 42 (1991) 532–64, esp. 533–48.
14. Krister Stendahl, *Paul among Jews and Gentiles and Other Essays* (Philadelphia: Fortress, 1976); E. P. Sanders, *Paul and Palestinian Judaism: A Comparison of Patterns in Religion* (Philadelphia: Fortress, 1977); Martin Hengel and Anna Maria Schwemer, *Paulus zwishen Damaskus und Antiochien: Die unbekannte Jahre des Apostles*, WUNT 102 (Tübingen: Mohr Siebceck, 1998).

15. See Sean Freyne, "The Jesus-Paul Debate Revisited and Re-Imaging Christian Origins," in *Christian Origins: Worship, Belief, and Society,* Journal for the Study of the New Testament, Supplement Series 241, ed. Kieran O'Mahoney (Sheffield: Sheffield Academic, 2003) 143–62.
16. Sean Freyne, "Jesus and the Servant Community in Zion: Continuity in Context," in *Jesus from Judaism to Christianity: Continuum Approaches to the Historical Jesus,* ed. Tom Holmén (New York: T. & T. Clark, 2007) 109–24.
17. Mark A. Chancey, *The Myth of a Gentile Galilee,* Society for New Testament Studies Monograph Series 118 (Cambridge: Cambridge University, 2002).
18. Sean Freyne, "Archaeology and the Historical Jesus," in John R. Bartlett, ed. *Archaeology and Biblical Interpretation* (New York: Routledge, 1997) 117–44.
19. Rafael Frankel et al., *Settlement Dynamic and Regional Diversity in Ancient Upper Galilee,* Israel Antiquities Authority Reports 14 (Jerusalem: Israel Antiquities Authority, 2001) 110–14.
20. Gerd Theissen, *The Gospels in Context: Social and Political History in the Synoptic Tradition,* trans. Linda M. Maloney (Edinburgh: T. & T. Clark, 1992) 61–80.
21. Elaine Mary Wainwright, *Shall We Look for Another? A Feminist Rereading of the Matthean Jesus* (Maryknoll, N.Y.: Orbis, 1998) 84–100.
22. Tomas Schmeller, "Jesus im Umland Galiläas: zu den Markinischen Berichten zum Aufenthalt Jesu in den Gebieten von Tyros, Caesarea Philipppi und der Dekapolis," *Biblische Zeitschrift* 38 (1994) 44–66.
23. Daniel Marguerat, "Jésus le juif selon la troisième Quête du Jésus de l'histoire" (paper presented at the conference, La recerca del Jesús historic, Barcelona, May 15–17, 2008) 5–7 (forthcoming 2009).
24. Denis Edwards, *Jesus the Wisdom of God: An Ecological Theology (*Maryknoll, N.Y.: Orbis, 1995).
25. Leo G. Perdue, 'The Wisdom Sayings of Jesus," *Forum* 2 (1986) 3–35.
26. Freyne, *Jesus, a Jewish Galilean* 40–48.

Jesus and the Undocumented Immigrant
A Spiritual Geography of a Crucified People

Daniel G. Groody, C.S.C.

> *The article explores the spirituality of undocumented immigrants along the U.S./Mexico border. It first examines the connection between the outer geography of the immigrant journey and the inner landscape that shapes immigrant spirituality. It then explores how this journey gives rise to the theological concept of the crucified peoples. Finally it looks at this christological concept in light of Christian mission and discipleship. As the article explores what strengthens and empowers immigrants, it also examines how the immigrant experience offers new ways of seeing some core elements of the Gospel narrative.*

MORE THAN TWELVE MILLION PEOPLE live in the United States without official authorization.[1] Each year about 500,000 individuals enter the country as undocumented immigrants. The vast majority of these are Mexican, totaling almost 60 percent of those who are irregular immigrants. Another 24 percent come from other Latin American countries, and the remaining from other parts of the world. Political controversies surrounding immigration continue unabated, but regardless of one's position, it is transforming not only the social, cultural, and economic landscape of the nation, but the theological, ecclesial, and spiritual as well.

Along the U.S./Mexico border, a few groups offer humanitarian aid to immigrants who make the grueling trek of 40 miles or more across deserts, mountains, and other dangerous terrain. One summer in Arizona, as temperatures reached 120 degrees, a group called the Samaritans sent volunteers to keep watch for any immigrants who might be in need or distress. After a group of 20 immigrants came walking along a dry river bed, a volunteer called out to them from a ledge on a hill and asked, "Is anybody injured?" "Do you need any food?" "Do you have any water?" Suddenly the group of immigrants stopped. Unsure of who was speaking to them, they huddled together and deliberated for awhile. Then slowly the leader began walking toward the Samaritan volunteers and said, "We don't have any more food. And we only have a little bit of water. But if you are in need of it, we will share what we have with you."

This story reveals as much about the inner journey of these immigrants as it does about the outer one. The inspiration for this article emerges from my years in Hispanic ministry and conversations with Mexican immigrants in the borderlands of the American Southwest. In the course of my research in the deserts, mountains, canals, and rivers of the U.S./Mexico border, and in various apostolic settings, immigrants have shared many stories about external and internal migration. Some themes of these conversations include the immigrants' reasons for leaving their homeland, the challenges of their border-crossing, their search for dignified lives, the importance of their relationships, the spirituality that sustains them, and their views of Jesus Christ.

In all these discussions, no immigrant has ever articulated in a comprehensive, systematic way the contours of their spirituality, the shape of their Christology, or their understanding of Christian mission. In many cases the theological concepts that emerge from their narratives are inchoate and embryonic, although they emerge often out of profound faith convictions. Yet not all the immigrants I talked with were necessarily deeply spiritual or close to God. Sometimes heroic tales, deep devotion, and great virtue were mixed with tales of exploitation, infidelity, and betrayal. At other times I encountered and was intrigued by the mysterious capacity to believe in God amidst many seemingly godless situations.

My own university-based social location in the United States, however, made me honestly question whether I could make enough of a "cognitive migration" into the world of the immigrant so that I could understand it from the inside. North American academic culture is powerfully shaped by rationalist, pragmatic, logical, systematic, linear, categorical, and individualistic imperatives, while the cultural world of Mexican immigrants is generally more at home with the symbolic, the literary, the lyrical, the interpersonal, the contemplative, the intuitive, and the providential. Formulating theological concepts that do justice to the christological spirituality of these immigrants is a complicated process. My aim here is not to digress into epistemological and anthropological differences, methodological controversies, or definitions about spirituality and its role in the academy.[2] Rather, I intend first to revisit some of the most powerful images and narratives that have emerged in my conversations with Mexican immigrants to the United States; second, to formulate these into a provisional, constructive account of this immigrant spirituality; and third, to consider the ways in which this particular Christian spirituality gives rise to a theological vision suited to the social challenges of our own day and age.

The Journey of the Immigrant: A Spiritual Geography

This contextualized, constructive account of the spirituality of undocumented Mexican immigrants to the United States begins with the immigrant journey itself and the land through which they travel. The physical terrain of the immigrant journey, the inner landscape of immigrants' mind and spirit, and the wells of biblical imagery from which immigrants often draw to express their hope in God, all interact in ways reminiscent of scriptural analogies in early Christian spirituality. In his Homily 27 on Numbers, about the emigration of Israel out of Egypt, Origen sees a parallel between the names of the places along Israel's sojourn and the stages of the spiritual journey.[3] The third century Christian theologian offers an allegorical interpretation of Numbers and lays out spiritual parallels to the physical geography of the Exodus. He writes, "When the soul sets out from the Egypt of this life to go to the promised land, it necessarily goes by certain roads and . . . observes certain stages that were made ready with the Father from the beginning."[4] Origen goes on to explain how the biblical geography reveals a spiritual geography, asserting that what is chronicled on the surface as a physical journey is in fact an archetypical elaboration of the soul's journey to God. I want to suggest, in a similar way, that the topography and geography of the U.S./Mexico border has many parallels to the spiritual journey of the immigrant.[5] In their arduous journey across a deadly border, which takes many of them through vast stretches of Latin America, Native America, and North America, immigrants speak spontaneously of a spirituality of sacrifice, a spirituality of the desert, and a spirituality of the cross.

Altar, Mexico, and the Land of Latin America: A Spirituality of Sacrifice

The cultural landscape and social fabric of Mexico, with its roots in Mesoamerica, is shaped in large part by notions of the heart and of sacrifice.[6] For many undocumented immigrants from Latin America, a popular road to the United States begins at a staging area in Mexico about 60 miles south of the border at the town of Altar, Sonora. The name "Altar," which is spelled identically in Spanish and English, symbolizes in part the physical and emotional costs paid by many immigrants for people they love. It marks the beginning of a dangerous and difficult road on which they offer their lives for the hope of a better future for themselves and their families.

At the center of the town plaza in Altar is the Church of Our Lady of Guadalupe where, before they depart, many immigrants participate in a Eucharistic celebration and pray for help, guidance, and safety. Few of them would know the work of French anthropologist and Jesuit theologian Pierre Teilhard de Chardin, but his words, spoken in the Ordos Desert of China while celebrating "The Mass On the World," fuse the universal struggle for work and faith in Jesus Christ in a powerful Eucharistic metaphor that captures much of the christological essence of the immigrant narratives that follow. Chardin, who believed that all work, all striving, and all human effort is related to the consummation of all things in Jesus Christ, writes, "I . . . will make the whole world my altar and on it will offer you all the labors and sufferings of the world."[7]

Immigrants walk or ride the sixty miles from Altar, Mexico to the U.S./Mexico border, which in some areas is marked by a dilapidated, barbed wire fence but increasingly is sealed off by an imposing, 15-foot wall. Then shouldering 24 to 32 pounds of water and as many provisions as they can carry, the immigrants begin an arduous trek on foot across 40 miles or more of rugged and unforgiving terrain. They migrate toward a "promised land," but it is a perilous journey.[8] The parallels of the immigrant narrative to the Exodus story are striking (Exod 13:17–17:7). The conditions of economic oppression, the burdensome yoke of poverty, and the hope of freedom lead migrants to wander through deserts or cross over bodies of water to evade border guards, and to struggle to believe that they are moving toward a better future. Some will run out of food and eat from the feeding troughs of desert livestock. Others will run out of water and drink their own urine. Every day at least one will die in the desert, drown in the canals, or freeze to death in the mountains. Even by conservative estimates, thousands of immigrants have died crossing this border since 1993, when more restrictive policies were put into place.[9]

"When we started the journey," said Mario, "the first thing we did was make the sign of the cross. We asked for protection from the snakes and from other dangers."[10] Immigrants like Mario are acutely aware that the price of providing for their families means leaving home, and the cost of living from the heart may entail the sacrifice of their own lives. "We abandon everything," said Gustavo, "our families, our children, and our people. I'm [migrating] more than anything for them."[11] It is a sacrifice often mixed with guilt. For all their good intentions, there is often the underlying regret in not being there to see children grow up, not being able to return home for a funeral, not being there for one's spouse. Their spirituality is first and foremost about relationships and providing for others, sometimes through their presence but often in their absence.

The physical and emotional demands of migrating are a difficult part of the journey, but they are only part of the sacrifice. Their long-term sacrifice is their labor, and the spirituality of the undocumented immigrant is grounded on work. "Nobody comes to the States for sightseeing or to get rich," said a 15-year-old immigrant named Mario. "I'm thirsty out here in the desert, but I'm even more thirsty to find work. My family is very poor, and they depend on me. We have nothing to eat, really just beans and tortillas, and I am anxious to respond to their needs."[12]

Immigrants face many obstacles in their journey northward, one of which is the physical barriers. A 700-mile fence symbolizes a nation's inhospitality toward them, and, like Lazarus at the rich man's gate (Lk 16:19-31), they will take any scrap of employment offered them, even though it is difficult, dangerous, and demanding (thus often called "3D jobs"). More than one immigrant per day will also die in the workplace—cutting North Carolina tobacco, processing Nebraska beef, chopping down trees in Colorado, welding a balcony in Florida, trimming grass at a Las Vegas golf course, or falling from scaffolding in Georgia.[13]

Immigrants go to these great lengths to offer themselves, but, even so, many find their sacrifice shunned. "We don't understand why Americans treat us this way," said Enrique. "Even though Americans treat us like oxen, all we want to do is work here legally.... Even though we want to work for them, they won't let us. We cross over the border, but they make us out to be criminals. It's like being poor is a crime."[14]

Tohono O'odham and the Land of Native America:
A Spirituality of the Desert

After leaving the town of Altar, many immigrants cross through the Tohono O'odham Indian reservation. It is a Native American territory about the size of Connecticut that spans both sides of the U.S./Mexico border, and for many years people circulated freely and crossed the border in this area without restriction. Tohono O'odham means "people of the desert"[15] in the language of the indigenous people who bear that name; it is a territory that names and symbolizes much of what they experience.

The desert is a physical place with spiritual significance. No immigrant said they went out into this territory to get a deeper understanding of the mystical writings of St. Antony or any of the desert fathers or mothers,[16] yet, like the ancient monks, immigrants discover that the desert is a place that often strips them of illusions about life, opens a place for purification, and helps them realize central truths about who they are before God. The spirituality of these migrants is shaped by the earth, by the elements, and by this arid terrain. Like the geography of desert trails, this dry, spiritual territory is often diffuse and capillary, sometimes fragmentary and difficult to follow. Some say the desert teaches them how to suffer. Others say it makes them come to terms with their vulnerability. Most speak about how the desert helps them appreciate their relationships, sometimes after having taken them for granted. This desert becomes their arena of struggle, a barren territory seemingly bereft of life, except that which threatens it, like snakes, scorpions, and other wild animals and desert reptiles.

Some immigrants say the desert gives them a heightened sense of the struggle between good and evil. With temperatures sometimes exceeding 120 degrees in the shade, some refer to this territory as the "devil's highway."[17] Others say the desert brought out their worst side, put them in touch with their own inner darkness, or brought them face to face with temptation. After a grueling journey, Caesar collapsed on the road and came within hours of dying when the Border Patrol rescued him. From his hospital bed he said:

> When I was in the desert, I thought about Jesus' temptation. It was like God was testing me in some way.... For me the temptation was to not trust God, to give up, to admit defeat, to allow myself to die in the desert. But I couldn't do it. Christ went into the desert for our sakes, not his. I felt God was calling me to fight, to keep going, to suffer for my family. I did not want to let myself be conquered by death least of all. At times I wanted to just stay there in the desert and die, but then I would think about my wife and my family who need me.... I just kept thinking of them, and this is what gave me strength.[18]

Manuel had a related experience. Four days after he began his journey he was lost, standing on a roadside, and waving an empty water jug in the air. Although he started with six friends, they left him behind when he could not keep up. He said, "I was scared. I got lost and then sick, and I wondered if I would ever make it out alive." In the midst of his weakness and vulnerability he also became more aware of the presence of God. When I asked him what he learned in the desert, he said, "I simply prayed. After my friends left me and I was out there all alone, I learned that all I have is God, and he is the one friend who will never leave me."[19]

Crucifixion Thorn, U.S.A., and the Land of North America: A Spirituality of the Cross

In the course of my research in the desert, the Border Patrol allowed me into one of their surveillance facilities and showed me the cameras and other technology used to monitor the border. When looking at a wide panorama of television screens, the agents zoomed in on one region and said, "Yesterday in this spot we found three immigrants who died after crossing the border." When I asked the name of the area, an agent replied, "It's called Crucifixion Thorn. It's a nature preserve that has a rare, spiny plant, like the one used to crown Jesus' head."[20] He was simply recounting a basic geographical fact, without any apparent awareness of the theological ramifications of this statement.

Many immigrants speak about Jesus as their refuge and the one who is not afraid to accompany them as they struggle to move forward.

They speak about how Jesus, like many of them, faced misunderstanding, rejection, ridicule, insults, temptation, and even death. He becomes a source of hope not only as they make the demanding journey across a deadly border but also as they establish their lives in a new land and endure the many abuses and indignities that diminish their humanity. What sticks, and pricks, and cuts, and wounds the deepest are the insults and humiliations, the fear that they are no one to anyone, that they are no more than dogs to other people. "We just want to be human, and they treat us like we are animals," said Maria, who crossed over with a group of 40 people. "Or worse—insects!"[21]

"When we moved a little farther north from the border, we thought we were OK," said Juan, one of Maria's traveling companions, "but then the helicopter came."[22] "They started shining its spotlight on us, and I just stood there . . . frightened," added Mario. "They started playing the song *La Cucaracha* [over the helicopter intercom]. We were terribly insulted," he continued.[23] "We felt worse than cockroaches . . . like we were truly being stepped on . . . ," said Margarita.[24] "I fell down again, and they kicked me twice or three times. I thought I wanted to die," Maria added. "No, dear God," she prayed, "I've gone through so much sacrifice to come this far. . . . I just asked God that we would be OK, that they wouldn't hurt us even more, that they wouldn't send us back where we came from."[25]

Setbacks and difficulties are frequent, but the goal of the immigrant is clear. Theirs is a journey marked often by surrender to God as they sojourn into unknown, unmarked, and unwelcoming territory: "All I can do is put myself in the hands of God and trust he will light my path," said Carlos. "I do not know where I am going, or what is ahead of me, but I have to take the risks because our needs are great."[26]

Amid the dangers that threaten their lives, some immigrants rediscover that life is not a possession or accomplishment but a gift, lent to them (*prestado*) by a benevolent God. Immigrants have few illusions of self-sufficiency. Aware they could lose everything in a moment, some come to an increasing awareness that all they have comes from God. For some this realization gives birth to a spirituality of gratitude, which is most remarkable, given the painful dimensions of their social location. "I have come to see that one of the greatest miracles is simply that I am alive, that I exist at all," said Ricardo. "Through this whole process [of migrating], I've come to see just how beautiful life is."[27]

Immigrants as "Crucified Peoples" of Contemporary Society

In the spirituality of the immigrants, Altar, Tohono O'odham, and Crucifixion Thorn are geographical stations on a dangerous and costly journey of sacrifice, asceticism, and the cross. These categories give us an initial description of their inner journey, but further analysis is needed in order to develop a theological interpretation of this reality. The risk of interpretation, as David Tracy notes, must be faced in trying to offer a constructive account of the rich christological images that arise from the experience of these immigrants.[28] But how and where do we begin? My argument is this: the spirituality that sustains Mario, Maria, Cesar, Magarita, Manuel, Gustavo, and countless other Mexican immigrants takes us beyond the anecdotal accounts of a particular group who cross the border, because their experience names something that is more universal in scope. In recent interviews with immigrants and refugees at the borders of Slovakia/Ukraine, Malta/Libya and Morocco/Spain, I have found similar stories that resonate with these themes.

Robert Lassalle-Klein gives us a possible clue to a more universal approach in pointing to "the crucified peoples" and "the mestizo Jesus" as two of the most promising images for formulating a "Christology grounded in the needs of a global church."[29] Noting that "Euro-American Christology has barely registered, much less accepted" these images, he explains how the "luminescent faith, hope, and communal solidarity" they embody "have helped desperate communities to survive in the face of overwhelming odds" at the dawn of the new millennium.[30] While the mestizo Jesus is certainly relevant to any discussion of Mexican immigrant spirituality (and is explored elsewhere in this issue),[31] I will limit myself here to a discussion of the "crucified peoples." In what follows I will argue that this image, which Lassalle-Klein correctly asserts has found broad resonance with global Christians interested in the "option for the poor,"[32] is a suitable theological metaphor for speaking about the arduous journey of undocumented Mexican immigrants through Altar, Tohono O'odham, and Crucifixion Thorn.[33]

Lassalle-Klein explains that this christological image was formulated in 1978 by Ignacio Ellacuría, extrapolating on a famous homily by Archbishop Oscar Romero of El Salvador.[34] Ellacuría understands the crucified people as "that vast portion of humankind, which is actually and literally crucified by natural . . . historical and personal oppressions."[35] Contextualizing Ellacuría's approach, Lassalle-Klein explains elsewhere that this Spanish Jesuit, who studied under Karl Rahner at Innsbruck from 1958 to 1962, just before Vatican II, "frames his entire theological project as a 'theology of sign,' his own development of Rahner's 'theology of symbol.'"[36] He adds that "the emphasis has been shifted from 'symbol' to 'sign,' in part, to cohere with the Council's mandate to 'the Church . . . of reading the signs of the times and of interpreting them in light of the Gospel (*Gaudium et spes* 4).'"[37]

Building on this fundamental theology of sign, Ellacuría makes the remarkable assertion that the crucified peoples can be seen as the defining "sign of the times," which perennially embodies the tragic consequences of sin, and the rejection of God's self offer in human history. He writes:

> Among so many signs always being given, some identified and others hardly perceptible, there is in every age one that is primary, in whose light we should discern and interpret all the rest. This perennial sign is the historically crucified people, who link their permanence to the ever distinct form of their crucifixion. This crucified people represents the historical continuation of the servant of Yahweh, who is forever being stripped of his human features by the sin of the world, who is forever being despoiled of everything by the powerful of this world, who is forever being robbed of life, especially of life.[38]

The key idea here for our purposes is that crucifixion is not limited to biblical times, and that crucifixion can serve as a suitable metaphor, or historical sign, for the unjust human suffering in all generations. Further, the crucified peoples of the world have been at the heart of the church's mission and the gospel message since Jesus first proclaimed the reign of God.

In this connection, Lassalle-Klein explains that Jon Sobrino appropriates the image or sign of the crucified people as the centerpiece of his two-volume Christology, following what he calls, "the fundamental methodological choice running right through Latin American Christology: to go back to Jesus in order to rethink all theological realities in terms of him."[39] Working carefully through the two volumes, Lassalle-Klein shows how Sobrino wants to "draw a fundamental analogy"[40] between, on the one hand, today's crucified peoples' struggle to believe and to survive amidst poverty, inequality, structural injustice, and violence, and, on the other hand, the life, death, and resurrection of Jesus Christ. Lasalle-Klein explains that Sobrino elevates this image or sign from popular religiosity to the level of a formal theological concept: "The term *crucified peoples* is also useful and necessary language in Christology."[41] Sobrino argues, "The *crucified peoples* are those who fill up in their flesh what is lacking in Christ's passion, as Paul says about himself. They are the actual presence of the crucified Christ in history." Citing the aforementioned words of Archbishop Romero to the terrorized survivors of the 1977 Aguilares massacre—"You are the image of the pierced savior"—Sobrino continues, "These words are not rhetorical, but strictly Christological. They mean that in this crucified people Christ acquires a body in history and that the crucified people embody Christ in history as crucified."[42]

Lassalle-Klein reminds us that Sobrino's language is analogical, grounded in Ellacuría's theology of sign; this allows Sobrino to argue that when followers of Jesus witness the crucifixion of the innocent, this encounter functions as a real sign drawing us into the reality of the paschal mystery ("Truly, I say to you, as you did it to one of the least of my brethren, you did it to me" [Mt 25:40]). Sobrino then concludes that "when followers of Jesus take the crucified people down from their cross, they become a living sign for the universal church of both the coming of the Kingdom of God and the resurrection of the crucified Jesus from the dead."[43] Sobrino insists that it is not that we are literally "repeating God's action," or "bringing the Kingdom of God," but rather "giving signs—analogously—of the resurrection and the coming of the Kingdom."[44] Emphasizing the connection to Ellacuría's theology of sign, he concludes, "This is what Ignacio Ellacuría meant when he ... used the expression 'taking the crucified people down from the cross' as a formulation of the Christian mission."[45] Building on this theology of sign, then, I would argue that migration must certainly be considered a complementary sign of the times. In some ways, immigration can be considered a more specific historical manifestation or sign of the crucified people in the ways it so often robs them of their human dignity, if not their very lives.

The reality of the journey of the immigrant today can be interpreted precisely as a way of the cross. In the process of leaving Mexico, crossing the border, and entering the United States, undocumented Mexican immigrants experience nothing short of a walk across a border of death. Even when they do not die physically, they undergo a death culturally, psychologically, socially, and emotionally. Their journey involves an economic sentencing, whereby they have to shoulder the difficult responsibilities of leaving family, home, and culture for an unknown future in the United States and the search for a job with meager wages. The Mexican immigrant experiences an agonizing movement from belonging to nonbelonging, from relational connectedness to family separation, from being to nonbeing, from life to death. Economically, undocumented Mexican immigrants experience a movement from poverty in Mexico to poverty and exploitation in the United States. Politically, they experience oppression. Legally, they are accused of trespassing. Socially, they feel marginalized. Psychologically, they undergo intense loneliness. And spiritually, they experience the agony of separation and displacement.[46] The suffering of the immigrant points not only to the reality of their personal struggles, but also to the socioeconomic conditions that contribute to this suffering.

As Gioacchino Campese observes: "Immigrants are dying by the thousands in the dangerous deserts of Arizona, but, most importantly, they are being 'crucified.' This was the fate of Jesus of Nazareth." [47] The undocumented immigrants who cross the border also can be legitimately portrayed as a historical incarnation of Christ crucified today. They are crucified not only in their trek across the border, but in the jobs they must take, which César Chávez likewise compared to a crucifixion:

> Every time I see lettuce, that's the first thing I think of, some human being had to thin it. And it's just like being nailed to a cross . . . [Like working with sugar beets,] that was work for an animal, not a man. Stooping and digging all day, and the beets are heavy—oh, that's brutal work. And then go home to some little place, with all those kids, and hot and dirty—that is how a man is crucified.[48]

The notion of the crucified peoples, then, is analogical language for speaking about the social reality of undocumented immigrants in terms of Christian theology, a way to conceptualize what immigrants are experiencing in the contemporary world. The immigrant poor see their own story in the Jesus story, and from their story we can also reread the Jesus story. Even if they do not always see themselves as a crucified people, for many, their human and spiritual journey gives rise to a relationship with the historical Jesus that is laden with theological meaning, and their struggles and difficulties can be understood as a way of participating in the paschal mystery.[49]

Moreover, what is crucial to my discussion here is that the identification with the historical Jesus that defines this spirituality, and the image of the crucified people that forms the basis for the christological concepts I have discussed above, not only describe and interpret the afflicted reality of the undocumented Mexican immigrant but also confront it. In the present case, the injustice related to such crucifixion necessitates challenging the disordered reality and policies that result in the death of so many innocent people. Lassalle-Klein insists on the importance of Sobrino's "insight that the crucified people functions for many Salvadorans as the root metaphor of a truly Christological theodicy."[50] So too, the Mexican immigrants I have considered here see in Jesus that God has taken on their human weakness, journeys with them in their anguish and distress, and even enters into the depths of hell to strengthen them as they move forward.

Christian Mission: Taking the
Crucified People Down from the Cross

The claim that the undocumented Mexican immigrants travelling through Altar, Tohono O'odham, and Crucifixion Thorn belong to the crucified peoples of this world gives rise to a challenging understanding of Christian mission and discipleship. Building on a deeply incarnational and trinitarian view of the world, Sobrino asserts, "To do theology means, in part, to face reality and raise it to a theological concept," and that, to carry out this task, "theology should be honest with the real."[51]

Expanding on Ellacuría's "noetic," "ethical," and "praxis-oriented" acts by which intelligence comes to terms with reality,[52] Sobrino elaborates four precise steps for apprehending and confronting historical reality. The follower of Jesus, the theologian, or anyone who wishes to deal with the historical reality of the risen Jesus today must therefore: (1) *hacerse cargo de la realidad*: immerse oneself in the midst of the presence of the risen Jesus in the historical reality of his followers today, and not just try to understand it cognitively from a distance; (2) *cargar con la realidad*: take responsibility for the ongoing crucifixion of Christ in his followers by taking the crucified people down from the cross; (3) *encargarse de la realidad*: help make real changes and achieve real transformations in the structures of historical reality that ensure the ongoing crucifixion of the risen Jesus in his followers today; and (4) *dejarse cargar por la realidad*: allow oneself to be carried along by the grace and hope at work in the lives of both the crucified peoples and those trying to take them down from their cross.[53]

Put another way, the idea that the undocumented immigrants dying in the deserts are part of the crucified people implies that, unless we act to alleviate their suffering, we are like those who stood by and watched Jesus die on the cross. At the heart of the gospel message is the conviction that the crucified Jesus has been raised from the dead by his Father and has breathed on us the Holy Spirit, who lives in us and unites us as sisters and brothers under one Father. This is the root of Sobrino's claim that we become living signs of faith in the resurrection of Jesus and the coming of the kingdom of God when we take the crucified peoples of our day down from their cross. Despite our callous lack of awareness and the pervasive character of sin in the world today, God's grace is always active, sowing seeds forgiveness, insight, and solidarity, which are ready to yield a hundredfold harvest anytime we open ourselves to God's constant self-offer mediated to us through the invitation to love our neighbor.

From the perspective of the immigrant, we have seen that interpreting their journey as a *Via de la Cruz* can be a source of strength and consolation. The resurrection of Jesus from the dead offers them hope that they will also overcome all that threatens their lives as well, even as they surrender in trust without knowing the final or even intermediate outcome of their journey. From the perspective of the inhospitable host, taking the crucified people down from the cross begins with meeting the basic needs of immigrants for food, shelter, and employment—in short, all that is necessary to live in dignity. Some organizations like Samaritans and Humane Borders in Tuscon, Arizona, which draw their inspiration from the gospel narrative, live out this mission by providing aid for immigrants who cross the deserts of the American Southwest. When aid workers speak about their mission as a call to "take death out of the immigration equation," they are demonstrating that taking the crucified peoples down from the cross is a way of working for a more just and peaceful world and proclaiming in word and deed that the kingdom of God is at hand.[54]

In addition to offering direct aid to immigrants in need, however, the same christological spirituality that animates these organizations also leads them to challenge a disordered reality that creates social structures and political policies that precipitate their migration in the first place. An unjust trading system, the continuing debt crisis, insufficient development aid, and especially flawed border policies are not ways of mixing faith with politics but rather serve as challenges that draw out the political implications of Christian commitment. Despite spending billions of dollars to control its border with Mexico, the U.S government has not actually reduced irregular migration.[55] It has simply diverted immigrant crossings to more dangerous areas like deserts and mountainous terrain, which have increased the death toll exponentially. When examined in this light, the cross of Jesus is not only a comfort to the crucified peoples but a challenge to the structures and systems that continue to regularize and legitimize such crucifixion.

Ellacuría's methodological approach to reality is particularly important when we consider that government officials still fail to take any responsibility for the immigrant deaths at the border—it sees them as "unintended" consequences of a nation's right to control its borders. The Mexican government must also become involved in this process by taking responsibility for its own failures. But the point here is that, regardless of our nationalities, we are called to immerse ourselves in the reality of these immigrants' deaths (*hacerse cargo de la realidad*), to take responsibility for this reality (*cargar con la realidad*), and to actively work to transform this reality by taking people down off the cross (*encargarse de la realidad*) by challenging those people, systems, and forces that contribute to these deaths. At the same time, if we consider migration as a sign of the times, we are left to discover how this sign can offer us new ways of understanding Jesus. Sobrino reminds us that we must allow ourselves to be carried along (*dejarse cargar por la realidad*) into new ways of living by our encounter with the grace and hope that is at work in the lives of crucified peoples and those trying to take them down from the cross.

Jaroslav Pelikan observes that it is the task of every generation to offer its own image of Jesus, much of which is shaped by the hopes and struggles of each historical epoch.[56] Given that some scholars refer to today as the "age of migration," one wonders if the notion of Jesus as the immigrant God is an appropriate icon for our age.[57] This image speaks not only to those who are physically on the move, but also all human beings who see life as a pilgrimage and a journey of hope. More palatable presentations of Jesus might emerge from social locations of comfort and affluence, but immigrants bring out one final element of the Jesus story that helps ground our recovery of the historical Jesus on the authentic tradition of *kenosis*. They see in the Jesus story a person who not only was born into marginality and forced into exile but who also ultimately surrenders everything for the sake of those he loves and appears to lose everything on the cross. The spirituality of Jesus is one of self-sacrifice, self-emptying, and self-offering for the sake of others.

Walking in hope toward an uncertain future, immigrants also relinquish everything they own, knowing that their one companion and lasting security is God and God alone. The immigrant experiences the utter vulnerability of human existence, but at the same time the cross is a sign of the fact that God has entered into the vulnerability of the human condition, even to the point of dying with them. Not limited by the borders created by society, Jesus is not ashamed to walk with those who are crucified today. He offers hope to all, especially those who are dying so that others may live, like so many immigrants today.

More theological reflection is needed on the immigrant reality today. Arguably no text in the New Testament better describes the social location and christological importance of that immigrantreality than Matthew 25:31–46. This text offers a particularly important hermeneutical perspective for Christology because of the parallels between those considered "least" (Greek *elachistōn*) in the last judgment account and the social location of undocumented immigrants today.[58] Many immigrants are people who are hungry in their homelands, thirsty in the deserts, naked after being robbed at gunpoint, sick in hospitals, imprisoned in detention centers, and, if they make it across the border, estranged in the United States.

Seen in this light, immigrants are not simply suffering people who depend on the charity of others but people who manifest in their flesh the real presence of Christ. The eschatological reversals of the gospel reveal that immigrants are not just passive recipients of the church's mission, but, in a mysterious way, active agents in the world's redemption. The face of Jesus, in whom we shall one day read our judgment, already mysteriously gazes on us, especially through the faces of those we see as the "other." It remains to be seen whether such a reality can be perceived as graced, but when we contemplate the reality of the undocumented Mexican immigrant who faces death in the desert so that others may live, we catch a glimpse of the crucified peoples whose arduous journey is a place of Christian revelation and human transformation. The eschatological horizon of the immigrant reality also leads us to consider ways in which the crucified peoples of today are integrally related to the salvation of the world and how, as Lydio Tomasi perceptively puts it, "It's not . . . the Church [that] saves the immigrant, but the immigrant who saves the Church."[59]

DANIEL G. GROODY, C.S.C., earned his Ph.D. from the Graduate Theological Union, Berkeley, Calif. He is assistant professor of theology and director of the Center for Latino Spirituality and Culture at the University of Notre Dame. In 2007 and 2008 he was a visiting research fellow at the Refugee Studies Centre at Oxford University. His recent publications indicate his special competencies: *Border of Death, Valley of Life: An Immigrant Journey of Heart and Spirit* (2002); *Globalization, Spirituality, and Justice: Navigating the Path to Peace* (2007); and edited works: *The Option for the Poor in Christian Theology* (2007); and, with coeditor Gioacchino Campese, *A Promised Land, A Perilous Journey: Theological Perspectives on Migration* (2008). He is currently working on a theology of migrants and refugees and the spirituality of immigrants at various borders around the world.

The author gratefully acknowledges the support of research grants from ATS/Lilly, the University of Notre Dame's Kellogg Institute for International Studies, and the Nanovic Institute for European Studies.

Notes

1. Depending on the counting method, the number of undocumented immigrants varies, ranging from seven million to twenty million. In this article I draw on the Pew Hispanic Center's research, which is based on the March 2005 Current Population Survey (CPS) and the monthly Current Population Surveys that run through January 2006. The Center defines the term "unauthorized migrant" (which I refer to above as "immigrants") to mean a "person who *resides* in the United States but who is *not* a U.S. citizen, has *not* been admitted for permanent residence, and is *not* in a set of specific authorized temporary statuses permitting longer-term residence and work" (emphases original). The report notes, "Two groups account for the vast majority of this population: (a) those who entered the country without valid documents, including people crossing the Southwestern border clandestinely; and (b) those who entered with valid visas but overstayed

their visas' expiration or otherwise violated the terms of their admission. Some migrants in this estimate have legal authorization to live and work in the United States on a temporary basis. These include migrants with temporary protected status (TPS) and some migrants with unresolved asylum claims. Together they may account for as much as 10% of the estimate." See Jeffrey S. Passel, "The Size and Characteristics of the Unauthorized Migrant Population in the U.S. (Washington: Pew Hispanic Center, March 7, 2006) i–ii.

2. Sandra Schneiders defines spirituality as "the experience of conscious involvement in the project of life-integration through self-transcendence toward the ultimate value one perceives." Drawing on her work, but nuancing her formulation of the topic, I define spirituality as how one lives out what one most values, and Christian spirituality as how one lives out what Jesus most valued. My method is sociotheological in nature in that it uses in-depth interviews and participant-observation approaches and then brings them into dialogue with tradition and the lived experience of Christian faith. See Sandra M. Schneiders, "The Study of Christian Spirituality: The Contours and Dynamics of a Discipline," *Christian Spirituality Bulletin* 1:1 (1998) 3–12, and "Religion vs. Spirituality: A Contemporary Conundrum," *Spiritus* 3 (2003) 163–85, emphasis added.

3. Rowan A. Greer, ed., *Origen*, (New York: Paulist, 1979) 245–69. I am grateful to Brian Barrett, who first introduced me to this connection between the physical and spiritual journey in patristic theology. For a critical overview of contemporary scholarship on Origen's exegetical method, with an emphasis on its moral and spiritual benefit for his audience, see Elizabeth Ann Dively Lauro, *The Soul and Spirit within Origen's Exegesis* (Boston: Brill, 2005). In Homily 27 on Numbers, Origen interprets the historical journey of Israel through the desert along two distinct but inseparable lines: (1) our moral growth in virtue, which begins at our conversion, and (2) our spiritual ascent to God, which culminates in the resurrection as our entry into the promised land. By applying Origen's method to a contemporary theology of migration, this article seeks not only to interrelate their spiritual journey to their physical journey but also to reframe the moral imagination with a view to human dignity, the challenge of making a cognitive migration in regard to "the other," and to highlight the core issue of human solidarity.

4. Ibid. 250.

5. A distinctive quality of patristic exegesis is that it is generally preached. The Church Fathers, particularly Origen, developed methods of interpreting Scripture precisely for the moral and spiritual benefit of their hearers. For contemporary introductions to patristic exegesis and its relevance for today, see Charles Kannengiesser, "Avenir des traditions fondatrices: La Christologie comme lâche au champ des études patristique," *Reserches de Science Religieuse* 65 (1977) 139–68; John J. O'Keefe and R. R. Reno,

Sanctified Vision: an Introduction to Early Christian Interpretation of the Bible (Baltimore: Johns Hopkins University, 2005); Robert Louis Wilken, *The Spirit of Early Christian Thought: Seeking the Face of God* (New Haven, Conn.: Yale University, 2003); Frances Young, *Biblical Exegesis and the Formation of Christian Culture* (New York: Cambridge University, 1997).

6. Daniel G. Groody, *Border of Death, Valley of Life: An Immigrant Journey of Heart and Spirit* (Lanham, Md.: Rowman & Littlefield, 2002) 115–36; Davíd Carrasco, *City of Sacrifice: The Aztec Empire and the Role of Violence in Civilization* (Boston: Beacon, 1999) 180.
7. Pierre Teilhard de Chardin, *The Heart of Matter*, trans. René Hague (New York: Harcourt Brace Jovanovich, 1979) 119–21. See also Pierre Teilhard de Chardin and Ursula King, *Pierre Teilhard de Chardin: Writings* (Maryknoll, N.Y.: Orbis, 1999) 80–81.
8. For more on this topic see Daniel G. Groody and Gioacchino Campese, eds., *A Promised Land, A Perilous Journey: Theological Perspectives on Migration* (Notre Dame, Ind.: University of Notre Dame, 2008).
9. Karl Eschbach, Jacqueline Hagan, and Nestor Rodríguez, "Deaths During Undocumented Migration: Trends and Policy Implications in the New Era of Homeland Security," *In Defense of the Alien* 26 (2003) 37–52; and United States Government Accountability Office, "GAO-06-770 Illegal Immigration: Border-Crossing Deaths Have Doubled Since 1995" (August 2006), http://www.gao.gov/new.items/d06770.pdf (accessed February 18, 2009).
10. Mario, interview by author, June 29, 2004, Altar, Sonora, Mexico. All quotations of immigrants are from the author's personal interviews in the deserts, mountains, and canals along the U.S./Mexico border, particularly in the towns of Altar and Sasabe, Sonora, Mexico, and various parts of Arizona and California. Transcripts of interviews are in the author's personal files. In some cases the names have been changed to preserve anonymity.
11. Gustavo, interview by author, June 26, 2003, Altar, Sonora, Mexico.
12. Mario, interview by author, July 14, 2003, Altar, Sonora, Mexico.
13. Immigrant deaths in the United States was the subject of an Associated Press story published March 21, 2004: http://customwire.ap.org/dynamic/stories/D/DYING_TO_WORK?SITE=LALAF&SECTION=HOME:3/21/2004. Unfortunately the link is no longer active.
14. Enrique, interview by author, June 29, 2004, Altar, Sonora, Mexico.
15. Alan J. McIntyre, *The Tohono O'Odham and Primeria Alta* (San Francisco, Calif.: Arcadia, 2008) 9.
16. Throughout the history of Judeo-Christian faith, the desert has been understood as a physical place with religious meaning. Often it is understood as a place of purification and testing, where one either succumbs to temptation or emerges victorious. The classic treatment of the desert spirituality is found in Athanasius, *Life of Antony* (New York: HarperOne, 2006). See also *The Sayings of the Desert Fathers*, trans. Benedicta Ward (Collegeville, Minn.: Cistercian, 1987); and Derwas Chitty, *The Desert a City: An Introduction to the*

Study of Egyptian and Palestinian Monasticism under the Christian Empire (Oxford: Blackwell, 1966).
17. Louis Alberto Urrea, *The Devil's Highway: A True Story* (New York: Little, Brown, 2004).
18. Cesar, interview by author, July 20, 2003, Tucson, Ariz. .
19. Manuel, interview by author, June 23, 2003, Arivaca, Ariz. .
20. Border Patrol Agent, interview by author, October 18, 2004, near Calexico, Calif.
21. Maria, interview by author, June 28, 2003 Altar, Sonora, Mexico.
22. Juan, interview by author, June 28, 2003, Altar, Sonora, Mexico.
23. Mario, interview by author, June 28, 2003, Altar, Sonora, Mexico.
24. Margarita, interview by author, June 28, 2003, Altar, Sonora, Mexico.
25. Maria, interview by author, June 28, 2003, Altar, Sonora, Mexico.
26. Carlos, interview by author, July 7, 2003, Altar, Sonora, Mexico.
27. Ricardo, interview by author, July 7, 2003, Altar, Sonora, Mexico.
28. David Tracy, *The Analogical Imagination: Christian Theology and the Culture of Pluralism* (New York: Crossroad, 1981) 103.
29. Robert Lassalle-Klein, "A Postcolonial Christ," in *Thinking of Christ: Proclamation, Explanation, Meaning*, ed. Tatha Wiley (New York: Continuum, 2003) 135–53, at 135–36.
30. Ibid.
31. Various forms of what Virgilio Elizondo has called the "mestizo Jesus" are taken up in this issue of *Theological Studies* by Elizondo, Michael Lee, Sean Freyne, and Robert Lassalle-Klein.
32. Lassalle-Klein, "A Postcolonial Christ" 142. He cites the following brief list of examples: James H. Cone, "An African-American Perspective on the Cross and Suffering," in *The Scandal of a Crucified World*, ed. Yacob Tesfai (Maryknoll, N.Y.: Orbis, 1994) 48–60; Kwesi A. Dickson, *Theology in Africa* (Maryknoll, N.Y.: Orbis, 1984) 81–98; Kosoke Koyama, "The Crucified Christ Challenges Human Power," in *Asian Faces of Jesus*, ed. R. S. Sugirtharajah (Maryknoll, N.Y.: Orbis, 1993) 149–62, at 156 ; Chung Hyun Kyung, "Who is Jesus for Asian Women?" in ibid. 223–46, at 224; Salvador T. Martinez, "Jesus Christ in Popular Piety in the Philippines," in ibid. 247–57; Elizabeth Moltmann-Wendel, "Is There a Feminist Theology of the Cross?" in *Scandal of a Crucified World* 87–98; John M. Waliggo, "African Christology in a Situation of Suffering," in *Faces of Jesus in Africa*, ed. Robert J. Schreiter (Maryknoll, N.Y.: Orbis, 1991, 1995) 164–80.
33. Jon Sobrino notes that "The crucified peoples of the Third World today are the great theological setting, the locus, in which to understand the Cross of Jesus," in Jon Sobrino, *Jesus the Liberator: A Historical-Theological View* (Maryknoll, NY: Orbis, 1999) 196. See also Ignacio Ellacuría, *Escritos Teológicos*, 2 vols., Colección latinoamericana 25–26 (San Salvador, El Salvador: UCA, 2000) 1:187–218; Jon Sobrino, "La Teología y el 'Principio Liberación,'" *Revista Latinoamericana de teología* 12 (1995) 115–40; Jon Sobrino,

Witnesses to the Kingdom: The El Salvadoran Martyrs and the Crucified Peoples (Maryknoll, N.Y.: Orbis, 2003); Michael E. Lee, "Liberation Theology's Transcendent Moment: The Work of Xavier Zubiri and Ignacio Ellacuría as Noncontrastive Discourse," *Journal of Religion* 83 (2003) 226–43; Kevin Burke and Robert Lassalle-Klein, *Love That Produces Hope: The Thought of Ignacio Ellacuría* (Collegeville, Minn.: Liturgical, 2006); Gioacchino Campese, "Cuantos Más: The Crucified Peoples at the U.S./Mexico Border," in *A Promised Land, A Perilous Journey: Theological Perspectives on Migration*, ed. Daniel G. Groody and Gioacchino Campese (Notre Dame, Ind.: University of Notre Dame, 2008) 271–98; and Groody, *Border of Death*, esp. 13–39.

34. Robert Lassalle-Klein, introduction to *Love That Produces Hope: The Thought of Ignacio Ellacuría*, xxix n. 2.
35. Ignacio Ellacuría, "The Crucified People," in *Mysterium Liberationis: Fundamental Concepts of Liberation Theology*, ed. Ignacio Ellacuría and Jon Sobrino (Maryknoll, N.Y.: Orbis, 1993) 580–604, at 580; trans. of "El pueblo crucificado, ensayo de soteriologia historica," in Ignacio Ellacuría, et. al., *Cruz y Resurreccion* (Mexico City: CTR, 1978) 49–82, at 49.
36. Robert Lassalle-Klein, "Rethinking Rahner on Grace and Symbol: New Proposals from the Americas," in *Rahner beyond Rahner: A Great Theologian Encounters the Pacific Rim*, ed. Paul G. Crowley (Lanham, Md.: Rowman & Littlefield, 2005) 87–99, at 95. Citations from Ignacio Ellacuría, *Teología política* (San Salvador: Secretariado Social Interdiocesano, 1973) esp. 9–10, 44–69; translated by John Drury as *Freedom Made Flesh: The Mission of Christ and His Church* (Maryknoll, N.Y.: Orbis, 1976) 15–18, 82–126; and Karl Rahner, "Theology of the Symbol," *Theological Investigations*, vol. 4 (Baltimore: Helicon, 1966) 221–52.
37. Lassalle-Klein, "Rethinking Rahner on Grace and Symbol" 95.
38. Ellacuría, *Escritos Teológicos* 2:133–35. The title of this article, originally published in 1980, is "Discernir el 'Signo' de los Tiempos." The English translation is from Kevin F. Burke, "The Crucified People as 'Light for the Nations': A Reflection on Ignacio Ellacuría," in *Rethinking Martyrdom*, ed. Teresa Okure, Jon Sobrino, and Felix Wilfred, *Concilium* 2003 no. 1(2003) 123–30, at 124.
39. Jon Sobrino, *Jesus the Liberator: A Historical-Theological Reading of Jesus of Nazareth* (Maryknoll, N.Y.: Orbis, 1993) 266; trans. of *Jesucristo liberador: Lectura historica-teologica de Jesus de Nazaret* (San Salvador: UCA, 1991) 443.
40. Sobrino, *Jesus the Liberator* 254–73; Jon Sobrino, *Christ the Liberator: A View from the Victims* (Maryknoll, N.Y.: Orbis, 2001) 3–8; trans. of *La fe en Jesucristo: Ensayo desde las víctimas* (Madrid: Trotta, 1999).
41. Sobrino, *Jesus the Liberator* 255; the Romero quotation is from Oscar Romero, *Voz de los sin voz* (San Salvador: UCA, 1980) 208.
42. Ibid.
43. Robert Lassalle-Klein, "A Postcolonial Christ," in *Thinking of Christ: Proclamation, Explanation, Meaning*, ed. Tatha Wiley (New York: Continuum, 2003) 143.

44. Sobrino, *Christ the Liberator* 48.
45. Ibid.
46. Daniel G. Groody, *Border of Death, Valley of Life: An Immigrant Journey of Heart and Spirit* (Lanham, Md.: Rowman & Littlefield, 2002) 32–33.
47. Gioacchino Campese, "Cuantos Más: The Crucified Peoples at the US/Mexico Border," in *A Promised Land, A Perilous Journey* 287–88.
48. Frederick John Dalton, *The Moral Vision of César Chávez* (Maryknoll, N.Y.: Orbis, 2003) 64.
49. Lassalle-Klein, "A Postcolonial Christ" 143.
50. Ibid. 142.
51. Jon Sobrino, *Witnesses to the Kingdom: The Martyrs of El Salvador and the Crucified Peoples* (Maryknoll, N.Y.: Orbis, 2003) 13.
52. Ignacio Ellacuría, "Hacia una fundamentación filosófica del método teológico Latinoamericano," *ECA Estudios Centroamericanicos* 322–323 (Agosto, Septiembre, 1975) 419; and Jon Sobrino, "Ignacio Ellacuría as a Human Being and a Christian: 'Taking the Crucified People Down from the Cross,'" in Kevin Burke and Robert Lassalle-Klein *Love That Produces Hope: Essays on the Thought of Ignacio Ellacuria* (Collegeville, Minn.: Liturgical, 2006) pp. 1-67, at 18.
53. Jon Sobrino, "La Teología y el 'Principio Liberación,'" *Revista latinoamericana de teología* 12 (Mayo–Agosto 1995) 115–40. I am indebted to Gioacchino Campese, who has helped me understanding the importance of Ellacuría's and Sobrino's thought for interpreting the immigrant reality. See Campese, "Cuantos Más" 271–98.
54. Robin Hoover, "The Story of Humane Borders," in *A Promised Land, A Perilous Journey* 160–73, at 160.
55. Douglas S. Massey, "Backfire at the Border: Why Enforcement without Legislation Cannot Stop Illegal Immigration," *Trade Policy Analysis* 29 (Washington: Cato Institute, June 13, 2005) 1; http://www.freetrade.org/node/32 (accessed February 18, 2009). An extended discussion of this research is available in Douglas S. Massey, *Beyond Smoke and Mirrors: Mexican Immigration in an Era of Economic Integration* (New York: Russell Sage Foundation, 2002).
56. Jaroslav Pelikan, *Jesus through the Ages: His Place in the History of Culture* (New Haven, Conn.: Yale University, 1999) 1–8.
57. Stephen Castles and Mark J. Miller, *The Age Of Migration: International Population Movements in the Modern World* (London: Guilford, 2003).
58. Scholars throughout history have debated the meaning of *elachistōn*. For differing accounts of Matthew 25:31–46 and its implications for ethics, see John Donahue, "The 'Parable' of the Sheep and the Goats: A Challenge to Christian Ethics," *Theological Studies* 41 (1986) 3–31.
59. Lydio F. Tomasi, "The Other Catholics" (Ph.D. diss., New York University, 1978) 301.

The Option for the Poor Arises from Faith in Christ

Gustavo Gutiérrez

Translated by Robert Lassalle-Klein
with Susan Sullivan and James Nickoloff

The author argues that the preferential option for the poor (1) constitutes a part of following Jesus that gives ultimate meaning to human existence and thus gives believers "reason to hope"; and (2) helps us see understanding faith in terms of a hermeneutics of hope, an interpretation that must be constantly enacted and reenacted throughout our lives and human history.

IN MAY OF LAST YEAR the 5th General Conference of the bishops of Latin America and the Caribbean took place in Aparecida, Brazil. The meeting explicitly and insistently situated itself in the open pastoral and theological line of thinking of the years of the Council and of the bishops' 2nd General Conference at Medellin, Colombia (1968). Aparecida makes the preferential option for the poor—which it considers "one of the characteristic features of the face of the Latin American and Caribbean Church" (*Aparecida* n.391)—the focal point of its conclusions.

The presence of this commitment at Aparecida owes much to the emphasis that Benedict XVI placed on the subject in his speech at the conference. He clearly and firmly located his remarks in the following theological context: "the preferential option for the poor is implicit in the Christological faith in the God who became poor for us, so as to enrich us with his poverty" (cf. 2 Corinthians 8:9)" (*Discourse* n.3). Its root is faith in Christ, which, Aparecida lucidly reiterates: "This commitment is born out of our faith in Jesus Christ, the God who became man" (n.392).

The vision of Christian life manifested in this statement and the placing of this commitment into practice are, in effect, the most substantial contributions from the life and theological reflection of the Church in Latin America to the universal Church. The option for the poor took its first steps in the years before Medellín, was affirmed in the period after the conference, and was invoked in the episcopal conferences of the following years and the recent teachings of Benedict XVI and Aparecida, which have provided an impact and a place that it would not have without them.

The Church's option for the poor is not limited to the assignment of pastoral workers to areas where the poor are found. This is often the case, which is good, but the option for the poor is more global and demanding. Some years ago Gregory Baum described it as "the contemporary form of discipleship"[1] In the following pages I intend to present some points with respect to this perspective, which goes to the marrow of Christian life. The option for the poor is deployed in three arenas: spirituality, theological work, and announcing the Gospel. This triple dimension gives vitality and perspective to the preferential option for the poor.

It deals with a commitment that implies leaving one's path, as the parable of the Good Samaritan teaches, and entering the world of the other, of the insignificant person, of those who do not fit into today's dominant social sectors, people, viewpoints, and ideas. It is a long and difficult, but necessary process, and a precondition for true authenticity. The priority of the other is a distinguishing mark of a gospel ethic, and nobody embodies this more clearly than the poor and the excluded. A poem by Antonio Machado speaks to us about this otherness:

> "Christ teaches: your neighbor
> you will love as yourself,
> and you will never forget that he is an other.[2]

Following Jesus

To be a Christian is to walk, moved by the Spirit, following in the footsteps of Jesus. This following, traditionally known as *la sequela Christi*, is the root and the ultimate meaning of the preferential option for the poor.

This commitment—the expression "preferential option for the poor" is recent and its content is biblical—is an essential component of discipleship. At its core is a spiritual experience of the mystery of God, that—according to Meister Eckhart—is both the "unnamable´ and the "omninamable." One must reach this point in order to understand the deeper meaning of this commitment to the absent and anonymous of history. The free and demanding love of God is expressed in the commandment of Jesus: "love one another as I have loved you" (John13:34). This implies a universal love from which no one is excluded, and at the same time a priority for the lowest of history, the oppressed, and the insignificant. Living, both universality and preference reveals the God of love, and makes present the mystery hidden for all time and now revealed: as Paul says, the proclamation of Jesus as the Christ (cf. Romans16:25-26). The preferential option for the poor points to this: finding out how to walk with Jesus the Messiah.[3]

For this reason, Puebla reminds us that "the service of the poor is the best, though not exclusive, means for following Christ" (n.1146). The lifestyles lived by many Christians undertaking different journeys in solidarity with the marginalized and insignificant of history have made us see that, in the last analysis, the eruption of the poor—their new presence on the historical scene—signifies a true eruption of God in our lives.

Saying this does not deprive the poor of the historical flesh of their suffering, or their human, social, cultural characteristics, and their cry for justice. And it is not a short sighted "spiritualization" that forgets about these human dimensions. It makes us truly see what is at stake according to the Bible in the commitment to one's neighbor. Precisely because we value and respect the density of the historical event of the eruption of the poor as such, we are in a position to treat it as a faith-based interpretation of this reality. It is worth saying that this implies understanding the option for the poor as a sign of the times, which we must scrutinize in light of the faith in order to discern the will of the God who has pitched his tent among us, according to John (John 1:14). Solidarity with the poor is a source for a spirituality of walking collectively—or communally if you prefer—toward God. This takes place in a history where the inhumane situation of the poor is being revealed in all of its cruelty, but which also allows its possibilities and hopes to be discovered.

Following Jesus is a response to the question about the meaning of human existence. It is a global vision of our own life, which also influences life's small and everyday aspects. Discipleship allows us to see our lives in relation to the will of God and gives us goals that are lived and towards which we strive through a daily relationship with the Lord, which implies relationships with other persons. Spirituality moves on the area of the practice of Christian life, of thanksgiving, prayer and an historical commitment to solidarity, especially with the poorest. Contemplation and solidarity are two sides of a spiritual practice inspired by a global sense of human existence as a source of hope and joy.

The deepest meaning of the commitment to the poor is the encounter with Christ. Echoing the passage in Mathew of the Final Judgment, Puebla invites us to recognize in the face of the poor, "the suffering features of the face of Christ, the Lord, who questions and addresses us," (n.31), a discovery that calls us to personal and ecclesial conversion. This much-abused text is, without doubt, a key to Christian spirituality, and provides us with a fundamental principle for discerning and discovering the road of fidelity to Jesus.

Archbishop Romero said in one of his homilies: "There is a criteria to know whether God is close to us or far away: all those who worry about the hungry, the naked, the poor, the disappeared, the tortured, the imprisoned and all who suffer are close to God" (February 5th, 1978). The gesture toward the other determines the proximity or distance of God, and makes us understand the why of this judgment, and the meaning of the term "spiritual" in a gospel context. "Love of God and love of neighbor have become one," says the Pope (*Deus caritas est*, n.15). The identification of Christ with the poor teaches one to see the fundamental unity of these two loves, and poses demands to his followers. The rejection of injustice and oppression it presupposes is anchored in faith in the God of Life. This commitment has been ratified by the blood of those who, as Archbishop Romero said (and this was true in his own case) died under "the sign of martyrdom." Aparecida has given a moving recognition to the testimony of these Christians: "the brave testimonies of our male and female saints, and even those who have not been canonized, who have radically lived the Gospel and have offered their lives for Christ, for the Church, and for his people" (n.98).

The option for the poor is a key part of a spirituality that refuses to be a kind of oasis, or still less, an escape or a refuge in difficult times.

At the same time it involves a walking with Jesus that, without disconnecting from reality and without distancing oneself from the rough roads tread by the poor, helps us maintain trust in the Lord and keep our serenity when the storm gets worse.

A Hermeneutics of Hope

If the following of Jesus is marked by the preferential option for the poor, so is the understanding of the faith that unfolds from these experiences and emergencies.[4] This is the second dimension of the option for the poor that that I would like to highlight.

Faith is a grace; theology is an understanding of this gift. It is a language that tries to say a word about this mysterious and ineffable reality that we believers call God. It is a *logos* about *Theos*. Faith is the ultimate source of theological reflection, giving theology its specificity and delimiting its territory. Its purpose is—or should be—to contribute to making the gospel present in human history through Christian testimony. A theology that is not nourished by treading the path in which Jesus preceded us loses its bearings. Those we call Fathers of the Church, for whom theology was spiritual theology, understood this very well.

On the other hand, neither the faith nor the reflection about how the faith is being lived in community is simply an individual task. This makes discourse on faith a labor that is related to the preaching of the gospel, a task that gives this community its reason to be. Every discourse on faith is born at a precise time and place in which it tries to respond to the historical situations and questions amidst which Christians live and proclaim the Gospel. For that reason it is tautological, strictly speaking, to say that a theology is contextual, for all theology is contextual in one way or another. It is not that some theologies are contextual and others are not. The difference, rather, is that some theologies take their context seriously and recognize it, while others do not.

To postulate with the theology of liberation and other reflections on the Christian message that arise from the world of social insignificance that discourse on faith signifies recognizing and somehow emphasizing its relationship with human history and people's everyday life—being alert to the question of poverty—presupposes an important change in the task of theology. In fact, we have long pigeonholed poverty as a social question. Today our perception is deeper and more complex.

Poverty is not limited to its economic dimension, as important as this may be. Instead it represents a situation of social insignificance which may be due to ethnic, cultural, gender, or economic reasons. Its inhumane and anti-evangelical character, as Medellin and Puebla put it, and its final outcome of early and unjust death makes it totally clear that poverty goes beyond the socio-economic sphere to become a global human problem, and therefore a challenge to living and preaching the gospel. Poverty thereby becomes a theological question, and the option for the poor makes us aware of it and provides a way to think about the issue.

Like all challenges to faith the condition of poor poses questions and makes arguments, while at the same time providing principles and categories that provoke new approaches to understanding and deepening the Christian message. It is critical to consider the counterpart and the other side of every question. Theological work consists of looking at challenges face to face, as radical as they may be, in order to identify the signs of the times residing there and to discern in them by the light of the faith new areas appearing there for interpreting and thinking about the faith and for talking about God that will speak to the people of our age.

From this perspective the preferential option of the poor plays an important role in theological reflection. Theology is faith seeking understanding, as is stated in the classic formula: *fides quaerens intellectum*. Given that faith "operates through charity" according to Paul (Galatians 5:6), theology is a reflection that tries to accompany a people in their sufferings and joys, their commitments, frustrations and hopes, both in becoming aware of the social universe in which they live and in their determination better understand their own cultural tradition. A theological language that does not take unjust suffering into account, and does not loudly proclaim the rights of each and every person to be happy, does not acquire depth and betrays the God of whom it speaks, the God precisely of the beatitudes.

In the end, all theology is a hermeneutics of hope, an understanding of the reasons we have to hope. Hope is, in the first place, a gift from God. Accepting that gift opens us to the future and to the trust of a follower Jesus. Seeing theological work as an understanding of hope makes it more demanding when it begins with the situation of the poor and solidarity with the poor. It is not an easy hope. But as fragile as it may seem, it is capable of planting roots in the world of social insignificance, in the world of the poor, and of breaking out and remaining creative and alive even in the midst of difficult situations. Nonetheless, hoping is not waiting, for it must carry the burden of actively building reasons for hope.

Paul Ricoeur says that theology is born at the intersection of "an experiential space" and "a horizon of hope." It is a space where Jesus invites us to follow him in the experience of the encounter with the other, especially with smallest of his brothers and sisters, and in the hope that this encounter which is open to every person, believer or not, will place us in the horizon of service to the other and communion with the Lord.

A Prophetic Announcement of the Good News

The preferential option for the poor is also an essential component of the prophetic announcement of the Gospel, which includes the connection between the gratuitous love of God and justice. Working so that the excluded might become agents of their own destiny is an important part of this.

It is not possible to enter into the world of the poor who live in an inhumane situation of exclusion without becoming aware of the liberating and humanizing aspect of the Good News. For that very reason it is a standard bearer of the cry for justice, such as the equality of all human beings. This is a core theme in the prophetic tradition of the first testament, which we meet again in the middle of the Sermon on the Mount as a command summarizing and giving meaning to the life of the believer: "seek first the kingdom of God and his righteousness" (Matthew 6:33).

The heart of the message of Jesus is the announcement of the love of God that is expressed in the proclamation of his kingdom. The kingdom is the final meaning of history, its total fulfillment takes place beyond history, and at the same time, it is present from this moment on. The Gospels speak to us precisely of its closeness to us today. This double dimension to which the parables of the kingdom point is expressed in the classic formula of the "already, but not yet," already present, but not yet fully so. For this reason the kingdom of God manifests itself as a gift, a grace, and also as a task, a responsibility.

The life of the disciple of Jesus is situated in the arena of the sometimes tense but always fertile relationship between free gift and historical commitment, and therefore includes talk about the God of the kingdom, which we accept in faith. The passage from the beatitudes of Matthew contains a promise of the kingdom to all those who upon accepting the free gift that is offered to them in their daily lives become Jesus' disciples. The kingdom is considered in a multitude of ways in the Gospels through expressions and images of great Biblical richness: the land, consolation, thirst, mercy, the vision of God, and family relations with the divine. The dominant theme of these terms is life, life in all its aspects. For its part, the nature of a disciple is fundamentally stated in the first and most critical blessing: the poor in spirit; the other blessings offer variations and shades of the first. Disciples are those who make the promise of the kingdom their own, placing their lives in God's hands. Their recognition of the gift of the kingdom sets them free from any other good. And it prepares them for the mission of evangelization, which is linked to "remembering the poor" (Galatians 2:10), according to the advice that Paul received in Jerusalem.

Theological thinking during the last decades has insisted upon the relationship between evangelization and the promotion of justice as seen in various texts of the magisterium: the conference of Medellín, the Roman Synod of 1971, *Evangelii Nuntiandi* by Pablo VI, and a variety of speeches by John Paul II. One can see an increasingly global and exclusive orientation toward these two aspects in these documents.

The promotion of justice is seen in a growing way as an essential part of announcing the gospel. It's not all of evangelization, though it is an aspect; but, neither is it situated on the doorstep of the proclamation of the Good News for it is not pre-evangelization as was once held. Rather, it constitutes part of the proclamation of the Kingdom, even though it does not exhaust its content. The path was long, but its current formulation clearly avoids both impoverishing divisions and possible confusions. Benedict XVI, in a text cited by the Aparecida conference stated that "evangelization has always been united to the promotion of humanity and authentic Christian liberation" (n.3, cf. Aparecida n.26).[5]

Solidarity with the poor also asserts a fundamental demand: the recognition of the full human dignity of the poor and their situation as daughters and sons of God. In fact, the conviction grows amidst the poor that, like all human beings, they have the right to take control of the reigns of their lives. This is not a theoretical proposition or a rhetorical appeal, but rather a truly difficult and costly, but obligatory lifestyle. And it is urgent, if we take into account that today in Latin America and the Caribbean the so called "sole thought" [*pensamiento unico*] idea is trying to sow skepticism with respect to the capacity of the poor to do this, in order to persuade them that the new and inescapable realities of globalization, the international economic situation, and political and military unipolarity leave room for no alternative but to accept the vision those realities set forth, and to radically change the trajectory of their own demands.

There is not a true commitment to solidarity with the poor if one just sees them as people passively waiting for help. Respecting their situation as actors in their own destiny is an indispensable condition for genuine solidarity. For that reason the goal is not to become, except in cases of extreme urgency or short duration, the "voice of the voiceless" as is sometimes said—undoubtedly with the best of intentions—but rather to make a contribution so that those who are without voice today might have it in the future. Being an agent of one's own history is for all people an expression of freedom and dignity, a beginning point, and a source of authentic human development. The historically insignificant were—and still are in large part—those who are silent in history.

For this reason it is important to note that the option for the poor is not something that should be done only by those who are not poor. The poor themselves are called to make a priority option for the insignificant and oppressed. Many do so, but it must be recognized that not all commit themselves to their sisters and brothers by race, gender, social class, or culture. The path that they must take to identify with the least of society will be different from those of people belonging to other social strata, but it is a necessary and important step toward becoming subjects of their own destiny.

But it is good to specify that the preferential option for the poor, if it aims at the promotion of justice, equally implies friendship with the poor and among poor. Without friendship there is neither authentic solidarity, nor a true sharing. In fact, it is a commitment to specific people. Aparecida says in this regard: "Only the closeness that makes us friends allows us to profoundly appreciate the values of the poor today, their legitimate desires and their own way of living the faith. The option for the poor should lead us to friendship with the poor" (n.398).

In this essay, then, I have distinguished three dimensions of the preferential option for the poor (spiritual, theological, and evangelizing) so that I might address them one by one, and be able to sketch their characteristic profile. On the other hand, it is clear that if we separate them we distort and impoverish them. They are interwoven and nourish each other; when they are treated as watertight compartments they lose their meaning and their power.

The preferential option for the poor constitutes a part of following Jesus that gives ultimate meaning to human existence, and which gives us "reason to hope" as believers (1 Peter 3:15). It helps us see the understanding of faith as a hermeneutics of hope, an interpretation that must be constantly enacted and re-enacted throughout our lives and human history, building up reasons for hope. It drives us to find the appropriate paths for prophetic proclamation of the kingdom of God; for a respectful and creative message of communion, brotherhood, and equality among all people; and for social justice.

GUSTAVO GUTIÉRREZ received his Ph.D. from the Université Catholique, Lyon, France. He holds the John Cardinal O'Hara Chair in Theology at the University of Notre Dame, where he plies his specializations in liberation theology, spirituality, and biblical foundations. Among his recent publications are: "Poverty, Migration, and the Option for the Poor," in *A Promised Land, A Perilous Journey*, ed. Daniel G. Groody and Gioacchino Campese (2008); "Memory and Prophecy," in *The Option for the Poor in Christian Theology*, ed. Daniel G. Groody (2007); and "Liberation Theology for the Twenty-First Century," in *Romero's Legacy*, ed. Pilar Hogan Closkey and John P. Hogan (2007).

Notes

1. Gregory Baum, *Essays in Critical Theology* (Kansas City, Sheed and Ward, 1994) 67.
2. Antonio Machado, "Campos de Castilla" (Proverbios y cantares XLII) in *Poesías Completas* (Espasa-Calpe, Madrid, 1979) 273.
3. The source for this position is biblical, but the immediate reference is the well known phrase of John XXIII: " . . . the church of all, and particularly the church of the poor." See John XXIII, "Radio message to all the

Christian faithful one month before the opening of the Second Vatican Ecumenical Council (September 11, 1962)."
4. A few decades ago Marie-Dominique Chenu accurately stated, "Finally, theological systems are nothing but an expression of spiritualities." See Marie-Dominique Chenu, *Le Saulchoir: Une école de theologie* (Kain-lez-Tournai, Belgium; Etiolles, France: Le Saulchoir, 1937). Spirituality is, in effect, the key unifying force of theology.
5. A little further on he says that the Church is called to be "a lawyer for justice and a defender of the poor." See Benedict XVI, "Discurso Inaugural," n.4, Aparecida n.395.

Galilee

A Critical Matrix for Marian Studies

Elizabeth A. Johnson

Historical imagination can open a powerful door helping situate Mary of Nazareth depicted in the Gospels and relate her to the quest for justice today. Galilee as a geographic region and social location is a marker of Mary's time and place that serves as shorthand for the scandal of God's preference for the lowly of the earth. To illuminate the significance of God's preference, this article traces four areas of Galilee research that impinge on Marian interpretation and underscores resulting theological ramifications.

"THE DOOR WHEREBY *one enters on* a question decides the chances of a happy or a less happy solution," observed Yves Congar, because the concepts one uses in starting out largely determine what follows.[1] For Christian faith, the life of the first century woman Miriam of Nazareth is woven into the story of salvation coming from God in Jesus through the power of the Spirit. Over time many different doors have served as portals for theological interpretation of her significance. In the first Christian centuries when docetic tendencies attempted to blot out the genuine humanity of Jesus Christ, Mary's genuine female pregnancy and birthgiving protected his identification with the human race. It was even written into the creed that he was born *of* the Virgin Mary, *ex Maria Virgine*, out of her very stuff, not *through* her, like water passing through a tube, as Gnostic opponents wished to maintain.[2] A very different door opened in the late Middle Ages when the church's juridical practice and its attendant theology divided the so-called kingdoms of justice and mercy. While the lion's share of justice went to Christ, Just Judge of sin, Mary ruled the realm of mercy. As a mother, she did not want one of her children to be lost; as Jesus' mother, she could and would intercede with him on their behalf; as at the wedding in Cana, she would succeed. The experience of divine mercy survived under the outstretched folds of her protective mantle.[3]

Theology with a Historical Imagination

In our day yet another door has opened to Marian studies, an approach through critical history. Part of a larger shift in contemporary theology, this approach ramifies out from the insight that God's self-revelation takes place in history, in specific times and places, rather than in the Platonic realm of eternal ideas. The postconciliar renewal of biblical scholarship underscored this insight, with significant impact on all areas. Consider Christology as a prime example. Critical studies of the Gospels emphasize that since these writings reflect the kerygmatic interests of the early church, they are not biographical but profoundly theological in character. At the same time, their witness to the grace and truth of God's saving love keeps a sound link to historical time and place as the locus of this gracious revelation. In addition to work on the genre, literary formation, and social contexts of the Gospels, broader literary studies of extrabiblical writings along with historical studies of the political, economic, social, and religious conditions of Roman-ruled first century Palestine have lent concreteness to Gospel depictions of the Messiah's life and ministry. As a result, interpretations of Jesus as Word and Wisdom of God have arisen that have their roots in time and place. Broadly speaking, Christology now operates with a historical imagination.

As part of this project, Galilee research has proved to be a potent tool. The very idea that Galilee is a distinct region with its own viable subculture to be investigated is itself relatively recent, much previous archeological work having centered on Jerusalem and other centers of ancient Israel.[4] Scholarly attention focused on this district in recent decades has brought to light salient concrete conditions of the immediate world in which Jesus lived and ministered. This knowledge in turn forms part of the matrix in which the salvific good news of the gospel can be construed.

In an analogous development, this scholarship spills over to limn an evocative picture of the person of Mary, embedded in this same location. Each of the canonical Gospels places her there: "After being warned in a dream, he (Joseph) went away to the district of Galilee. There he made his home in a town called Nazareth" (Mt 2:22–23); "In those days Jesus came from Nazareth of Galilee and was baptized by John in the Jordan" (Mk 1:9); "In the sixth month the angel Gabriel was sent by God to a town in Galilee called Nazareth, to a virgin engaged to a man whose name was Joseph, of the house of David. The virgin's name was Mary" (Lk 1:26–27); "On the third day there was a wedding in Cana of Galilee, and the mother of Jesus was there" (Jn 2:1). Entering through the door of Galilee allows theology of Mary to construe her as an actual historical woman in the concrete. In turn, this insight guides interpretation of her significance within the revelatory narrative of God's self-gift in history.

The trajectory of scholarship to date affords something of a surprise. While Galilee research has been largely the province of white, educated men of First World nations, its results have intersected with theologies being done by new practitioners of this ancient craft, not persons of the dominant race, class, or sex, but people in poor, marginalized communities and women the world over. From the vantage point of their distinctive experiences of struggle, these groups inevitably raise questions and see connections that eyes trained by classical forms of privilege have missed. People in Latin American *comunidades eclesiales de base*, for example, have grasped the concrete similarity of their lives with that of the Galilean Mary, a poor village woman who suffered from state violence. With this identification, they interpret her *Magnificat*, omitted from traditional Mariologies, as an anthem of fierce hope in God and countercultural resistance to oppression. "For poor women," explains Latina theologian María Pilar Aquino, "Mary is not a heavenly creature but shares their lives as a comrade and sister in struggle."[5] Indeed, in her own person as a Galilean woman she becomes a lodestone of hope for those who have been cheated of their lives.

Insofar as such theologies start out with conscious reference to their own social location which then plays a guiding role in their understanding of Christian faith and praxis, they can be called contextual theologies. Whether liberation theology done out of Latin American, southern Asian, or African communities; or theology done in black, Hispanic, or Asian communities in the United States; or theology done from the experience of women in feminist, womanist, *mujerista*

Latina, or Asian women's formats, all allow the specificity of their situation and its attendant suffering to filter the meaning of the gospel. In the light of human finitude, of course, all theology is contextual; no universal viewpoint is possible. Theologies that assume the contrary almost always emanate from positions of privilege and historically have had the effect of making poor, marginalized groups and women as a whole virtually invisible and silent in their deliberations. By contrast, contextual theologies claim their particularity precisely as an honest and humble way of reading the good news that leads to universal significance for the whole church. Their resulting construals bring the liberating intent of God's saving actions in Jesus through the Spirit unmistakably to the fore.

Galilee: both a geographic region and a social location, it serves as shorthand for the scandal of God's compassionate preference for the lowly of the earth. To illuminate its significance as a door for Marian studies, this article first presents the earthy results of four areas of Galilee research that impinge on the interpretation of Mary, and then notes the resulting theological ramifications.

Galilee Research

Archeological/Cultural Research

Forming the northern part of the ancient land of Israel, Galilee is a distinct region from Judea in the south. Its most obvious geographic features are four continuous hilly ranges that march across the land like stripes in an east-west direction. In between are broad valleys dotted with farming villages that worked the fertile soil. In John Dominic Crossan's description, the 470 square miles of Lower Galilee are "rich with grain and cereal on valley floor and with vine and olive on hillside slope."[6] At the region's eastern boundary the land sinks down into a basin that contains the Sea of Galilee, a fresh water lake flowing into the Jordan River. The lake, river, and their surrounding lands are all below sea level, creating a subtropical zone in an otherwise generally Mediterranean climate.

Since the 1980s, scientifically-conducted archeological excavations have produced an explosion of information about ancient Galilee in Roman times. This painstaking work uncovers the material culture of the place, which in turn helps scholars reimagine everyday life. Jonathan Reed, a key practitioner of this science, points out that unlike literary texts, which intentionally set out to tell a story or make a plea from a definite point of view, archeological evidence uncovers not only the intentional witness of public architecture but also many unintentional witnesses to everyday life in antiquity. "Sherds from pots and pans, hidden coins, discarded kitchen scrap ~ all afford a glimpse behind closed doors of antiquity."[7] Scholars have married this knowledge to studies of cross-cultural anthropology, economic systems, and literary, political, military, and historical sources to help reconstruct a general picture of village society.[8]

The village that interests Christian theologians most is Nazareth, a small place located on the slope of a broad ridge in southern Galilee. Though only three to four miles from the gleaming regional city of Sepphoris, it was situated off the main road that funneled most people to that administrative center. Most of the hard archeological remains point to farming as the villagers' main occupation: olive presses, wine presses, millstones for grinding grain, cisterns for holding water, holes for storage jars. These findings indicate that the inhabitants were either peasants who worked their own land, tenant farmers, or craftspersons who served the inhabitants' needs. To date, nothing that indicates wealth has been uncovered in Nazareth: no public paved roads or civic buildings, no inscriptions, no decorative frescoes or mosaics, no luxury items such as perfume bottles or even simple glass.

As in villages all over Galilee, the homes were small and clustered. Each family occupied a domestic space or "house" of one or two small rooms built of native stone held together by a mortar of mud and smaller stones. Floors were made of packed earth. The roofs were thatched, constructed of thick bundles of reeds tied over beams of wood, most likely covered with packed mud for additional protection. Instead of standing alone, three or four of these small dwellings were clustered around a courtyard open to the sky. Surrounded by an outer stone wall, they formed a secure living space. The enclosed family rooms were used for sleep and sex, giving birth and dying, and taking shelter from the elements. In the unroofed, common courtyard, inhabitants of the domestic units, most likely an extended family, shared an oven, a cistern, and a millstone, indicating that this was the kitchen where food was prepared. Domestic animals also lived here.

Alleyways or "streets" skirted the domestic enclosures. Reed notes that "none had channels for running water or sewage, which must have been tossed in the alleyways. Instead, the roads bend at the various clusters of houses, and were made of packed earth and dirt, dusty in the dry hot seasons and muddy in the short rainy seasons, but smelly throughout."[9] Living at a subsistence level, households by and large grew their own food, did their own building, and sewed their own clothes from cloth (mostly woolen) that they spun and wove. The identity of Nazareth as an agricultural hamlet of little consequence would seem to be born out in the literary record. The Hebrew Scriptures do not mention this place, nor does Josephus who names 45 villages in Galilee, nor does the Talmud which refers to 63 Galilean villages: "from Jewish literary texts, then, across almost one thousand five hundred years, nothing."[10] As Richard Horsley observes, "Judging from its somewhat out of the way location and small size, it was a village of no special importance."[11] Mary of Nazareth spent most of her life in this village and its environs.

Galilee at this time was a multilingual world. Latin was the native tongue of the Romans; Greek was the *lingua franca* of the educated, business, and ruling classes throughout the empire and had made massive inroads in Palestine; and Hebrew was the ancient language of the Bible, heard when the Torah scrolls were read and their fine points debated. In the households and villages of Galilee, the ordinary, everyday language was Aramaic, spoken, it would appear, in a distinct style. During Jesus' trial a bystander accosts Peter in the courtyard saying, "Certainly you are one of them, for your accent betrays you" (Mt 26:73). It is fair to assume that like her neighbors, Mary spoke Aramaic with a Galilean accent.[12] Her location in this village also indicates that rather than the fair-haired, blue-eyed, svelte figure of popular Western art, she, along with the people of her class and ethnic heritage, would have had Semitic features and Mediterranean coloring of skin, hair and eyes. Given her everyday life, she would also have had a strong body shaped by the routines of hard daily labor. Commenting on how the ruling classes of the Renaissance had turned the mother of Jesus into "Our Lady," a fair, gentlewoman like themselves, pioneering biblical scholar John L. McKenzie commented: "About Palestinian housewives they knew nothing. If they had, they would have found her like the maids of their palace kitchens or the peasant women of their domains."[13] Reflecting on this cultural research, poet Kathleen Norris has called on artists to produce more work that envisions Mary as a strong peasant woman, "capable of walking the hill country of Judea and giving birth in a barn."[14]

According to custom Mary entered into an arranged marriage with her husband Joseph. At some point her household consisted of her son Jesus, the ones whom the Gospels call his brothers James, Joseph, Simon and Judas, and his sisters, unnamed by the Gospels but numbering at least two (Matthew says "all his sisters" 13:56; see Mk 6:3). The Catholic Church teaches that these were Jesus's cousins. The Orthodox Church sees them as Joseph's children by a previous marriage. Protestants by and large see them as the natural children of Mary and Joseph. Even if they did not live in the immediate household but perhaps shared a courtyard, their repeated presence yoked to the mother of Jesus in the Gospels indicates a closeness of multiple children in this extended family. Given these brothers and sisters, the romanticized picture of an ideal "holy family" composed of an old man, a young woman, and one perfect child needs to be revised.

Given this Galilean location, contextual theologies' identification of Mary as a poor woman of the people gains further traction in the light of studies of Galilean economics.

Economic Research

Starting in 63 BCE the Roman empire had expanded to conquer the land of Israel. As a province within this vast empire, Galilee was technically a peasant agrarian society, meaning not only that most people worked the land but also that their productivity was extracted for the benefit of rulers without an equivalent economic recompense. In other words, the basic economic structure of this society was that of a redistributive network. "This means that taxes and rents flowed relentlessly away from the rural producers to the storehouses of cities (especially Rome), private estates, and temples."[15] According to the influential model developed by Gerhard Lenski, mature agrarian societies have basically two major classes, upper and lower, with an enormous gap between them.[16] The upper class consisted of the ruler, his administrators, and the scribes, military personnel, merchants and priests who all helped him govern. These comprised ten percent of the population. On the other side of the chasm was the peasant class, consisting mainly of the farmers and fishers who worked the land and the sea, and also artisans who served their needs. These were the great majority of the population whose energy produced what was necessary for life. Below these on the economic ladder was the unclean class, separated from the mass of peasants and artisans by circumstances of birth or occupations such as prostitution. Finally, most terribly, was the expendable class, about five to ten percent of the population. "These included a variety of types, ranging from petty criminals and outlaws to beggars and underemployed itinerant workers, and numbered all those forced to live solely by their wits or by charity."[17]

The social stratification based on wealth described in this model was not absolute, but, given the relative power of the upper classes and the relative powerlessness of the lower, downward mobility was much more frequent than upward. Lenski's observation alerts us to the dynamic at work: "One fact impresses itself on almost any observer of agrarian societies. . . . This is the fact of *marked social inequality*. Without exception, one finds pronounced differences in power, privilege, and honor associated with mature agrarian economies."[18] The mechanism that maintained this inequality was taxation. During the period of Roman occupation, Galilean villagers were triply taxed. They had to pay the traditional tithe for the Temple in Jerusalem, tribute to the Roman emperor, and a third tax to the local Jewish client-king through whom Rome ruled by proxy. These monies were skimmed off as a certain percentage of the villagers' crops, flocks, or fish hauls. In lean years, needing to borrow to pay taxes, many fell into increasing indebtedness to the wealthy. Over time villagers too easily lost their land and became truly impoverished. In this context, Jesus' proverb rings bitterly true: "I tell you that to everyone who has, it shall be given, but from the one who has not, even what he has will be taken away" (Lk 19:26).

As the wife of a village *tekton*, the Greek word used in the Gospels to designate a carpenter, stonemason, cartwright, and joiner all rolled into one, Miriam of Nazareth belonged to this peasant world and, using Lenski's model, to its lower bracket of artisans. In addition to plying their craft her family probably also cultivated some plot of land for basic foodstuffs. This might explain why many of the images in Jesus' parables are taken from farming rather than carpentry, though he was himself a *tekton* (Mk 6:3) and son of a *tekton* (Mt 13:55).[19] We need to guard against romantic images of the carpenter shop, for being an artisan in an agrarian society like that described by Lenski did not give one the same economic and social standing that being a skilled craftsman in an advanced, industrial market economy like our own bestows. Consulting an ancient "lexicon of snobbery," MacMullen found *tekton* among the slurs the literate upper classes could throw to those of plebeian origins.[20]

This family was a village family of the artisan class, no more respectable than anyone else. They belonged to the poor who had to work hard for their living. It is true, as Meier argues, that theirs "was not the grinding, degrading poverty of the day laborer or the rural slave."[21] But it would seem equally misleading to compare their economic status, as Meier does, to "a blue-collar worker in lower-middle-class America."[22] The analogy does not work insofar as structural analysis indicates there was no middle class. The family of Miriam of Nazareth lived on the underside of a two-sided system. Occupying a lower rung of the economic ladder, her situation is typical of that of countless people throughout the ages, including countless women, who experience the civic powerlessness, low social status, and lack of formal education that result from poverty.

Political Research

The poverty and hunger in Galilee acted as a spawning ground of first-century revolts against the repressive Roman occupation and taxation. Rome customarily appointed client-kings from the conquered population, rulers charged with subduing their own people. This policy of indirect rule through native aristocracies backed by Roman military might brought three generations of the Jewish Herod family to power. The first, Herod the Great, came to power in 37 BCE and ruled until his death in spring of 4 BCE, during Mary's childhood and young adulthood. Politically savvy in dealing with the Romans, Herod was a cruel tyrant at home and ruled with an iron fist. The incident recounted in Matthew's Gospel of Herod's killing all the male children under the age of two in Bethlehem, even if not strictly speaking historical, fits with the way he was remembered. His brutality was matched only by his love of luxury and the hate he engendered in the people.[23]

This King of the Jews took the already existing town of Sepphoris, four miles from Nazareth, beautified it, and fortified it as the center from which to administer the region. To the peasants in the villages the already burdensome triple tax became next to unbearable as Herod's portion was increased to pay for this and other massive building projects. The prayer Jesus taught his disciples, with its plea to "give us this day our daily bread" (Mt 6:11), had critical resonance as many cascaded from subsistence living into penury and loss of family land. People yearned for a messianic king who would do justice for the poor. Rebellion was in the air.

When Herod died, resentment exploded in revolt all over Palestine. In Galilee the insurrection was organized by a popular leader named Judas, son of the brigand-chief Ezekias, who led a large number of desperate men in a raid on the royal fortress in Sepphoris. Having seized all the weapons stored there, he armed his followers and made off with all the military and food supplies. Facing widespread uproar, the Romans responded with brutal efficiency to quash the uprising. In Jerusalem they crucified 2,000 Jewish men outside the city walls. In Galilee they recaptured Sepphoris, set fire to homes and shops, and enslaved many inhabitants. Recent excavations at Sepphoris do not as yet show evidence of total fiery destruction from this period. But the city and the surrounding villages were severely damaged to punish the rebels among their inhabitants. Horsley points out that, "in the villages around Sepphoris such as Nazareth the people would have had vivid memories both of the outburst against Herod and the Romans, and of the destruction of their villages and the enslavement of their friends and relatives. . . . The mass enslavement and destruction would have left severe scars on the social body of the Galilean village communities for generations to come."[24]

While this incident is not recorded in Scripture, the basic chronology of Jesus' life indicates that his mother would have been around 15 or 16 years old at the time, a married woman with a young child. She and her husband obviously survived the depredations of the rampaging Roman legions. But what terror did they experience, either directly or vicariously through what was done to their neighbors? How much rebuilding absorbed their energy when psychically they were at a low ebb and materially they had so little to begin with? Sad to say, the wretched wars of the late 20th and early centuries 21st centuries leave little work for the imagination. Watching village women in Vietnam, El Salvador, Bosnia, Congo, Iraq, and Darfur flee with their children from forces intent on their destruction conjures up such suffering in real time. Miriam of Nazareth was no stranger to violence and social disruption. Horsley explains, "From the Roman point of view, the slaughter of people, devastation of towns and countryside, and enslavement of able-bodied survivors after the rebellions in 4 BCE and the widespread revolt in 66 CE were all pointed attempts, finally, to terrorize the populace into submission."[25] The crucifixion of Mary's firstborn son midway between these two Jewish uprisings can be understood historically in this context as one more dose of violence meted out to control an occupied people.

Religious Research

As this picture of the cultural-economic-political world of Galilee indicates, Miriam of Nazareth was a member of the Jewish people. This is meant not only in the ethnic sense that she was born into the people who trace descent from Abraham and Sarah, but also in the religious sense. Jewish faith in God was shaped by the covenant forged at Mount Sinai, nourished by dramatic narratives of God's liberating deeds, oriented by the prophets' announcement of God's loving-kindness to the poor, and expressed in the prayers, rituals, and ethical observances of Torah. Diversity was a hallmark of Jewish religion before 70 CE, with many different interpretations of the tradition advocated by different groups. For all this documented pluralism, however, a relatively clear combination of belief and practice identified the Jews as a single religious community, recognized as such by Rome even when they became Hellenized and widely scattered in the cities of the empire.

Scholars dispute over just how Jewish the village residents of Galilee actually were. A history of warfare starting in the eighth century BCE had decimated the ten tribes of Israel that had settled in the north, leaving Galilee open to foreign inhabitants. In addition, Roman rule coupled with Herod's building projects had imported Hellenistic culture to the province. How deeply did this overlay of pagan culture run? Based on diggings in village households, Jonathan Reed argues for an indigenous Jewish population: "wherever archeologists have excavated, Jewish religious indicators permeate Galilean domestic space in the Early Roman Period."[26] He lists four archeological indicators of Jewish religious identity: numerous *miqva'ot* or baths used for ritual immersion;

stone vessels made of soft limestone rather than clay also tied to a concern for ritual purity; ossuaries indicating the Jewish burial practice of collecting and reburying a corpse's bones after the flesh has decomposed; and a diet without pork, as indicated by analysis of those human bones. The first three of these have been found in Nazareth. When this evidence from private life is coupled with the absence of pagan cultic shrines in the public setting, it seems right to conclude that the people of Galilee in the north shared the same pattern of religious belief as the Jews of Judea in the south.

One relevant structure that archaeology might be expected to turn up, but which is almost entirely missing, is the synagogue. The remains of one have been found in Gamla, a village near Capernaum, and possibly one or two more. But constructed synagogues as a whole in Galilee before 70 CE are absent (so far). Given the hypothesized Jewish character of the region, this is puzzling. It is equally curious in view of the Gospels' picture of Jesus of Nazareth preaching and healing in the synagogues of Galilee. Scholars explain that while our imagination conjures up a building when we hear the word synagogue, the original Greek term *synagōgē* actually means an assembly or a congregation of people. It is similar to the word "church," *ekklesía*, which, though it now usually denotes a building used for Christian worship, originally referred to the assembly of persons consecrated by baptism: the people are the church. Thus the synagogue in first-century Galilean villages was the local village assembly: the people were the synagogue.[27] On the Sabbath they would meet in an open space, a public square, under the trees, or in a private house to read and interpret Torah, offer prayers of praise and petition, and take care of other religious business. Since there were no priests in Galilee, these being clustered around the Jerusalem Temple to perform sacrifice, leadership was taken by villagers, most likely men but with women's contributions expected in this assembly of village people who shared a common faith.[28]

Centered on covenant with the one God, incomparable Creator of the universe who acts in history to redeem, this was the religion of Jesus, which he never repudiated, and of his own family. The immediate world that the Gospels portray and the style and content of Jesus' adult teaching, healing ministry, and personal religious behavior is saturated with Jewish belief and custom and cannot be understood apart from this religion. Turning this research on Miriam of Nazareth allows the reasonable supposition that she and her husband, like their neighbors, ran an observant household. The years of her life would be marked by the rhythm of daily prayer and conduct, weekly Sabbath observance, and, occasionally, festival pilgrimages to the Temple in Jerusalem, as ordained in the Torah.

Miriam of Nazareth lived and died as a faithful Jew. Placing her in the Christian community is not without basis insofar as the last we see of her in the New Testament, she is praying with the disciples assembled in Jerusalem after Jesus' death, awaiting the Spirit (Acts 1:14). While this community indeed developed into a religious organization separate from Judaism and can even be called the "early" church, it was in those first decades still a recognizably Jewish group. The definitive split came after the destruction of the Temple in 70 CE when rabbinic leaders tightened the borders of Jewish identity in order for the community to survive. As an Aramaic-speaking Galilean Jew, Mary's faith was not shaped by the belief and devotion to Christ characteristic of the post-Nicene church 300 years later. Rather, she was a Jewish believer who trusted in the God of Israel through whose mercy she had borne the child now seen to be the Messiah who would soon return: Miriam of Nazareth, on the cusp of the divide between two world religions.

Entering a theology of Mary through the door of Galilee offers at the outset a rather definite portrait. Occupying a lower rung of the social ladder, Miriam of Nazareth's life was lived out in an economically poor, politically oppressed, Jewish peasant culture marked by continuous exploitation and occasional publicly violent events.

Theological Significance

Catching a glimpse of the Galilean Mary is the first step through the door of contextual Marian studies. The relevance of this particular information becomes clear when theology reflects on the biblical affirmation that it is precisely to such a woman that God has done great things (Lk 1:49). Then the second step can be taken, which interprets her story as both revelatory of God and significant for the church. This two-step method entails shifting from a primarily doctrinal or devotional approach to one colored by history that draws on a picture of the historical Mary culled from the Gospels read within the matrix of her Galilean context. This shift does not mean that doctrine and liturgy have no part in interpretation, but that their symbolizing should arise from and be tethered to her concrete reality at every point.

Lest this approach be seen as a collapse of the transcendence proper to any theological interpretation, it must be reiterated that history is the locus of God's saving encounters with humanity. "The great salvific, revealing, and communicating acts of God have taken place in history," underscores Ignacio Ellacuría, even though this cannot be proved scientifically by historical research.[29] From the freeing of the Hebrew slaves in the Exodus to the life, death, and resurrection of Jesus Christ, people can point to moments and places and concrete events where the ineffable graciousness of God becomes more present, knowable, and effective than usual. The same experience of God is kept alive for later generations who relive these events in word and anamnetic ritual. This emphasis on history, coherent with the *logos* of our age, in no way ignores divine transcendence or reduces it to a merely inner-worldly reality. Rather than conceiving of divine transcendence as distance, absence, or separateness from the world, however, contextual theology understands transcendence to be the freely-given presence of God amidst historical events. Transcendence refers to the whole rich, mysterious reality of God gratuitously present and accessible, creating scandal and giving hope, in theophanies that nourish life. Here the essential mystery of divine nature is not safeguarded by placing God beyond time and space, but by recognizing God's free theopraxis of life embracing everything.

As appropriated by contextual theologies, Galilee research discloses that not just any history bears the key to divine ways in the world, but a particular concatenation of events that reveal the Creator God to be freely on the underside of history, identified as source of hope with those ground down by oppression and death. The Galilean context of Miriam of Nazareth's life provides rich material for this line of thinking.

Revelatory of God

Reflecting on the *Magnificat*, Gustavo Gutiérrez underscores at the outset the lowliness of Mary's situation, described by the term *tapeinōsis* which in other biblical usages connotes affliction and oppression. God has looked upon her suffering with a gaze of love, the canticle continues, which causes her spirit to exult for joy. But this mercy is not for herself alone. It is intended for all who suffer humiliation and hunger, even to the point of starvation. For God "has put down the mighty from their thrones and exalted the lowly . . . has filled the hungry with good things and sent the rich away empty" (Lk 1:52–53). This is the paradoxical truth proclaimed in Mary's canticle: divine holiness which freely creates and redeems the world acts by doing justice out of the same freely given, unmerited love. If we strip this song of its historical sting, Gutiérrez warns, our exegesis is fruitless, because "Mary's song tells us about the preferential love of God for the lowly and abused, and about the transformation of history that God's loving will implies."[30] At the same time, the spiritual power of her words consists in their ability to make us see that the quest for justice must be located within the dynamism of God's holy love or it loses its meaning in Christian life. Take Galilee out of this analysis, and it loses its strength.

An analogous approach to the modern Marian dogmas has been worked out by Brazilian theologians Ivone Gebara and María Clara Bingemer. The Immaculate Conception and the Assumption carry the memories of other generations, they write, and true though they be, their relevance is not immediately apparent today on a continent marked by the suffering of millions of poor people. Yet these doctrines carry a liberating impulse and can be made to work as allies in the struggle for life. For the *Immaculata* venerated on church altars is the poor Mary of Nazareth, insignificant in the social structure of her time. She embodies the confirmation of God's preference for the humblest, the littlest, the most oppressed. Similarly, the Assumption exalts the woman who gave birth in a stable, lived a life of anonymity, and stood at the foot of the cross as the mother of the condemned. "The Assumption is the glorious culmination of the mystery of God's preference for what is poor, small, and unprotected in this world," Gebara and Bingemer write; the Assumption sparks hope in the poor and those in solidarity with them "that they will share in the final victory of the incarnate God."[31] These dogmas reveal the unrepentant ways of the living God whose favor shines on those whom the worldly elite see as insignificant or indeed, do not see at all.

Similarly, for theologians of Latino/Latina communities in the United States, Mary's historical roots in poverty and oppression create a strong connection between people's devotion to her and hope for their own lives. While the plethora of Marian images and titles defies neat systematization, they are always and everywhere a symbol of grace, of God's faithful solidarity in the midst of struggle. As Miguel Díaz observes, "Whether understood as the female face of God (Rodriquez, Elizondo), a symbol of the Holy Spirit (Espín), the poetry of the trinitarian God (García), or the *mestizo* face of the divine (Goizueta), it is clear that U.S. Hispanic theologians understand Marian symbols as mediators of the life of grace, especially to and within the experience of the poor and marginalized."[32]

Women theologians the world over note that many women engaged in the struggle for equality and human rights find themselves repelled by traditional theologies of Mary, shaped as these are by patriarchal expectations. The passive, obedient, woman who stands ready to do whatever men in authority direct; the desexualized figure whose lack of experience is taken as a sign of holiness; the woman whose *sole* purpose in life is to bear a child (which is not to downplay the value of women's ability to give life); or the silent embodiment of the so-called feminine ideal of sweetness and nurture: none of these construals promotes women's flourishing in an age of expanding social roles and independent notions of the female self. None offers a firm ground for resisting male dominance with its frequently physically violent manifestations. By contrast, reading the Gospel stories of Mary's life through a Galilean lens offers a different view of this woman through whom God became a child of earth, and a concomitantly different understanding of the holy God whom she praised.[33] The village woman who proclaims the *Magnificat* stands in the long Jewish tradition of female singers, from Miriam with her tambourine to Deborah, Hannah, and Judith who sang dangerous songs of salvation. Once an analysis of patriarchy is in place, Mary's song of God's victory over those who dominate others rings with support for all women in their struggle against sexism in combination with racism, classism, heterosexism, and other demeaning injustice. "Mary's song is precious to women and other oppressed people," writes Jane Schaberg, "for its vision of their concrete freedom from systemic injustice ~ from oppression by political rulers on their 'thrones' and by the arrogant and rich."[34] As in society, so in the Catholic Church: women in whose tradition Mary has been a significant figure wrestle with the significance of this canticle for their own subordinate ecclesial position. With unassailable logic Susan Ross argues that, since in many ways the mighty still occupy the Church's thrones, the lowly still await their exaltation. Indeed, Mary's prophetic song characterizes as nothing less than *mercy* God's intervention into such a scandalous social order.³⁵

Mary preaches as a prophet of the poor and marginalized. She represents their hope, as a woman who has suffered and been vindicated. These several examples illuminate how Galilee forms a matrix for contextual theologies' interpretation of Mary's story that is revelatory of the liberating God of life.

Significant for the Church

With a firm grasp of Mary's historical circumstances, contextual theologies understand her relationship to the church today in dynamic terms: she walks with the community, accompanies us, relates to us as a fellow traveler, a *compañera*. True, the world races along today in ways she never dreamed of. But her reality as a Galilean woman creates the possibility for a deep solidarity with those who strive for life here and now. Far from being an exercise in fantasy, this connection has a solid foundation in the Christian teaching of the communion of saints, which connects people across the generations. Down through the centuries, as the Holy Spirit graces persons of every race and nation, they form together a grand company of the "friends of God and prophets" (Wis 7:27). Geographically this company encircles the globe in space. Historically, it stretches backward and forward in time to encompass those living on earth and those who have died, alive now in the embrace of God.

As a first-century Jewish woman of faith who responded full-heartedly to the Spirit, Mary is a friend of God and prophet who belongs in this company of grace. In no way does this placement among the friends of God and prophets diminish her unique historic vocation to be the mother of the Messiah or the specific grace that accompanies this vocation. It remains true, however, that a woman's maternal function does not exhaust her identity as a person before God. While honoring her unique relationship with Jesus, therefore, relating to Mary as "truly our sister" within the communion of saints refocuses her significance for he church today in terms of her whole graced life lived before God.

The question then arises of how to relate to her. Broadly speaking, two possibilities lie open.³⁶ One, more continuous with the biblical notion of the holy people of God, envisions the living and the dead forming a company of mutual companions in the one Spirit-filled community. The other, influenced by the civil system of patronage, structures this relationship according to patron-client dynamics. While at first the two interacted with each other in an ever-changing cultural context, eventually the patronage model took a commanding lead and carried the torch of the communion of saints into the medieval period and beyond.

The ground of the companionship pattern is a lively sense of the presence of the Holy Spirit in the people as a whole, shaping them into a holy people. When through a combination of personal giftedness and historical circumstance some individuals stand out, the church receives their lives with profound gratitude because of how powerfully their witness nourishes the faith of the rest. This companionship model situates the saints in heaven not *between* God and those on earth but *alongside* their sisters and brothers in Christ. The letter to the Hebrews envisions them as a great "cloud of witnesses" up in the stands of the stadium cheering on those who are still running the race (Heb 12:1). In this spirit, speaking of the company of martyrs now joined by their beloved bishop Polycarp, the church at Smyrna exclaimed, "May we too become their comrades and fellow disciples."[37] Comparing the martyrs to jars of aromatic ointment whose fragrance fills a house, Augustine eloquently preached: "Blessed be the saints in whose memory we are celebrating the day they suffered. They have left us lessons of encouragement."[38] Since they did what they did by the outpouring of the gift of God, in their company we find courage and hope in our own struggles to be faithful: "The fountain is still flowing, it hasn't dried up."[39] In this paradigm, the living and the dead form a circle of hope centered on the graciousness of the living God.

By contrast, the patronage system arises when concentrations of wealth and political power in the hands of the few, coupled with neediness of the many and lack of democratic processes, conspire to create permanent social stratifications. According to Carl Landé, whose definition reflects a wide consensus, "a patron-client relationship is a vertical dyadic alliance, i.e., an alliance between two persons of unequal status, power or resources each of whom finds it useful to have as an ally someone superior or inferior to himself."[40] The purpose of this relationship is an exchange of benefits, whether material or intangible. The Roman empire was no stranger to the structure of patronage, which formed a linchpin of its social, economic, and political organization. A mass of little pyramids of influence, each one nested in one of greater power, cascaded upward to form the warp and woof of public life, with not only individuals and families but even towns and whole regions seeking benefit by subservient alliance with personages more powerfully placed than themselves.

Given the church's inculturation into this system, it is perhaps not surprising that the patronage pattern also began to govern transactions with the realm of heaven. According to a study by G. E. M. De Ste. Croix, "by the later fourth century the term *patrocinium* [patronage] has begun to be applied to the activity of the apostles and martyrs on behalf of the faithful.... Just as the terrestrial patron is asked to use his influence with the emperor, so the celestial patron, the saint, is asked to use his influence with the Almighty."[41] Being far from the distant throne, people need more important personages to plead their cause; they need friends in high places, so to speak.

The rise of patronage left the companionship pattern largely undeveloped in the theology of the saints. The presence of this more collegial paradigm, however, can still be discerned in ancient texts and practices, where it now serves as a fruitful resource for contextual theologies. In the companionship relationship with its lively sense of mutuality, one key practice entails *remembering* those who have gone before us. This is not sentimental reminiscence that bathes the past in a rosy glow. Rather, it recalls the course, defeats, and victories of those who toiled before us in order to unlock their "lessons of encouragement." In a provocative turn of phrase, Johann Baptist Metz calls this kind of remembrance "dangerous."[42] Why dangerous? Because it interrupts both complacency and discouragement, disclosing that "something more" is possible. Remembering the saints this way creates a moral force that propels the church out of passivity into compassionate, active engagement on behalf of those in agony. This is memory with the seed of the future in it. Empowered by their memory, we become partners in hope.

One concrete example of how this pattern of veneration "works" comes from El Salvador. In the villages and cities, people recite the traditional litany of the saints, adding the names of their own martyrs for the cause of justice. To each name the people respond *Presente*, be here with us. Oscar Romero: *Presente*; Ignacio Ellacuría: *Presente*; Celina Ramos: *Presente*; young catechists, community workers, and religious leaders of the *pueblos*: *Presente*. This prayer summons the memory of these martyrs as a strong, enduring presence that commits the community to emulate their lives. The fire of each martyred life kindles a new spark in the next generation.

Within this great cloud of witnesses stands Miriam of Nazareth, a Galilean woman of faith who heard the word of God and kept it. Remembering her story releases dangerous power in the life of the church. While the precise circumstances of her life cannot be repeated, the style and spirit of her life reverberate through the centuries to propel us forward in today's different cultural contexts. In solidarity with her, we find strength to face our own encounters with the Spirit and go forward with the best of our faithful wits. This impetus receives a critical edge when we remember Mary historically as poor, female, and endangered in a violent society. Then the vital memory of this woman has the quality of "danger" insofar as it awakens courage for the struggle for the reign of God, that is, for a just and peaceful world in which poor people, women, indeed all humans and the earth, can flourish as beloved of God.

Interpreting Mary as a historical Galilean woman who kept faith with God and now abides in the communion of saints broadens Marian studies beyond the parameters of doctrinal Christology where it has long been situated. Indeed, as the mother of Jesus who is the crucified and risen Savior, Mary's meaning took shape according to developments in Christology, all the way up to the title *Theotokos*, God bearer or Mother of God. Without diminishing the importance of this pattern, glimpsing the Galilean Mary opens yet another trajectory, one that emphasizes her own faith journey in response to the Spirit of God throughout her adult life. A pneumatological Mariology understands her significance in light of the actual life she lived as a poor woman in a world awash in violence. With a bracing jolt of reality, it roots grace in the vagaries of her history rather than treating the Spirit's presence in an abstract manner.[43]

With this move, contextual theologies invite the whole church to connect with this friend of God and prophet and honor her memory with its Galilean colors, to practical and critical effect. Resisting the tendency to privatize and overspiritualize devotion to Mary, which may allow first-world Christians placidly to neglect the world's poor, and resisting romantic construals of her femininity which legitimate women's subordination in male-designed systems, such theologies of Mary work positively to illuminate the liberating God of life and the justice that is a hallmark of God's holy reign.

Conclusion

Galilee, as geographic region and social location, functions in contextual theologies not as mere historical background but as the warp and woof of the world in which the revelation of God took place. It is precisely in this cultural, economic, political, and religious setting, living out her Jewish belief as a peasant woman of the people, that Mary walked her journey of faith with enormous consequence. It is here that God poured out divine favor on a marginalized female villager, calling her to participate in the great work of redemption. It is precisely such a woman who sings with joy that the mercy of God overturns oppression in favor of the poor of the earth. Allowing the matrix of her actual world to shape theological imagination is one way to make certain that when the church remembers and honors her and theologizes about her significance, it serves the power of the God of life. Miriam of Nazareth: *Presente*.

ELIZABETH A. JOHNSON received her Ph.D. from The Catholic University of America and is Distinguished Professor of Theology at Fordham University, New York. Specializing in systematic theology, she has recently published, among other works, *Quest for the Living God: Mapping Frontiers in the Theology of God* (2007). In progress is an essay on Christology in an ecological framework.

Notes

1. Yves Congar, "My Path-findings in the Theology of Laity and Ministry," *Jurist* 32 (1972) 169–88, at 176, emphasis original.
2. Irenaeus, *Adversus Haereses* 1.7,2; cf. 3.11,3; describing the Valentinians.
3. For historical information see Hilda Graef, *Mary: A History of Doctrine and Devotion* (Westminster, Md.: Christian Classics, 1990); and Jaroslav Pelikan, *The Emergence of the Catholic Tradition: 100–600*; and Pelikan, *Reformation of Church and Dogma: 1300–1700* (Chicago: University of Chicago, 1971 and 1983).
4. See the groundbreaking work by Sean Freyne, *Galilee from Alexander the Great to Hadrian, 323 B.C.E. to 135 C.E.: A Study of Second Temple Judaism*

(Notre Dame, Ind.: University of Notre Dame, 1980), esp. chap. 3, "Galilee under the Romans" 57–97.
5. María Pilar Aquino, *Our Cry for Life: Feminist Theology from Latin America* (Maryknoll, N.Y.: Orbis, 1993) 176–77.
6. John Dominic Crossan, *The Birth of Christianity: Discovering What Happened in the Years Immediately after the Execution of Jesus* (San Francisco: HarperSanFrancisco, 1998) 219.
7. Jonathan Reed, *Archaeology and the Galilean Jesus: A Re-examination of the Evidence* (Harrisburg, Penn.: Trinity Press International, 2000) 19.
8. See Douglas Edwards and C. Thomas McCollough, eds., *Archaeology and the Galilee: Texts and Contexts in the Graeco-Roman and Byzantine Periods* (Atlanta: Scholars, 1997), esp. James Strange, "First Century Galilee from Archaeology and from Texts" 39–48. A helpful study that applies knowledge of Galilee to Jesus is Bernard Lee, *The Galilean Jewishness of Jesus* (New York: Paulist, 1988).
9. Reed, *Archaeology and the Galilean Jesus* 153.
10. John Dominic Crossan, *The Historical Jesus: The Life of a Mediterranean Jewish Peasant* (San Francisco: HarperSanFrancisco, 1991) 15.
11. Richard A. Horsley, *Archaeology, History, and Society in Galilee: The Social Context of Jesus and the Rabbis* (Harrisburg, Penn.: Trinity Press International, 1996) 110.
12. See the lucid presentation by John Meier, *A Marginal Jew: Rethinking the Historical Jesus*, 3 vols. (New York: Doubleday, 1991) 1:255–68.
13. John L. McKenzie, "The Mother of Jesus in the New Testament," in *Mary in the Churches*, ed. Hans Küng, Jürgen Moltmann, and Marcus Lefébure (New York: Seabury, 1985) 9.
14. Kathleen Norris, *Meditations on Mary* (New York: Viking Studio, 1999) 16–17.
15. Douglas Oakman, "The Countryside in Luke-Acts," in *The Social World of Luke-Acts: Models for Interpretation*, ed. Jerome Neyrey (Peabody, Mass.: Hendrickson, 1991) 156.
16. Gerhard Lenski, *Power and Privilege: A Theory of Social Stratification* (New York: McGraw Hill, 1966). John Kautsky's idea of a commercializing agrarian society (see his *The Politics of Aristocratic Empires* [Chapel Hill: University of North Carolina, 1982]) has nuanced Lenski's view of traditional agrarian society. The Lenski-Kautsky model now appears in numerous studies of Galilee. See also Sean Freyne, "Herodian Economics in Galilee: Searching for a Suitable Model," in his *Galilee and Gospel: Collected Essays* (Tübingen: Mohr Siebeck, 2000) 86–113.
17. Lenski, *Power and Privilege* 281.
18. Ibid. 210, emphasis original.
19. See illuminating description of this work by Meier, *A Marginal Jew* 278–85.
20. Ramsay MacMullen, *Roman Social Relations, 50 B.C. to A.D. 384* (New Haven, Conn.: Yale University, 1974) 107–8.

21. Meier, *A Marginal Jew* 1:282.
22. Ibid.
23. It took Herod three years to quash popular resistance to his reign, especially in Galilee where people already knew of his brutality. See Peter Richardson, *Herod, King of the Jews and Friend of the Romans* (Columbia: University of South Carolina, 1996).
24. Horsley, *Archaeology, History, and Society* 32, 112.
25. Richard A. Horsley, *Galilee: History, Politics, People* (Valley Forge, Penn.: Trinity Press International, 1995) 123.
26. Reed, *Archaeology and the Galilean Jesus* 53; Freyne renders a similar judgment; see *Galilee from Alexander the Great to Hadrian* 112–31.
27. While the "synagogue" is mentioned in texts about Galilee from Jesus' period, archeologists have uncovered almost no synagogal structures. The much-visited one in Capernaum dates from the fifth century CE. See Horsley, *Archaeology, History, and Society* 131–53; and Reed, *Archaeology and the Galilean Jesus* 154–57.
28. Horsley, *Archaeology, History, and Society* 131–53; see also Horsley, "Synagogues: The Village Assemblies," in his *Galilee* 222–37.
29. Ignacio Ellacuría, "The Historicity of Christian Salvation," in *Mysterium Liberationis: Fundamental Concepts of Liberation Theology*, ed. Ignacio Ellacuría and Jon Sobrino (Maryknoll, N.Y.: Orbis, 1993) 251.
30. Gustavo Gutiérrez, *The God of Life* (Maryknoll, N.Y: Orbis, 1991) 185.
31. Ivone Gebara and María Clara Bingemer, *Mary, Mother of God, Mother of the Poor* (Maryknoll, N.Y: Orbis, 1989) 120–21.
32. Miguel Díaz, *On Being Human: U.S. Hispanic and Rahnerian Perspectives* (Maryknoll, N.Y: Orbis, 2001) 125.
33. For an overview, see Anne M. Clifford, *Introducing Feminist Theology* (Maryknoll, N.Y.: Orbis, 2001), chap. 5. Also Chung Hyun Kyung, *Struggle to Be the Sun Again: Introducing Asian Women's Theology* (Maryknoll, N.Y.: Orbis, 1994), chap. 5; and Sally Cuneen, *In Search of Mary: The Woman and the Symbol* (New York: Ballantine, 1996).
34. Jane Schaberg, "Luke," in *Women's Bible Commentary*, ed. Carol Newsom and Sharon Ringe (Louisville, Westminster John Knox, 1998) 373.
35. Susan A. Ross, "He Has Pulled Down the Mighty from Their Thrones and Has Exalted the Lowly," in *That They Might Live: Power, Empowerment, and Leadership in the Church*, ed. Michael Downey (New York: Crossroad, 1991) 145.
36. For full discussion, see Elizabeth A. Johnson, *Friends of God and Prophets: A Feminist Theological Reading of the Communion of Saints* (New York: Continuum, 1998).
37. "The Martyrdom of Polycarp" 17, in *The Acts of the Christian Martyrs*, ed. Herbert Musurillo (Oxford: Oxford University, 1954) 17.
38. Augustine, Sermon 273.2, *Sermons*, 10 vols., trans. Edmund Hill (Hyde Park, N.Y.: New City, 1990–1995) 8:17.

39. Augustine, Sermon 315.8 (*Sermons* 9:133).
40. Carl Landé, "Introduction," in *Friends, Followers, and Factions*, ed. Steffen Schmidt et al. (Berkeley: University of California, 1977) xx.
42. Johannes Baptist Metz, *Faith in History and Society: Toward a Practical Fundamental Theology*, trans. David Smith (New York: Seabury, 1980) 88–118.
43. For a pneumatological theology of Mary in the communion of saints, with abundant references to Galilee and contextual theologies, see Elizabeth A. Johnson, *Truly Our Sister: A Theology of Mary in the Communion of Saints* (New York: Continuum, 2003).

Jesus of Galilee and the Crucified People

The Contextual Christology of
Jon Sobrino and Ignacio Ellacuría

Robert Lassalle-Klein

THE fundamental theology of Ignacio Ellacuría and the allied Christology Jon Sobrino form what I believe may be the most fully developed contextual theology written since Vatican II.[1] This remarkable collaboration reflects epoch-shaping events in Latin America and the Catholic Church in El Salvador, as well as long years of Jesuit friendship, shared ministry, persecution, and finally martyrdom at the University of Central America. The impressive corpus produced by these Jesuit "companions of Jesus"[2] is unified by its shared conviction that the *analogatum princeps* of the life, death, and resurrection of Jesus of Nazareth is to be found today among the "crucified peoples" of Latin America, and the billions of victims of poverty, inequality, structural injustice, and violence around the globe.

Sobrino summarizes the central themes associated with this claim in an evocative passage on Galilee published not long after the brutal assassination of Ignacio Ellacuría with five Jesuit colleagues and two lay coworkers on November 16, 1989.

> Galilee is the setting of Jesus' historical life, the place of the poor and the little ones. The poor of this world—the Galilee of today—are where we encounter the historical Jesus and where he is encountered as liberator. And this Galilee is also where the risen Christ who appears to his disciples will show himself as he really is, as the Jesus we have to follow and keep present in history: the historical Jesus, the man from

Nazareth, the person who was merciful and faithful to his death on the cross, the perennial sacrament in this world of a liberator God.³

This analogy embodies Sobrino's response to Vatican II's mandate "of reading the signs of the times and of interpreting them in light of the Gospel"⁴ and introduces his hope-filled volume on the meaning of the Jesus' resurrection, the sending of the Spirit, and his call to faith-filled discipleship. Methodologically, the analogy reflects 40 years of living with the "preferential option for the poor" discerned by Latin American bishops shortly after Vatican II as God's will for the Church, and places that discernment in a hermeneutical circle with the life, death, and resurrection of Jesus Christ.⁵ Substantively, it reflects Sobrino's claim that "we have done nothing more than—starting from Jesus—elevate the reality we are living to the level of a theological concept, to theorize about a christological faith that we see as real faith."⁶ And as an icon of Christian discipleship, it reflects the influence of Archbishop Oscar Romero on the Jesuits of El Salvador as a model of the call by Ignatius Loyola to discern and collaborate with the work of the Trinity in the world. I will say more about this near the end of the essay.

What, then, is the significance for contextual theologies around the world of the *substance* and *methods* informing the analogy drawn by Sobrino and Ellacuría between the historical reality of Jesus Christ and the "crucified peoples" of today? In this article I will identify two elements defining their approach that I believe should and likely will help shape other fundamental and christological contextual theologies in the years ahead. First, Ignacio Ellacuría develops a profound historical realism (a Christian historical realism, if you prefer⁷) that is manifested in his concepts of "historical reality" and the "theology of sign," which he uses to frame a Latin American fundamental contextual theology. Second, building on Ellacuría, Sobrino integrates these concepts in what I will call a contextualized Latin American "saving history" Christology, which starts "from below" with the historical reality of Jesus.

The Christian Historical Realism of Ignacio Ellacuría

Historical Reality

History and metaphysics have long been considered antinomies, yet Catholic and Christian contextual theologies and philosophies need both. In this section I will briefly summarize the meaning and the philosophical and theological roots of the term "historical reality," the defining concept of Ellacuría's (Christian) historical realism wherein the antinomy is overcome. Building on the work of Spanish philosopher Xavier Zubiri, Ellacuría claims that "historical reality" is the proper object of a contextualized Latin American approach to philosophy and theology.[8]

Ellacuría's magnum opus, *Filosofía de la realidad histórica* (1990, posthumous), summarizes the philosophical arguments for this core element of his 30-year effort to develop a Latin American philosophy and theology capable of conceptualizing the faith, hope, and struggle for life of the Continent's "poor majorities."[9] I have argued elsewhere that Ellacuría is Rahner's most important Latin American interpreter, building on Zubiri's groundbreaking work on Heidegger and Continental phenomenology in order to historicize Rahner's supernatural existential and his theology of sign.[10] While I cannot do justice to Zubiri's arguments here, a word is warranted on this work and its implications for Ellacuría's understanding of the historical reality of Jesus.

Zubiri attempts to preserve the insights of Heidegger's ontology of being in the face of the claim that relativity theory and contemporary science have shown that, "space, time, consciousness, [and] being, are not four receptacles for things." For Zubiri, this insight leads to the potentially devastating conclusion that "modern philosophy . . . has been riding upon . . . four incorrect substantivations: space, time, consciousness, and being."[11] Taking a page from Heidegger's mentor, Edmund Husserl, Zubiri responds by creating a phenomenological definition of "reality" (or "reity"[12] as he calls it). Thus, Zubiri defines reality as the "thing" whose apprehension has the character of being something "in its own" right (*en propio*), as something "of its own" (*de suyo*), or "as something that already is what it is before its presentation, as a *prius*, more in a metaphysical than in a temporal sense."[13] Students of the emergence of systems theory during this period will notice that Zubiri's description of reality (or "reity") sounds like the phenomenological version of a "boundary-maintaining system."

Building on his studies of Einstein, Planck, Schrödinger, and others, Zubiri then describes "historical reality" as the most self-possessing (*de suyo* or "of its own") of the series of subsystems that comprise the natural and historical ecology of "the cosmos." Historical reality is the "last stage of reality" in which the material, biological, sentient, and personal and collective historical dimensions of reality are all made present, and "where we are given not only the highest forms of reality, but also the field of the maximum possibilities of the real."[14]

Focusing on the human person, Ellacuría asserts that historical reality "is where all of reality is assumed into the social realm of freedom." Elsewhere, he asserts: "The personal dimension of life . . . consists in achieving self-possession through defining oneself in terms of one way of being in reality when confronted with reality as a whole."[15] Zubiri explains, "When the human person, the reality animal, begets another reality animal, they do not only transmit their life, that is . . . certain psycho-organic characteristics, but they also, inexorably . . . , set them up in a certain way of being in reality."[16] Eventually, however, the demands of everyday life require us to interpret and to make choices about ways of being in the world that have been inherited, thereby forcing us to define our own historical reality. As a result of this process, Zubiri says, echoing Heidegger, the creation of historical reality involves "the constitution of a new kind of world," in which "reality becomes a world." Thus, if Heidegger can be said to understand *dasein* as the kind of being (i.e., the human person) that must take a stand on its being-in-the-world, then we could say by analogy that Zubiri and Ellacuría understand human *historical reality* as that reality that must take a stand on its historical-reality-in-the-world.[17]

Ellacuría and Zubiri then formulate the term "historicization" to refer to the appropriation and transformation of the historical (i.e., tradition-centered) and natural (i.e., the material, biological, and sentient) dimensions of reality[18] through which this process of human self-definition takes place. For Zubiri, historicization is driven by the fact that when something "is already given as a reality, I not only have to allow it to be [*dejar que sea*], but I am forced to realize the weight of it [*hacerse cargo de ella*] as a reality."[19] Ellacuría agrees, but argues that this process of "facing up to real things as real has a triple dimension."[20] Emphasizing the component of human freedom, he asserts that historicization involves not only (1) "becoming aware of," "understanding," or "realizing about reality" (*hacerse cargo de la realidad*); but also (2) an ethical demand to take responsibility for reality, or "to pick up reality" (*cargar con la realidad*); and (3) a praxis-related demand to change or "to take charge of reality" (*encargarse de la realidad*).[21]

Building on this foundation, Ellacuría and Sobrino apply the philosophical category of "historical reality" (and "historicization") to Jesus and to Christian discipleship in three key ways. First, Sobrino endorses Ellacuría's argument that a truly Latin American Christology must be shaped by a "new historical *logos* . . . which takes into account the historical reality of Jesus."[22] He explicitly cites Ellacuría's assertion, following Rahner, that "this new historical *logos* must start from the fact, indisputable to the eye of faith, that the historical life of Jesus is the fullest revelation of the Christian God."[23] Second, both authors assert that the historical reality of Jesus of Nazareth is defined or historicized (Sobrino says "created"[24]) in large part through the words and actions that define Jesus' basic historical stance toward the history and people of Israel, his relationship to the Father, his mission, and the affirmation in faith (by his disciples) that he is risen from the dead and glorified with the Father. And third, both Ellacuría and Sobrino assert that God's historical self-offer is definitively mediated by the historical reality of Jesus (Sobrino says "the human, Jesus, is the real symbol of the Word"[25]), which is described in the Gospels and forms the proper object of Latin American fundamental theology and Christology. In my second part I will address how each of these elements is taken up in Sobrino's Christology.

Theology of Sign

Ellacuría's philosophy of historical reality leads him to historicize Rahner's theology of symbol as a theology of sign.[26] His core claim here, that "God revealed himself in history, not directly, but in a sign: . . . the humanity of Jesus,"[27] is a contextualized reinterpretation of Rahner's famous assertion from his theology of symbol that "the incarnate word is the absolute symbol of God in the world."[28] The latter follows from Rahner's "basic principle" that "all beings are by their nature symbolic, because they necessarily 'express' themselves in order to attain their own nature."[29] But Ellacuría has shifted the emphasis from "symbol" to "sign" in part to cohere with Medellín's response to the council's mandate to read the signs of the times and interpret them in light of the Gospel. Accordingly, Ellacuría argues that the "mission of the Church" is to be "a sign, and only a sign, of the God who has revealed himself in history, . . . of Jesus, the Lord, the Revealer of the Father."[30]

In 1978 Ellacuría further historicized this theology of sign for a Latin American context with the startling claim that the "principal" sign of the times "by whose light the others should be discerned and interpreted" is "the historically crucified people."[31] Building on Archbishop Romero's famous 1977 homily to the terrified peasants of Aquilares,[32] Ellacuría defines the "crucified people" as that "vast portion of humankind, which is literally and actually crucified by natural, . . . historical, and personal oppressions."[33] He ties this terrifying sign to Jesus with the claim that it has defined "the reality of the world in which the church has existed for almost two thousand years, [literally] since Jesus announced the approach of the Reign of God." In the end, Ellacuría's closest friend and collaborator, Jon Sobrino, claims that Ellacuría defined "his life, and his vocation as a Jesuit and, deeper still, as a human being"[34] in terms of "a specific service: *to take the crucified people down from the cross.*"[35]

Sobrino and Ellacuría insist that this striking metaphor for Medellín's option for the poor ultimately places a claim on the universal church. Indeed, their whole project could be described as an attempt to show how followers of Jesus are drawn into a mystical "analogy"[36] between the life, death, and resurrection of Jesus Christ,[37] and the struggles of the crucified people to believe and to survive the "world of poverty . . . today."[38] This final point takes us into what the Greek Fathers of the Church called *"theosis,"* which, for Ellacuría and Sobrino, implies that following the historical reality of Jesus draws the disciple into a transformative participation in the divine mystery of the inner life of God. Building on the trinitarian mysticism of the Spiritual Exercises of St. Ignatius, Rahner's recovery of the economic Trinity in 20th-century Catholic theology, and Augustine's contributions to Christian semiotics and Western trinitarian theology, the two Jesuits offer us a deeply trinitarian theology of sign. This is emblemized by Sobrino's claim that the disciple who responds to the grace-filled call to take the crucified people down from the cross becomes a living sign of the life, death, and resurrection of Jesus Christ, the sending of the Spirit, and the ongoing work of the Trinity in the world. I will say more about this intriguing and potentially controversial metaphor below.

Sobrino's "Saving History" Christology

Jon Sobrino's two-volume Latin American Christology builds on the philosophical concept of historical reality and Ellacuría's theology of sign. Given what I have already said about the Rahnernian roots of Ellacuría's fundamental theology, it will come as no surprise that Sobrino defines his project in relation to Rahner's "two basic types of Christology."[39] Rahner distinguishes "the *saving history* type, a Christology viewed from below," which he finds in the New Testament; from what he calls "the *metaphysical* type, a Christology developing downwards from above,"[40] which he associates with Chalcedon and the early ecumenical councils. Rahner presciently predicts his typology will be misunderstood, particularly the affirmation that a Christology from below "understands, and must understand, this process of 'rising up' as an act proper to God himself." Certainly recent criticisms suggest that Sobrino's appropriation of this aspect of Rahner's approach to Christology has been misunderstood.[41]

Describing "saving history" Christology, Rahner argues that "the point of departure for this Christology . . . is the simple experience of the man Jesus, and of the Resurrection in which his fate was bought to its conclusion." He argues:

> The eye of the believer in his experience of saving history alights first on the man Jesus of Nazareth, and on him in his *fully human reality*, in his death, in the absolute powerless[ness] and in the abidingly definitive state which his reality and his fate have been brought to by God, something which we call his Resurrection, his glorification, his sitting at the right hand of the Father.[42]

Sobrino explicitly ties his Christology to this "undertaking of Karl Rahner . . . to restore to Christ his true humanity," which "insisted on thinking of the humanity of Christ "sacramentally."[43] And Sobrino adopts the "basically chronological" pattern of christological reflection "found in the New Testament," where "Jesus' mission of service to the Kingdom" raises "the question about the person of Jesus," ultimately answered by the disciple's "confession of his unrepeatable and salvific reality."[44] Reflecting Rahner's characteristic insistence on the unity of the historical Jesus and the Christ of faith, Sobrino concludes, "As a result the *real* point of departure is always, somehow, the whole faith in Christ, but the *methodological* point of departure continues to be the historical Jesus. This is objectively, the best *mystagogy* for the Christ of faith."[45] Sobrino and Ellacuría further insist that one comes to know the resurrected Jesus mainly by picking up and carrying the historical burden of his message about the Kingdom of God,[46] and by accepting the suffering that comes to those who try to historicize today the values of the Kingdom that defined the historical reality of Jesus.

The Historical Reality of Jesus Christ

Exactly what, then, do Sobrino and Ellacuría mean by the "historical reality" of Jesus? And how does Sobrino make the historical reality of Jesus the proper object for his contextualized Latin American "saving history" Christology? I address these questions in this and the following sections. Then, heeding Rahner's prescient warning, I will conclude by suggesting how Sobrino's "saving history" Christology makes the "process of 'rising up'" from the historical reality of Jesus to the Christ of faith into "an act proper to God himself."[47]

Sobrino asserts that the historical Jesus is both the way to Christ and the starting point for Latin American Christology. He says that Latin American Christology "presupposes . . . faith in the whole reality of Jesus Christ." But he notes that "the methodological problem" remains: "where does one start in giving an account of this whole?" So he argues, "I have chosen as my starting point the *reality* of Jesus of Nazareth, his life, his mission and his fate, what is usually called the *historical Jesus*."[48]

Here it is worth noting that, while Sobrino generally refers to the "reality" of Jesus rather than Ellacuría's more precise "historical reality" of Jesus, the meaning and the approach are generally the same. This conjunction of the terms *reality* and *historical Jesus* should also alert us to Sobrino's affinity with Rahner's insistence on the unity of history and transcendence in Jesus. This is clear in Sobrinos statement, "Jesus Christ is a whole that, to put it for now in a simplified way, consists of a historical element (Jesus) and a transcendental element (Christ), and the most characteristic feature of faith as such is the acceptance of the transcendental element: that this Jesus is more than Jesus, that he is *the* Christ."[49]

Sobrino outlines "the meaning of the *historical dimension of Jesus* in Latin American Christology," starting with what he calls "(1) the most *historical* aspect of Jesus: his practice with spirit."[50] He then moves "(2) from the practice of Jesus to the *person* of Jesus," and "(3) from the historical Jesus to the whole Christ."[51] While volume one, *Jesucristo liberador*, traces these themes through the New Testament from "the mission and faith of Jesus" to his crucifixion and death, volume two picks up the trail from the New Testament resurrection accounts through the development of Christology in the early church and the first ecumenical councils. In all this, Sobrino makes it clear that the deposit of faith remains normative, and that he is reading it from a Latin American ecclesial "setting"[52] defined by the option for the poor and the perspective of the victims of history. In the following three subsections, I will summarize the core claims of Sobrino's two volumes on each of the aforementioned points. I will also link them to his profound historical realism and to his vision of a Latin American "saving history" Christology that starts "from below" with the historical reality of Jesus.

"The Most Historical Aspect of Jesus: His Practice with Spirit"

Sobrino begins with the definition, "By 'historical Jesus' we mean the life of Jesus of Nazareth, his words and actions, his activity and his praxis, his attitudes and his spirit, his fate on the cross (and the resurrection)."[53] This inclusion of both the "spirit" and the resurrection of Jesus in what Sobrino calls his "historical" reality help us see that his understanding of the historical reality of Jesus transcends the positivism of historical facts. Indeed, he argues that "the most historical aspect of Jesus is his practice, and . . . the spirit with which he engaged in it and . . . imbued it." But what exactly does Sobrino mean by Jesus' "practice with spirit," and the "spirit" of the practice of Jesus?

Sobrino says this "spirit" refers to Jesus' "honesty toward the real world, partiality for the *little ones*, deep-seated mercy, [and] faithfulness to the mystery of God."[54] But what is "historical," observable, or empirical about this spirit? On the one hand, he argues "this spirit was defined and so became real, through a practice, because it was within that practice, and not in his pure inwardness, that Jesus was challenged and empowered." Thus, Sobrino contends that we can discover the spirit of Jesus by examining his practice.

"On the other hand," Sobrino insists, "this spirit was not merely the necessary accompaniment of Jesus' practice, but shaped it, gave it a direction and even empowered it to be historically effective."[55] The spirit that suffuses Jesus' practice cannot be captured by "what is simply debatable in space and time."[56] In fact, he argues, "the *historical* is . . . what sets history in motion." And this is precisely what has been "handed down to us as a trust . . . [in] the New Testament . . . as narratives published to keep alive through history a reality started off by Jesus." Thus, he concludes, the New Testament is less interested in empirically cataloguing Jesus' activities than in capturing and passing on the spirit of Jesus to his disciples, when this "spirit" is understood as the fundamental relationships, loves, commitments, and self-understanding that defined his life.[57]

After these introductory remarks on method, volume one provides two large sections on factors that define the historical reality of Jesus. "The first thing that strikes one in beginning to analyze the reality of Jesus of Nazareth," Sobrino writes, and what "emerges incontrovertibly from the Gospels" is that "Jesus' life was an outward-directed one, directed to something . . . expressed by two terms: 'Kingdom of God' and 'Father.'"[58] Both terms, Sobrino asserts, "are authentic words of Jesus" and "all-embracing realities." The "Kingdom of God" defines for Jesus "all of [historical] reality and what must be done," and that "by 'Father' Jesus names the personal reality that lends ultimate meaning to his life."[59] But, he concludes, "we begin with Jesus' relationship to the Kingdom, because this is how the Gospels begin . . . and because, I think, one gains better access to the whole reality of Jesus by starting from his external activities on behalf of the Kingdom and by moving from there to his inner relationship with God."[60] Sobrino's starting point, it must be noted, is not determined arbitrarily but is based on a trajectory he discovers in the Gospels.

Building on Ellacuría's three dimensions of historicization mentioned above, Sobrino then outlines how Jesus (a) understands the Kingdom of God, (b) takes responsibility for the Kingdom of God, and (c) carries out transformative activities on behalf of the Kingdom of God through his "practice with spirit." Each of these moments is summarized in the subsections below, including what each contributes to Sobrino's understanding of the "spirit," or the defining aspects of the person of Jesus historicized in his practice.

Jesus' Kingdom of God: A Hoped-for Utopia Addressed to the Suffering Poor

Sobrino says that Jesus articulates a specific "concept" of the Kingdom of God in the Gospels, and that he presents the Kingdom as primarily addressed to the poor.[61] He says the Synoptic Jesus understands the Kingdom as a "hoped-for utopia in the midst of the sufferings of history,"⁶² a view Jesus shares with the Hebrew Scriptures and John the Baptist. Jesus believes the Kingdom is "possible" and "something good and liberative,"⁶³ which reflects not only the common "expectation" of the country folk of Galilee and first-century Israel, but also the hopes and aspirations of oppressed people throughout the ages.

On the other hand, Sobrino asserts that Jesus breaks with John the Baptist and the Hebrew prophets in three important ways. First, "Jesus not only hopes for the Kingdom of God, [but] he affirms that it is at hand, that its arrival is imminent, [and] that the Kingdom should be not only an object of hope, but of certainty."⁶⁴ Second, Jesus insists that, while the Kingdom is God's initiative, gift, and grace, its actual coming "demands a conversion, [or] *metanoia*." This creates "a task for the listener" that differs according to his or her location in the cycle of oppression. Thus, "the hope the poor must come to feel" must not be confused with "the radical change of conduct required of the oppressors." In either case, "demands [are] made on all to live a life worthy of the Kingdom." ⁶⁵

Third, while the Kingdom implies a "crisis" and/or "judgment on the world and history,"⁶⁶ Jesus presents it as "good news" for the poor that "has to be proclaimed with joy and must produce joy."⁶⁷ This spirit of joy and hope "is why Jesus aroused undoubted popular support throughout the whole of his ministry."⁶⁸

Fourth, Sobrino argues that, while Jesus "did not exclude anyone from the possibility of entering into the Kingdom," he primarily addressed the Kingdom of God to the poor.⁶⁹ Accordingly, for Jesus, "proclaiming good news *to the poor* of this world cannot be a matter of words alone," since "what the poor need and hope for" is a change in their historical reality.⁷⁰ Therefore, while Jesus' understanding of the Kingdom as liberating good news for the poor provokes hope and requires conversion, it also demands a commensurate "messianic practice" capable of historicizing this spirit.

Jesus Assumes Responsibility for the Kingdom of God through His "Messianic Practice"

Sobrino sees Jesus as driven by a spirit of ethical responsibility for the Kingdom, which he historicizes through a "messianic practice"⁷¹ as "*proclaimer* and *initiator* of the Kingdom of God."⁷² To appreciate the role of Jesus' miracles in this practice, Sobrino says we must see them through the eyes of the poor country folk of Galilee as liberative signs and expressions of God's compassion. The miracles arouse faith "in a God who, coming close, makes us believe in new possibilities actively denied to the poor in history." They elicit "a faith that overcomes fatalism . . . so that believers, now healed, are converted so as to become themselves principles of salvation for themselves."[73]

Second, Sobrino says that when Jesus casts out devils, his Galilean audience appreciates Jesus' recognition that "the Kingdom implies, of necessity, actively struggling against the anti-Kingdom."[74] Third, Jesus' welcoming and forgiving common sinners simultaneously liberates them from themselves and overcomes their marginalization.[75] He calls the powerful to "an active cessation from oppressing" and asks the poor to accept "that God is not like . . . their oppressors and the ruling religious culture."[76] Fourth, Jesus tells parables about the Kingdom that similarly call the oppressor to conversion, defend the poor, and justify his actions on their behalf.[77] And fifth, Jesus gathers his followers for meals and other joyful events that "are signs of the coming of the Kingdom and of the realization of his ideals: liberation, peace, universal communion."[78]

In the end, Sobrino argues that Latin American liberation theology "makes the Kingdom of God central for strictly christological reasons"[79] grounded in the Kingdom's defining role in Jesus' messianic practice, and the conviction that his historical reality is the real sign of the Word made flesh. Sobrino argues that the messianic practice of Jesus historicizes his courageous confrontation of oppression, his spirit of compassion, forgiveness, the call to personal transformation, and joy. And he concludes that this messianic practice leads Jesus to a "prophetic praxis" that decisively alters the historical reality of first-century Israel.

"Prophetic Praxis": Jesus' Transformative Activities for the Kingdom of God

Jesus defends the first fruits of his messianic practice in service of the Kingdom of God through a "prophetic praxis" of "direct denunciation of the anti-Kingdom,"[80] which Sobrino says changes both Jesus' immediate context and the historical reality of Israel forever. He distinguishes this praxis from Jesus' "messianic practice" that produces "signs" of the Kingdom but is not "aimed at bringing about the total transformation of society."[81] On the other hand, in the controversies, unmaskings, and denunciations "Jesus denounces the scribes, the Pharisees, the rich, the priests, the rulers . . . [who] represent and exercise some kind of power that structures society as a whole." Jesus' prophetic actions, Sobrino affirms: (a) seek to reform and change the "realities (the law, the Temple) in whose name society is structured"; (b) expose structural abuses of institutional power as "an expression of the anti-Kingdom"; and (c) "show that the anti-Kingdom seeks to justify itself in God's name."[82] In this way, the prophetic activity of Jesus historicizes a spirit of transformative "'praxis' . . . because . . . its purpose [is] the transformation of society." He says this praxis demonstrates "that Jesus, objectively, faced up to the subject of society as a whole—including its structural dimension—and sought to change it."[83]

Sobrino then analyzes controversies, unmaskings of lies and other mechanisms of oppressive religion, and denunciations of oppressors and their idols, which are too numerous to review here. He concludes, however, by examining Jesus' expulsion of the traders from the Temple (Mk 11:15–19; Mt 21:12–17; Lk 19:45–48; Jn 2:14–16), which serves as an explanation for the crucifixion. I will say more about this below. He insists that in virtually all the controversies, unmaskings, and denunciations, "Jesus not only proclaims the Kingdom and proclaims a Father God; he also denounces the anti-Kingdom and unmasks its idols."[84] He concludes that "in this praxis, Jesus can be seen to be in the line of the classic prophets of Israel, of Amos, Hosea, Isaiah, Jeremiah, Micah . . . , and in that of the modern prophets, Archbishop Oscar Romero, . . . Martin Luther King, Jr." Thus, Jesus historicizes a prophetic spirit in keeping with the prophetic traditions of Israel through a prophetic praxis designed to confront, reform, and transform the current abuse of its ancient institutions and practices by contemporary first-century elites.

With this claim, Sobrino concludes his argument that (a) Jesus understands the Kingdom of God as justice, forgiveness, and mercy for the suffering poor and the marginated; (b) Jesus' "messianic practice" responds in a liberating manner to this suffering; and (c) Jesus' transformative "prophetic praxis" is both good news for the poor and leads inevitably to his crucifixion. Sobrino's point is that the merciful, liberating, and prophetic spirit that suffuses Jesus' proclamation and initiation of the Kingdom of God as good news for the poor, also provokes resistance by the forces of the anti-Kingdom. Sadly, the awful logic of the anti-Kingdom willingly sacrifices the poor and their defenders to preserve its treasures. Unfortunately, this logic also implies that those who share Jesus' spirit of service of the Kingdom as good news to the poor will be crucified as well.

"From the Practice of Jesus to the Person of Jesus"

I come, then, to what Sobrino calls the second *"historical dimension of Jesus* in Latin American Christology."[85] He argues that Jesus' "practice with spirit" of the Kingdom of God as good news for the poor (which includes his prophetic praxis) leads directly to his crucifixion, the defining moment of the life and "the *person* of Jesus."[86] Praising this dimension of Sobrino's work, biblical scholar Daniel Harrington argues that "Sobrino's 'historical-theological' reading of Jesus of Nazareth offers important methodological contributions to both the historical and theological study of Jesus and his death."[87] Harrington points out that Sobrino correctly eschews the "narrow version of historical criticism" found in many authors and formulates a "more adequate and fruitful way of treating ancient sources," which "involves taking seriously the historical data about Jesus and trying to do theology on the basis of and in light of these data."[88]

Harrington agrees with Sobrino that, "Jesus' death was not a mistake, tragic or otherwise," and that "what got Jesus killed . . . was the fact that he was a radical threat to the religious and political powers of his time."[89] Jesus "got in the way" by defending the victims of their policies, in the name of the Kingdom of God.[90] As evidence, Harrington cites the fact that, "the four Gospels are united in presenting Jesus as the victim of persecution and in suggesting that his death was . . . the logical consequence of who Jesus was and the circumstances in which he lived and worked."[91]

Harrington then asks, "Did Jesus know beforehand that he was going to suffer and die in Jerusalem?"[92] Noting that biblical scholars generally view the three passion predictions (Mk 8:31; 9:31; 10:33–34) as later insertions, Harrington says that Sobrino "wisely points to the fate of John the Baptist" to argue that Jesus went to Jerusalem ready to accept death "out of fidelity to the cause of the kingdom of God, out of confidence in the one whom he called 'Father,' and out of loyalty to his prophetic calling."[93] With this move, he argues, Sobrino correctly situates "the link between the historical Jesus and the Christ of faith" precisely at "the root of Jesus' resolve to go to Jerusalem . . . [and] his understanding of his life as service on behalf of others, even to the point of sacrificial service." This is Sobrino's explanation for how the divine economy of salvation is historicized through what the Gospels portray as the defining moment of the historical reality of Jesus: his decision to accept suffering and death in order to fulfill his messianic, prophetic, and priestly mission from the Father to bring the Kingdom of God as good news for the poor.

Citing the Temple incident (Mk 11:15–19) and Jesus' prophecy of the destruction of the temple (13:2), Harrington supports Sobrino's argument that "it is reasonable to conclude that at the 'religious trial' [before the Sanhedrin] Jesus was accused of wanting to destroy the Temple not only because he criticized certain aspects of it but also because he offered an alternative (the Kingdom of God) that implied that the Temple would no longer be the core of the political, social, and economic life of the Jewish people."[94] Similarly, Harrington endorses Sobrino's acceptance of Luke's charges in the "political trial" before the Roman governor, Pontius Pilate (23:2), as very likely historical: "We found this man perverting our nation, forbidding them to pay taxes to the emperor, and saying that he himself is the Messiah, a king."[95] Harrington argues that "the charge that Jesus made himself 'the Messiah, a king,' would have been especially incendiary in this context." Thus, the Evangelists' description of the inscription on the cross, "The King of the Jews" (Mk 15:26), not to mention the public torture itself, would have served as brutal public warnings to "would-be Messiahs . . . tempted to lead an uprising against the Roman occupiers."[96]

It is crucial to understand that Sobrino is arguing that Jesus' relationship with the Father ultimately guides and motivates the nature of his obedient service to God's call to initiate his Kingdom, which is historicized through a liberative prophetic practice that leads to Jesus' faith-filled death on the cross. Harrington notes appreciatively that Sobrino finds "strong analogies between first-century Palestine and late-twentieth-century El Salvador," which open up new insights "that other interpreters in other circumstances may miss."[97] Sobrino admits: "I have nothing to contribute to the exegetical elucidation" of scriptural accounts of the death of Jesus, but, he insists, "the point I want to make is that the cross that dominates the Third World greatly illuminates the coherence with which the passion and death of Jesus—as a whole—are described."[98] Thus, the received tradition clearly remains normative in Sobrino's analogical approach. But his work enters the hermeneutical circle initiated at Vatican II through the commitment to read the terrifying sign of the crucified people of Latin America in light of the historical reality of Jesus' "praxis with spirit, his crucifixion, and his resurrection,"[99] and vice versa. Harrington correctly argues that it is this perspective that defines Sobrino's primary contribution to the interpretation of the New Testament crucifixion narratives.

"From the Historical Jesus to the Whole Christ"

Volume two, *La fe en Jesucristo,* deals with what Sobrino calls the third element of *the historical dimension of Jesus,* shifting "from the historical Jesus to the whole Christ."[100] The perceptive reader will note that here Sobrino moves far beyond the bounds of the usual treatment of the "historical Jesus" (e.g., he includes the resurrection) precisely because his Rahnerian "saving history" approach to Christology leads him to interpret the historical reality of Jesus as the living sacrament of the Word of God.

Sobrino's approach is marked by the historical reality he attributes to the New Testament "paschal experience" and to its interpretation and acceptance in faith. Again, this emphasis on the historical dimension of the Resurrection emblemizes Sobrino's "saving history" approach to the historical reality of Jesus. His analysis is driven by what he calls the "reality principle,"[101] which he says is "the central presupposition of the Christologies of the New Testament." The reality principle is a kind of scribal exegetical standard that works to limit the addition of various titles and other elements to the story of Jesus in the New Testament so that "the real and historical subject is still Jesus of Nazareth."[102] The key point is that the reality principle allows the New Testament authors to credibly claim—given first century scribal standards—that "Faith . . . is referred back to 'what we have heard, what we have seen with our eyes, what we have looked at and touched with our hands' (1 John 1:1)."[103]

Sobrino observes that New Testament witnesses to the resurrection of Jesus are presented as firsthand accounts of a "paschal experience," which "claims to be based in a *reality* that happened to Jesus and was, in some way, observable."[104] But what exactly does Sobrino mean when he asserts that "the New Testament builds its reflection on this *reality of the historical Jesus and his resurrection*"?[105] Having outlined in the previous section the defining elements of his understanding of the historical reality of Jesus, I will focus in this section on Sobrino's answer to question, "What is historical in Jesus' resurrection?"[106]

Sobrino's observation that the canonical Gospels "never describe Jesus' resurrection" leads him to assert that "in order to know what happened to Jesus, we are of necessity referred to what happened to the disciples" and what he calls "the Easter experience."[107] He then examines the pre-Pauline kerygma that scholars place among the earliest summaries of what Christians believed (1 Cor 15:3b–5): "that Christ died for our sins in accordance with the scriptures, and that he was buried, and that he was raised on the third day in accordance with the scriptures, and that he appeared to Cephas, then to the twelve."

From this material Sobrino draws three properly historical claims. First, the kerygmatic texts "affirm that something happened to Jesus' disciples, something they attribute to *their encounter with Jesus*, whom they call the risen Lord."[108] Second, "a change was worked in the disciples . . . before and after Easter." The texts describe changes in "the places in which they were (from Galilee to Jerusalem); their behavior (from fear to bravery); [and] their faith (from 'We were waiting, but it is now the third day' to 'The Lord is risen indeed')." Third, the kerygma does not reflect the impact of Jesus on his followers during his life and death, but emerges from the disciples' experience of the resurrection. "The *objective* conclusion, therefore, has to be . . . [that] for them there was no doubt that this subjective faith had a corresponding reality that happened to Jesus himself."[109] Sobrino concludes, "From a historical point of view, I do not think one can go further than this."

This brings Sobrino face to face with the problem of the exact nature of the relationship of history and faith, his resolution of which ultimately defines his interpretation of the historical reality of Jesus from a Latin American context. Sobrino argues that "the proclamation of the message that 'God raised Jesus from the dead'" presents Christians with an historical "invitation" to a "reasonable faith."[110] Drawing an analogy between the claims of the resurrection and the Exodus, Sobrino notes that both accounts confront readers with historical events that some have believed can be reasonably interpreted as actions of the transcendent God. Sobrino agrees with John Henry Newman that the faith that God has acted in history through such events can in fact be seen as a "reasonable response" to a "sum total of [historical] indicators," which he says include credible texts, personal experiences, and the long-lasting impact on believers of faith. In the present case, Sobrino argues that Scripture first confronts the reader/hearer with testimonies to "the presence of the eschatological in history" from witnesses that "appear to be honest people." Second, readers/hearers judge these claims through analogies to their own "present-day" historical encounters with "something ultimate." And third, readers/hearers note that believing acceptance of these claims consistently (but not always) generates "greater personal humanization" and the creation of "more and better history."

These factors lead Sobrino to conclude "that understanding Jesus' resurrection as an eschatological event is an analogous problem to that of knowing God through any divine action."[111] The underlying idea, grounded in Ellacuría's Christian historical realism, is that history and faith are not opposites but are inextricably intertwined in human historical reality, which, as I have noted above, must take a stand on its historical reality in the world. Adapting the three questions that Kant says every person must face, Sobrino then asks what historical *knowledge*, what historical *praxis*, and what historical *hope* "are needed today in order to understand what is being said when we hear that Jesus has been raised from the dead?" As we will see in the next section, Sobrino predictably argues that "the replies will above all take account of what the scriptural texts themselves require," while at the same time reflecting what emerges when the story of Jesus is "reread from the Latin American situation."[112]

In this section, then, I have outlined important aspects of what Sobrino means by the "historical reality" of Jesus Christ, and have begun to suggest its place in his Christology. Here Sobrino clearly builds on the concept of "historical reality" developed by Ellacuría with his vision of a Latin American Christology guided by a historical logos capable of articulating the salvific significance of the historical reality of Jesus. Ellacuría's notion of historical reality as that reality that must take a stance on its history in the world is exemplified in Sobrino's claim that Jesus defines his life, his person, and the salvation he brings through his fundamental historical stance toward the Father, his people Israel, the mission that the Father gives Jesus to initiate the Kingdom of God, and his action of raising Jesus from the dead. These are the defining elements of the historical reality of Jesus Christ as witnessed by the Gospels, and Sobrino argues that they guide his contextualized rereading of the tradition.

But I have only begun to suggest the place of the historical reality of Jesus in Sobrino's overall reading of christological tradition from a Latin American perspective. In what follows I will allude to how Sobrino builds on Ellacuría's Rahnerian theology of sign, the trinitarian spirituality of Ignatius Loyola, and most especially Archbishop Romero's vision of the poor as the crucified image of Christ . . . in order to argue that it is the "victims of history" who help us understand and enter the historical reality of Jesus as the "real symbol" of the Word made flesh.[113]

The Faith, Hope, and Love of the "Victims" of History as the Hermeneutical Key to the Historical Reality of Jesus' Resurrection

The originality of Sobrino's approach to Christology is reflected in the question he adds to those of Kant mentioned above: "What can we celebrate in history?"[114] Sobrino contends that, "however scandalous this may seem," we must ask what there is to celebrate in the blood-stained history of "the Latin American situation." He answers with three "hermeneutical principles from the victims" of history, which he believes lay the foundation for understanding acceptance of the resurrection of Jesus in a Latin American context.[115] First, he says that the historical *hope of the crucified* in the victory of life over death is "the most essential hermeneutical requirement for understanding what happened to Jesus."[116] He begins by asserting: "If human beings were not by nature 'beings of hope' or were unable to fulfill this hope over the course of history with its ups and downs, the resurrection texts would . . . be incomprehensible. It would be like trying to explain colors to a blind person."[117] Historicizing this claim, he argues that Hebrew scripture calls Israel to faith and hope in the God of life and justice who has been revealed through Israel's history of oppression and liberation. Similarly, New Testament accounts of the resurrection of Jesus call for "hope in the power of God over the injustice that produces victims,"[118] and over the crucifixion and death that tries to defeat the promises of the Kingdom. Thus, he concludes, "Human transcendental hope is a necessary but insufficient condition for understanding Jesus' resurrection."[119]

But where in history do we actually find this hope, and how do we make it our own? Sobrino says the answer "is difficult; it requires us to make the hope of victims, and with it their situation, our own." [120] Like a parable of Jesus that turns the world on its head, hope "is like a gift the victims themselves make to us." In order to make it our own, however, "we have to slot ourselves into this hope, and by doing so we can rebuild—with different, through ultimately similar, mediations—the process followed by Israel's faith in a God of resurrection." Thus, by making the historical hope of history's victims into our own hope, "we progress in finding a God who is loving and on the side of the victims, so we can respond to this God with radical love for them." On the one hand, adopting the hope of the victims "makes the question of the ultimate fate of these victims more acute," which can be uncomfortable. On the other, however, it implies not only that "we can . . . 'hope' that the executioner will not triumph over them," but also that we are invited to "resign ourselves to a final and fulfilling hope."[121]

Second, Sobrino asserts that the hope of the victims in God's victory over death is only truly understood through a *praxis of love* that takes the crucified people down from the cross. This provocative assertion reflects Sobrino's idea is that if "the ultimate root of all hope is . . . always love," then "the Kingdom cannot be understood only as what is hoped for . . . but also . . . as what has to be built."[122] Sobrino argues that, just as love leads Jesus to initiate the Kingdom and to accept suffering and death on its behalf, so when he appears to his followers, "the risen Lord sends them out to preach, baptize, forgive sins, feed the faithful, and . . . (Matthew 28:19–20; John 20:23; 21:15, 17) . . . like the earthly Jesus, to heal and cast out demons (Mark 16:17–18)."[123] The point is that love of neighbor implies action on behalf of the beloved.

Similarly, Sobrino insists that "understanding today that Jesus has been raised by God entails [not only] the hope that we can be *raised*, but . . . that we also have to be, in some way, *raisers*."[124] Here it is important to appreciate the interlocking character of Sobrino's trinitarian theology of sign and the *analogatum princeps* he draws between the fate of the crucified people and the life, death, and resurrection of Jesus. Sobrino argues that, just as in due course God's "justice was done to the crucified Jesus, . . . so the course of action called for is [for us] to take the crucified people down from the cross."[125] He then makes the startling claim: "This is action on behalf of the victims, of those crucified in history, that tries in a small way—with of course no hubris—to do what God himself does: to take the victim Jesus down from the cross."[126]

Lest the reader miss the significance and potentially controversial nature of this claim, it is worth noting that in a private letter leaked and published in 1984, Joseph Ratzinger, head of the Congregation for the Doctrine of the Faith (CDF), mentions (citing an earlier work) "the impressive, but ultimately shocking interpretation of the death and resurrection of Jesus made by J. Sobrino . . . that God's gesture in raising Jesus is repeated in history . . . through giving life to the crucified."[127] Responding to what he sees as a misstatement of his claim, Sobrino cautions, "I hope it is clear that I am not talking of repeating God's action, any more than I talked of bringing in the Kingdom of God in the previous volume of this work." He argues, however, "What I do insist on is giving signs—analogously—of resurrection and coming of the Kingdom. And this is also what Ignacio Ellacuría meant when he . . . used the expression 'taking the crucified people down from the cross' as a formulation of the Christian mission."[128]

It is difficult, if not impossible, to understand Sobrino's claim (and Ellacuría's as well) without taking note of its roots in Ignatian spirituality, and how those are articulated in Sobrino's theology of sign and his understanding of the historical reality of Jesus.[129] In the famous meditation on the Trinity from Spiritual Exercises, Ignatius calls the retreatant to direct collaboration with the work of the Trinity in the world.[130] This meditation is cited by the 32nd General Congregation of the Society of Jesus (1974–1975)[131] as one of the defining elements of the mission and spirituality of Jesuits today in a document first drafted by the Central American Jesuits during the very years in which Sobrino wrote the text cited by Ratzinger. The meditation on the Trinity is also cited by the former novice master of both Ellacuría and Sobrino in the defining talk of the epoch-changing 1969 retreat at which the Central American Jesuits officially embraced the option for the poor professed by the Latin American Bishops at Medellin, Colombia (1968). Outlining the vocation of a Jesuit, Miguel Elizondo writes:

> The Ignatian vocational experience consists in a trinitarian experience, of the Trinity present and operative in this world, in all things . . . realizing its plan for the salvation of the whole world. In this experience Ignatius sees that all things are born from God and return to God through the presence and operation of God's self. And not only by means of the presence and operation of God, but through the insertion of humanity in history. Into this history of salvation comes the human "par excellence," Christ, and with him all persons chosen to actively cooperate in the operation of the Trinity, to realize the salvific plan of God.[132]

Here, then, we see the Ignatian roots of Sobrino's claim that Christians are called "to do what God himself does: to take the victim Jesus down from the cross." The disciple is called to collaborate with the work of the Trinity in the world. The initiative for this call originates with the incarnation of the Word in Jesus Christ and the call by the Holy Spirit to join him in discipleship and service. As a result, Elizondo says,"the definitive God of Ignatius is going to be the God of this world." For Ignatius and his Jesuits, "action becomes a totally different category. . . . Love will not be principally affective or contemplative, but a love that is realized in works, that translates into service, that is realized in this cooperation with God." "Thus," Elizondo argues, "action will be for St. Ignatius the response to this trinitarian God and the sign of the active presence of the Trinity in Ignatius and in the life of his Society."[133]

Sobrino's point, then, is that, when the disciple responds to a grace-filled call by Jesus Christ to take the crucified people down from the cross, he or she is caught up in what the Greek Fathers called *"theosis,"* becoming a living sign of God's work (including the resurrection) in Jesus Christ. Unfortunately, just as Jesus' prophetic praxis leads inevitably to his crucifixion, so "action on behalf of the crucified . . . is also automatically against the executioners and . . . conflictive."[134] Sobrino says this praxis implies, on the one hand, that "action at the service of the resurrection of the *dead*, [and] . . . the resurrection of the *many* . . . should also be social [and] political, seeking to transform structures, *to raise them up.*"[135] On the other hand, however, it also implies that such action will bring persecution and suffering to the disciples of Jesus, transforming them into living signs of his life, death, and resurrection. Thus, the disciple who responds to the call, embodied in the historical reality of Jesus, to loving action on behalf of the poor is destined to become, analogously, a living sign of the Kingdom and the economy of salvation carried out in Jesus Christ.

Third, Sobrino says that we learn from the victims of history that, "in the final analysis, to know Jesus' resurrection we have to accept that *reality is a mystery* that is being shown to us gratuitously."[136] Sobrino's point is that, "If . . . one confesses [the resurrection] . . . as something real, then it is necessary to have . . . faith in God's possibilities for intervening in history." He says this implies "an understanding of reality as that which bears within itself and points to[ward] an eschatological future."[137]

This conjunction of "history" and "reality" reflects Ellacuría's understanding of historical reality, including his rejection of the narrow focus of "nineteenth-century positivism"[138] on history as empirical events and its inability to conceptualize the possibility of radical historical discontinuity. Sobrino argues instead that the religious claim that the transcendent is known through history, like the more specific Christian claim that "the resurrection is the appearance of the eschatological in history,"[139] presupposes that events reveal a historical reality that is "more" than the empirical event itself. This "more" is epitomized in the aforementioned trinitarian Ignatian spirituality that suffuses the works of Sobrino, Ellacuría, and Rahner, and that leads them to suggest that the "more" revealed in history is the mystery of God and of the economy of salvation.

At the end of volume two Sobrino suggests: "On this journey through history, not going outside history but taking flesh and delving deep into history, it can happen that reality gives more of itself, and the conviction can grow (or decrease) that . . . the journey is enveloped in the mystery of the beginning and the end, a mystery that antedates us, from which we come, which moves us to good and leads us to hope for eternal life."[140] Here, he further historicizes for a Latin American context the Ignatian spirituality and the trinitarian theology of Ellacuría and Rahner. The originality of Sobrino's work, however, springs less from his interest in Ignatian spirituality or a Rahnerian fascination with the dialectic of history and transcendence than from the use by Ellacuría and Sobrino of these sources to articulate, after Vatican II, the experience of the Latin American church in living with the option for the poor.

Thus, the influence of Sobrino's Latin American context can be heard in the remarkable claim: "This mystery is grace, and the victims of this world, the crucified peoples, can be, and in my view are, the mediation of this grace. The victims provide the dynamism—the quasi-physical 'shove'—for carrying out the task of journeying that involves taking the crucified peoples down from their cross."[141] Sobrino finally concludes, however, that "the greatest encouragement comes from those who inspire with their actual lives, those who today resemble Jesus by living and dying as he did" (no matter who they are). These are the people like Archbishop Oscar Romero, who pick up this hope, take responsibility for it, and carry out Jesus' compassionate, loving, and transformative "practice with spirit." Reflecting his Ignatian preoccupation with discerning the practical means to collaborate with the historical work of the Trinity in the world, Sobrino concludes, "This is God's journey to this world of victims and martyrs, . . . it is the way to the Father and the way to human beings, [and] above all [it is the way] to the poor and the victims of this world."[142]

"Rising Up" from the Historical Reality of Jesus to the Christ of Faith: "An Act Proper to God Himself"

We are now in position to summarize how Sobrino's Christology embodies Rahner's notion that "saving history" Christologies make the "process of 'rising up'" from the historical reality of Jesus to the Christ of faith "an act proper to God himself."[143] Here Sobrino clearly builds upon the trinitarian character of Ellacuría's Rahnerian theology of sign.

Sobrino's trinitarian (and Ignatian) approach to Christology leads him to situate Chalcedon's teaching on the unity of humanity and divinity in Jesus Christ within the larger, more "holistic," framework of the divine economy of salvation (the ongoing work of the Trinity in the world). Sobrino rejects the tendency "to understand the unity of the divine and the human in Jesus Christ as . . . the union of two realities that . . . could exist independently of one another." He argues instead for "the sacramentality of the real," endorsing Rahner's claim that "the human, Jesus, is the real symbol of the Word."[144] For Sobrino and Rahner, this claim implies a dynamic understanding of role of human nature in the economy of salvation, which Rahner places under the heading of theological anthropology. Sobrino writes: "The Word . . . took on human nature in creating it and created it in taking it on." His point is that "the humanity of Christ is . . . that created reality which becomes the Word when the Word alienates itself, goes outward from itself." This means that what Ellacuría and Sobrino call the historical reality of Jesus Christ ultimately "remains the symbol of the Word for always, including in the beatific vision."[145] Sobrino's point here is that the historical reality of the life, death, and resurrection of Jesus is the real symbol, the definitive revelatory sign of the Word of God in history. Ellacuría emphasizes this point with his claim that "the historical life of Jesus is the fullest revelation of the Christian God."[146]

The key idea in all this is that the initiative in Sobrino's "saving history" approach to Christology originates with the work of the Trinity in the world. Ellacuría makes the point clearly when he states: "It is in the incarnation where one appreciates up to what point God has interiorized himself in history." Thus, Ellacuría concludes:

> Following St. Augustine and with greater truth than in his formulation—*nolite foras ire, in interiore hominis habitat veritas* [do not go outside, truth resides within humanity]—it should be said: *nolite foras ire, in interiore historiae habitat Verbum trinitarium* [do not go outside, the Word of the Trinity resides within history]. That is, the Word personally resides in history, and the historical incarnation of the Word makes the Father and the Holy Spirit present . . . in history in a radically distinct manner.[147]

The key point, then, is that the self-revelation and self-offer of the Word of God achieved in the historical reality of Jesus Christ is an action of the Trinity.

For Ellacuría (as for Sobrino), this notion of the Trinity acting through the historical reality of Jesus presumes that "the presence of God in the mediation of Jesus does not take place like a momentary docetist step."[148] Rather, "it is a real continuing presence, whose full reality will be given in the Second Coming." Thus, "the resurrection and the exaltation [of Jesus] in heaven manifest transcendence, but they are not a negation of history." And here I return to the question of what is historical in the resurrection of Jesus? For Ellacuría, in addition to what has already been said, the resurrection means "that [Jesus] sends the Spirit, who is his Spirit, the Spirit of Christ, precisely in order to continue dwelling among humanity until the end of the ages."[149] This spirit produces historical witnesses and living signs of the resurrection like Archbishop Oscar Romero, and the many thousands who have followed his example.

In the end, Sobrino is arguing that the historical reality of Jesus Christ is the very sacrament of God's self-revelation and self-offer, and that the acceptance of this offer raises up witnesses to the resurrection, and living signs of the work of the Trinity in the world. Thus, using Rahner's formulation, Sobrino's argument implies that the "process of 'rising up'" from the historical reality of Jesus to the Christ of faith must be seen as "an act proper to God himself."[150] The Holy Spirit empowers the disciple to respond in faith to the call to follow Jesus Christ, thereby fulfilling the will of the Father by saying *yes* to the historical self-offer of the Mystery of God in Jesus. Given this perspective, it seems only fair to suggest with Sobrino and Rahner that other contextual Christologies using this promising "saving history" approach might be expected to discover an analogous historical *logos* operating in their own particular historical context.

Conclusion

In concluding, I return to the question with which I began: What is the significance for contextual theologies around the world of the substance and the methods informing the *analogatum princips* drawn by Jon Sobrino and Ignacio Ellacuría between the historical reality of Jesus Christ and the "crucified peoples" of today? I have argued that Ellacuría develops a profound historical realism, providing key concepts from fundamental theology, which Sobrino uses to develop a contextualized Latin American "saving history" Christology that starts "from below" with the historical reality of Jesus Christ, and which he interprets as the real sign of the Word made flesh. More specifically, I first outlined how Ellacuría uses his concept of "historical reality" to formulate a "theology of sign" (historicized as a theology of the signs of the times), which claims (a) the "crucified people" are the defining sign of the times today,[151] and (b) that disciples of the Jesus are called to take the crucified people down from the cross. Second, I have tried to show how Sobrino's Latin American Christology builds on these claims to argue that, when followers of Jesus heed his call to take the crucified people down from the cross, they are transformed into living signs for the universal church of the Kingdom, the resurrection of Jesus, the sending of the Holy Spirit, and the ongoing work of the Trinity in the world.

In the end, I have highlighted the importance of a few key concepts developed by Sobrino and Ellacuría during 40 years of living with the "preferential option for the poor" discerned as God's will for the Church by the Latin American bishops after Vatican II. I have suggested that Ellacuría's fundamental theology and Sobrino's "saving history" Christology should be placed together, forming what I believe may be the most fully developed contextual theology written since Vatican II. More importantly, I hope that some of the key elements outlined here will contribute to the development of fundamental and christological contextual theologies now emerging around the globe.

Notes

1. The English titles of the Orbis editions of Jon Sobrino's two-volume Christology (which is the focus of much of this article) are seriously mistranslated from the Spanish, casting them in the model of Schillebeeckx's two volumes, *Jesus* and *Christ*, and obscuring the focus of *both* volumes on Jesus Christ. *Jesucristo liberador: Lecture histórica-teológica de Jesús de Nazaret* (San Salvador: UCA, 1991) becomes *Jesus the Liberator: A Historical-Theological View* (Maryknoll, N.Y.: Orbis, 1993); and *La fe en Jesucristo: Ensayo desde las víctimas* (San Salvador: UCA, 1999) becomes *Christ the Liberator: A View from the Victims* (Maryknoll, N.Y.: Orbis, 2001). Where I translate directly from the Spanish rather than quote the English, the Spanish version is cited first, followed by the English. It should be noted that the voluminous writings of Ignacio Ellacuría and Jon Sobrino cover many topics other than fundamental theology and Christology in considerable depth.

2. Ignatius Loyola named the order he founded on August 15, 1534 (officially approved September 27, 1540, by Paul III) *La Compañia de Jesus*, and referred to its members as "companions of Jesus." The spirituality and the mystical theology of Ignatius embodied in the order's name finds expression in the idea of Ellacuría and Sobrino that followers of Jesus are called not only to share the burden of his cross but also to take the crucified people down from the cross. This metaphor echoes the famous opening words of the 32nd General Congregation of the Society of Jesus (December 2, 1974 to March 7, 1975): "What is it to be a Jesuit? It is to know that one is a sinner, yet called to be a companion of Jesus as Ignatius was: Ignatius, who begged the Blessed Virgin to 'place him with her Son,' and who then saw the Father himself ask Jesus, carrying his Cross, to take this pilgrim into his company. What is it to be a companion of Jesus today? It is to engage, under the standard of the Cross, in the crucial struggle of our time: the struggle for faith and that struggle for justice which it includes" (Society of Jesus, "Jesuits Today" nos. 1 and 2, Decree 1, *Documents of the 31st and 32nd General Congregations of the Society of Jesus* (St. Louis: Institute of Jesuit Sources, 1977) 401.

3. Sobrino, *Jesus the Liberator* 273.

4. *Gaudium et spes* no. 4, *Vatican Council II*, ed. Austin Flannery, O.P. (Northport, N.Y.: Costello, 1975).

5. It is essential to evaluate the legitimacy and adequacy of Sobrino's methodological presuppositions in terms of the hermeneutical circle he seeks to create between the option for the poor of the contemporary church, and the church's normative tradition regarding Jesus Christ. Sobrino asserts, "Latin American Christology . . . identifies its setting, in the sense of a real situation, as the poor of this world, and this situation is what must be present in and permeate any particular setting in which Christology is done" (Sobrino, *Christ the Liberator* 28). Noted American Christologist William Loewe argues that Sobrino's Christology "admirably" represents

the kind of theological reflection approved in *Libertatis conscientia*, claiming that, "while he insists on the church of the poor as the ecclesial setting of his theology, what is received in that setting as the foundation of his theology is the apostolic faith of the church" (William Loewe, "Interpreting the Notification: Christological Issues," in *Hope and Solidarity: Sobrino's Challenge to Christian Theology*, ed. Stephen J. Pope [Maryknoll, N.Y.: Orbis, 2008]) 143–52, at 146.

6. Sobrino, *Jesucristo liberador* 30, my translation. See Sobrino, *Jesus the Liberator* 8.

7. In a handful of strictly philosophical works, where he develops the category of "historical reality," Ellacuría does not refer to explicitly Christian categories or to faith. However, in the majority of his writings (ethics, politics, education, and theology), he uses the category in reference to explicitly Christian concepts, norms, values, and ecclesial concerns.

8. Ignacio Ellacuría, *Filosofía de la realidad histórica* (San Salvador: UCA, 1990) 42. For book-length studies and collections on the philosophical roots of Ellacuría's theology see Kevin Burke, S.J., *The Ground Beneath the Cross: The Theology of Ignacio Ellacuría* (Washington: Georgetown University, 2000); Michael E. Lee, *Bearing the Weight of Salvation: The Soteriology of Ignacio Ellacuría* (New York: Crossroad, 2009); and Kevin Burke and Robert Lassalle-Klein, eds., *Love That Produces Hope: The Thought of Ignacio Ellacuría* (Collegeville, Minn.: Liturgical, 2006); Héctor Samour, *Voluntad de liberación: La filosofía de Ignacio Ellacuría* (Granada: Comares, 2003); José Sols Lucia, *La teología histórica de Ignacio Ellacuría*" (Madrid: Trotta, 1999); and Jon Sobrino and Rolando Alvarado, eds., *Ignacio Ellacuría, "Aquella libertad esclarecida"* (Santander: Sal Terrae, 1999.

9. Ignacio Ellacuría, "Función liberadora de la filosofía," *Estudios centroamericanos* 435–436 (1985) 45–64, at 46; also Ellacuría, *Viente años de historia en El Salvador (1969–1989): Escritos políticos*, 3 vols. (San Salvador: UCA, 1991) 1:93–121, at 94. For Ellacuría's efforts to develop a Latin American philosophy and theology see "Bibliography of the Complete Works of Ignacio Ellacuría," *Love That Produces Hope* 255–79.

10. I am indebted here to the early work of Martin Maier, which focuses on the Ellacuría-Sobrino collaboration, emphasizes Ellacuría as an important interpreter of Karl Rahner, especially through his efforts to "historicize" Rahner's supernatural existential, and asserts that Ellacuría seeks to develop "a theology of the signs of the times." My own work is more specific, however, in asserting (1) the "saving history" character of Sobrino's Christology and its roots in Ellacuría's work; (2) that Ellacuría subordinates Rahner's supernatural existential within the larger horizon of a human "historical reality" that has been transformed by grace; and (3) that Ellacuría reinterprets Rahner's theology of symbol as a theology of sign. See Martin Maier, "Theologie des Gekreuzigten Volkes: Der Entwurf einer Theologie der Befreiung von Ignacio Ellacuría und Jon Sobrino"

(doctoral dissertation, University of Innsbruck, 1992); and Maier, "Karl Rahner: The Teacher of Ignacio Ellacuría," in *Love That Produces Hope* 128–43. For my development of this theme, see Robert Lassalle-Klein, "Rethinking Rahner on Grace and Symbol: New Proposals from the Americas," in *Rahner beyond Rahner: A Great Theologian Encounters the Pacific Rim*, ed. Paul Crowley, S.J. (Lanham, Md.: Rowman & Littlefield, 2005) 87–99; and Robert Lassalle-Klein, "La historización de la filosofía de la religión de Rahner en Ellacuría y Zubiri," in *Historia, ética, y liberación: La actualidad de Zubiri*, ed. Juan A. Nicolás and Héctor Samour (Granada,: Comares, 2007) 113–230.

11. Xavier Zubiri, *Inteligencia sentiente: Inteligencia y realidad*,(Madrid: Alianza, 1980) 15.
12. Ibid. 57
13. Ignacio Ellacuría, "La superación del reduccionismo idealista en Zubiri," *Estudios centroamericanos* 477 (1988) 633–50, at 648.
14. Ellacuría, *Filosofía de la realidad histórica* 43.
15. Ibid. 493.
16. Xavier Zubiri, "La dimension histórica del ser human," *Siete ensayos de antropología filosófica*, ed. Germán Marquínez Argote, (Bogota: Universidad Santo Tomás, Centro de Enseñanza Desescolarizada, 1982) 117–74, at 127.
17. Zubiri argues that human persons individually (and communities as well) gradually define their own historical reality through the process of creating, transmitting, and actualizing or abandoning the "traditions" of "ways of being in reality" passed on to them by others. See Ellacuría, *Filosofía de la realidad histórica* 528; and Zubiri, *La estructura dinamica de la realidad* (Madrid: Alianza, 1989) 325.
18. For the two primary meanings of "historicization" see Ellacuría, *Filosofía de la realidad histórica* 169; and "La historización del concepto de propiedad como principio de desideologización," *Estudios centroamericanos* 335–336 (1976) 425–50, at 427–28; trans. as "The Historicization of the Concept of Property," in *Towards A Society That Serves Its People: The Intellectual Contribution of El Salvador's Murdered Jesuits*, ed. John J. Hassett and Hugh Lacey, foreword Leo J. O'Donovan (Washington: Georgetown University,1991) 105–37, at 109.
19. This is Ellacuría describing Zubiri in "La historicidad del hombre in Xavier Zubiri," 526. See Zubiri, *Sobre la esencia* 447.
20. Ellacuría, "Hacia una fundamentación" 419.
21. Ibid.
22. Ignacio Ellacuría, *Freedom Made Flesh: The Mission of Christ and His Church* (Maryknoll, N.Y.: Orbis, 1976) 27; trans. John Drury from *Teología política* (San Salvador: Secretaridado Social Interdiocesano, 1973); cited in Sobrino, *Jesus the Liberator* 46–47.
23. Ibid.; cited by Sobrino in *Jesus the Liberator* 47. Ellacuría criticizes Rahner's more transcendental focus, however, claiming that "the yardstick of

Christian living is not to be sought in some alleged supernatural grace whose presence eludes the objectivity of personal and social awareness; it is to be sought in the following of Jesus, which is a visible and verifiable reality" (*Freedom Made Flesh* 31).

24. Sobrino, *Christ the Liberator* 319.
25. Ibid.
26. Rahner argues that the representative character of the symbol must be distinguished from the "merely arbitrary" forms of reference suggested by other "concepts which point linguistically and objectively in the same direction: ειδos, μορπϕη, sign, figure, expression, image, aspect, appearance, etc." He says the symbol is "the highest and most primordial manner in which one reality can represent another ... from the ontological point of view," because "the symbol strictly speaking (symbolic reality) is the self-realization of a being in the other, which is constitutive of its essence" (Karl Rahner, "Theology of the Symbol," *Theological Investigations*, vol. 4 [Baltimore: Helicon, 1966] 221–252, at 224, 225, 234). Ellacuría's theology of *sign* is most fully articulated in *Freedom Made Flesh*. Laurence A. Egan, M.M., in the book's foreword (vii–ix, at viii) describes Ellacuría as a "former student of Karl Rahner" who "has tried to combine the insights of Rahner with those of the Theology of Liberation—a synthesis ... imbued with the reality of Central America."
27. Ellacuría, *Teología política* 9; *Freedom Made Flesh* 18.
28. Rahner, "Theology of the Symbol" 237. The argument of this section is developed more fully in Robert Lassalle-Klein, "Rethinking Rahner on Grace and Symbol" 93–96.
29. Ibid. 224–25.
30. Ellacuría, *Teología política* 48; *Freedom Made Flesh* 89.
31. Ignacio Ellacuría, "Discernir 'el signo' de los tiempos," *Diakonía* 17 (1981) 57–59, at 58. The crucified people first appears in Ignacio Ellacuría, "El pueblo crucificado, ensayo de soteriología histórica," in *Cruz y resurrección: anuncio de una Iglesia nueva*, ed. I. Ellacuría et al. (Mexico City, CTR, 1978) 49–82; translated as "The Crucified People," in *Mysterium Liberationis* (Maryknoll, N.Y.: Orbis, 1993) 580–604.
32. Two months after the assassination of Rutilio Grande, Archbishop Romero delivered this important homily to the Jesuit's former parishoners in Aguilares, El Salvador, telling the traumatized peasants, "You are the image of the pierced savior" ("Homilia en Aguilares [June 19, 1977], *La voz de los sin voz: La palabra viva de Monseñor Oscar Arnulfo Romero* [San Salvador: UCA, 1980] 207–12, at 208).
33. Ignacio Ellacuría, "The Crucified People," *Mysterium Liberationis* 580–603, at 580.
34. Jon Sobrino, "Ignacio Ellacuría, the Human Being and the Christian: 'Taking the Crucified People Down From the Cross,'" *Love That Produces Hope* 1–67, at 5, trans. Robert Lassalle-Klein from "Ignacio Ellacuría, el hombre

y el cristiano: Bajar de la cruz al pueblo crucificado," *Revista latinoamericano de teología* 32 (1994) 134.
35. Ibid. Throughout this article, emphases in quotations are original unless otherwise indicated.
36. See Sobrino, *Jesus the Liberator* 254–73; and *Christ the Liberator* 3–8.
37. Sobrino identifies three "typical situations" of "present-day deaths for God's Kingdom [that] are like Jesus' death" (*Jesus the Liberator* 268). There are priests, nuns, catechists, delegates of the word, students, trade unionists, peasants, workers, teachers, journalists, doctors, lawyers, etc., who structurally reproduce the martyrdom of Jesus—"they defended the Kingdom and attacked the anti-Kingdom" with a prophetic voice "and were put to death" (ibid. 269). There are those who die an ethical "soldier's death," defending the Kingdom by open struggle, using "some sort of violence." He believes such a person may "share in martyrdom by analogy" by "laying down one's life for love" (ibid. 270). Then, "finally, there are the [innocent and anonymous] masses who are . . . murdered, even though they have not used any explicit form of violence, even verbal." Sobrino notes that, "They do not actively lay down their lives to defend the faith, or even directly to defend God's Kingdom." For "they are the peasants, children, women, and old people above all who died slowly day after day, and die violently with incredible cruelty and totally unprotected." But, he argues, "their historical innocence," like that of the Suffering Servant, shows they "are unjustly burdened with a sin that has been annihilating them" (ibid. 270–71).
38. Sobrino, *Christ the Liberator* 4.
39. Karl Rahner, "The Two Basic Types of Christology," *Theological Investigations*, vol. 13, trans. David Bourke (New York: Seabury, 1975) 213–23.
40. "Two Basic Types" 213–14.
41. Sobrino's assertion that the historical development of dogma about Jesus Christ reflects the historical character of the divine economy of salvation appears not to have been considered in the recent notification issued by the CDF. The document clearly admits, on the one hand, that "Father Sobrino does not deny the divinity of Jesus when he proposes that it is found in the New Testament only 'in seed' and was formulated dogmatically only after many years of believing reflection." However, it criticizes a "reticence" that "fails to affirm Jesus' divinity with sufficient clarity," which, it asserts, "gives credence to the suspicion that the historical development of dogma . . . has arrived at the formulation of Jesus' divinity without a clear continuity with the New Testament" (CDF, "Notification on the Works of Father Jon Sobrino, S.J.," in *Hope and Solidarity* 256). Reading Sobrino's work as an example of what Rahner calls "saving history" Christology, however, supports the interpretation that what the notification sees as "reticence" is instead a reflection of Sobrino's analytical focus on the church's "process of 'rising up'" from its first generation faith-filled

response to the life, death, and resurrection of Jesus Christ to the fully elaborated fourth-century doctrinal claims of Chalcedon as an act inspired by the Holy Spirit and "proper to God himself." Referring to the criticism of the CDF, William Loewe correctly points out that "the Congregation does not insist that Sobrino *should* be read as saying this, nor does his text support such a reading. Rather the opposite is the case" (Loewe, "Interpreting the Notification" 146, 150).

42. Rahner, "Two Basic Types" 215, emphasis added.
43. Sobrino, *Jesus the Liberator* 45.
44. Sobrino, *Jesucristo liberador* 104; Sobrino, *Jesus the Liberator* 55.
45. Ibid.
46. Like many theologians, Ellacuría and Sobrino, from Medellín on, place great emphasis on the Kingdom of God as a defining element of the message and ministry of Jesus. Ellacuría, however, characteristically links the fundamental theological significance of the kingdom preached by Jesus to what he calls "the transcendental unity of the history of salvation," arguing that the kingdom reveals that "there are not two histories but one single history in which the presence of the liberator God and the presence of the liberated and liberator human being are joined together" (Ignacio Ellacuría, "La teología de la liberacion frente al cambio socio-historicao de America Latina," *Revista latinoamericana de teología* 4 [1987] 21.
47. Rahner, Two Basic Types 214.
48. Sobrino, *Jesus the Liberator* 36–63, at 36.
49. Ibid. 36–37.
50. Ibid. 50. Sobrino's notion of the "poor with spirit" goes back to an early essay by Ellacuría on the Beatitudes where he interprets the first beatitude of Matthew 5:3 as "Blessed are the poor with spirit" (Ignacio Ellacuría, "Las bienaventuranzas como carta fundamental de la Iglesia de los pobres," in *Iglesia de los pobres y organizaciones populares*, ed. Oscar Romero et al. (San Salvador, UCA, 1979) 105–18; repr. in Ellacuría, *Escritos teológicos* 2:417–37, see esp. 423.
51. Sobrino, *Jesucristo liberador* 96, 100, 102; *Jesus the Liberator* 50, 52, 54.
52. Sobrino, *Jesus the Liberator* 28.
53. Ibid. 50–52., esp. 50.
54. Ibid. 52.
55. Ibid.
56. Ibid. 51.
57. Ibid.
58. Ibid. 67.
59. Sobrino, *Jesucristo liberador* 121; *Jesus the Liberator* 67.
60. Sobrino, *Jesucristo liberador* 122; *Jesus the Liberator* 67.
61. Sobrino, *Jesus the Liberator* 69.
62. Ibid. 70.
63. Ibid. 75.

64. Ibid. 76.
65. Ibid. 76–77.
66. Ibid. 77.
67. Ibid. 78.
68. Ibid.
69. Ibid. 79.
70. Ibid. 87.
71. Ibid. 161.
72. Ibid. 87.
73. Ibid. 93.
74. Ibid. 95.
75. Ibid. 95–99.
76. Ibid. 97.
77. Ibid. 100–101.
78. Ibid. 103.
79. Ibid. 123.
80. Ibid. 161.
81. Ibid. 160.
82. Ibid. 161.
83. Ibid.
84. Ibid. 179.
85. Ibid. 50.
86. Ibid. 52–54.
87. Daniel J. Harrington, S.J., "What Got Jesus Killed? Sobrino's Historical-Theological Reading of Scripture," in *Hope and Solidarity* 79–89, at 81.
88. Ibid.
89. Ibid.
90. Ibid. 82.
91. Ibid.
92. Ibid.
93. Ibid. 82–83.
94. Ibid. 83.
95. Ibid.
96. Ibid. 84.
97. Ibid. 85.
98. Sobrino, *Jesus the Liberator* 196.
99. Sobrino clearly insists on the normativity of the received tradition (*Christ the Liberator* 36), while illustrating David Tracy's widely accepted definition of systematic theology as "the discipline that articulates mutually critical correlations between the meaning and truth of an interpretation of the Christian fact, and the meaning and truth of an interpretation of the contemporary situation." David Tracy, "The Foundations of Practical Theology," in *Practical Theology: The Emerging Field in Theology, Church and World*, ed. Don S. Browning [New York: Harper & Row, 1983] 61–82, at 62).

100. Sobrino, *Jesucristo liberador* 102–4, *Jesus the Liberator* 54–55.
101. Sobrino, *Christ the Liberator* 225.
102. Ibid. 225.
103. Ibid.
104. Sobrino, *Jesucristo liberador* 413; this sentence is part of a paragraph not translated in the English edition.
105. Sobrino, *Christ the Liberator* 226, emphasis added.
106. Ibid. 64, emphasis added.
107. Ibid. 55.
108. Ibid. 64, emphasis added.
109. Ibid. 64–65.
110. Ibid.
111. Ibid. 35.
112. Ibid. 36.
113. Ibid. 319.
114. Ibid.
115. Ibid. 35. Matthew Ashley asserts that Sobrino's principles are formulated in reference to "a hope that hopes first . . . for the raising to full life of the poor; a praxis devoted to raising them up now by striving for justice for the poor and . . . a knowing that is open to the surprise of finding God revealed in the poor" (J. Matthew Ashley, "The Resurrection of Jesus and Resurrection Discipleship in the Systematic Theology of Jon Sobrino," summarized in Tatha Wiley, "Christology," Catholic Theological Society of America, *Proceedings of the Sixtieth Annual Convention* 60 [2005] 104).
116. Sobrino, *Christ the Liberator* 45.
117. Ibid. 36.
118. Ibid. 42.
119. Ibid. 45.
120. Ibid.
121. Ibid.
122. Ibid.
123. Ibid. 46.
124. Ibid. 47.
125. Ibid. 48.
126. Ibid.
127. Originally published in *30 Giorni* 3.3 (1984) 48–55; republished. in *Il Regno: Documenti* 21 (1984) 220–223; cited in Sobrino, *Christ the Liberator* 48.
128. Sobrino, *Christ the Liberator* 48. The first instance of this metaphor is cited as Ignacio Ellacuría, "Las Iglesias latinoamericanas interpelan a la Iglesia de España," *Sal Terrae* 3 (1983) 230.
129. In his important essay on Ignacio Ellacuría as an interpreter of Ignatian spirituality, Ashley asserts that Ellacuría's "philosophy and theology had

as their goal the communication of a powerful 'fundamental intuition' from the *Spiritual Exercises*," which he later describes as a "mysticism of the historical event." In a related article, Ashley asserts that Ellacuría tried to put this spirituality "at the service of the church in Latin America . . . by seeking philosophical and theological language and arguments to articulate the encounter with Christ that is structured by Ignatius Loyola's *Spiritual Exercises*," and which is embodied in the Ignatian tradition of "contemplation in action." While I agree with and build upon Ashley's insights in this regard, my article places more emphasis on the trinitarian dimensions of Ignatian spirituality (which Ashley recognizes) and their influence on Ellacuría's theology of sign. See J. Matthew Ashley, "Ignacio Ellacuría and the *Spiritual Exercises* of Ignatius Loyola," *Theological Studies* 61 (2000) 16–39, at 37, 39; "Contemplation in the Action of Justice: Ignacio Ellacuría and Ignatian Spirituality," in *Love That Produces Hope* 144, 145, 164 n 54.

130. David L. Fleming, S.J., *The Spiritual Exercises of Saint Ignatius: A Literal Translation and a Contemporary Reading* (St. Louis: The Institute of Jesuit Sources, 1978) 70–74, 102–9.
131. "Our Mission Today: The Service of Faith and the Promotion of Justice" no. 14, *Documents of the 31st and 32nd General Congregations of the Society of Jesus* 414.
132. Miguel Elizondo, "La Primera Semana como comienzo indispensable de conversión," in *Reunion-Ejercicios de la Viceprovincia Jesuitica de Centroamerica, Diciembre 1969*," vol. 2 of *Reflexion teológico-espiritual de la Compañia de Jesus en Centroamerica* (San Salvador: Archives of the Society of Jesus, Central American Province, Survey S.J. de Centroamerica) 1–8, at 3.
133. Ibid. 3, 4.
134. Sobrino, *Christ the Liberator* 48.
135. Ibid.
136. Ibid. 53.
137. Ibid.
138. Sobrino, *Jesucristo liberador* 50.
139. Ibid. 52.
140. Sobrino, *Christ the Liberator* 340.
141. Ibid. 340.
142. Ibid.
143. Rahner, "Two Basic Types" 214.
144. Sobrino, *Christ the Liberator* 319.
145. Sobrino, "Jesus, Real Symbol of the Word," in ibid.
146. Ellacuría, *Freedom Made Flesh* 27.
147. Ignacio Ellacuría, "Fe y justicia," Escritos teológicos, vol. 3 (San Salvador: UCA, 2002) 307–73, at 319–20; repr. from *Christus* 42 (August 1977) 26–33, and (October 1977) 19–34.
148. Ibid.

149. Ibid.
150. Rahner, "Two Basic Types" 214.
151. Ellacuría, "Discernir 'el signo' de los tiempos," *Diakonía* 17 (1981) 58; also Ellacuría, "The Crucified People" 580–603.

Galilean Journey *Revisited*

Mestizaje, Anti-Judaism, and the Dynamics of Exclusion

Michael E. Lee

The article explores Virgilio Elizondo's Galilean Journey and its critiques, particularly the claim that he uses anti-Jewish rhetoric. While acknowledging the legitimacy of some concerns, the author argues that in both its object of study (the New Testament portrayal of Jesus as Galilean) and its hermeneutical location (marginalized contemporary believers), Elizondo's work provides regulative principles for interpretation that guard against the dangers of anti-Jewish, supersessionist readings of the Gospels. The key lies in viewing Jesus' prophetic ministry as a model of faithful dissent against forces of marginalization and exclusion.

"Surely you are not also from Galilee, are you?
Search and you will see that no prophet is to arise
from Galilee" (Jn 7:52).

RECENT DECADES HAVE SEEN critiques by scholars doing historical Jesus research of his portrayal in theologies inspired by the preferential option for the poor.[1] Virgilio Elizondo's landmark work, *Galilean Journey: The Mexican-American Promise*, has been criticized by some for anti-Jewish rhetoric in its portrait of Galilee, and of Jesus' conflicts with the Jewish religious authorities in Jerusalem.[2] Mary Boys treats Elizondo's work as emblematic of liberation theologies, asserting, "Scholarship simply does not support the sweeping generalizations they draw, and the anti-Judaism in their work is appalling."[3]

The basic tension that Elizondo identifies, however, is not his own invention. It is rooted, rather, in the Gospel narratives themselves and raises complex issues for certain readers of the Second Testament. The deadly conflict between Jesus and some Jerusalem authorities poses special problems for a culturally contextualized theology like *Galilean Journey*, which wrestles with experiences of marginalization in the Mexican-American experience. In what follows, I argue that Elizondo's focus on the critical-prophetic nature of Jesus' ministry fortifies and encourages Christian efforts toward justice, and (while granting some points of his critics) cannot be fairly said to advocate for the superiority of Christianity over Judaism. I suggest, rather, that the critiques serve to focus attention on the complex hermeneutics of interpreting (for a post-Holocaust world) the first century intra-Jewish conflicts that led to the death of Jesus. Thus, we are led to ask, How can Christians hold fast to the prophetic dimension of Jesus' ministry, portrayed in the Gospels as a confrontation with Jewish religious authorities, without falling into, or being vilified for, anti-Judaism?

On the one hand, if Christian accounts of Jesus omit his critical stance toward the religious hypocrisy, legalism, and exclusionism of important elements of first-century Jewish leadership, then significant dimensions of his preaching and ministry are lost. Indeed, it would seem these lessons should be at the forefront of Christian self-examination regarding the sad consequences of later efforts to establish Christian identity in contradistinction to Judaism. On the other hand, when such themes are linked to anti-Jewish caricatures and supersessionist theological ideas, the tragic legacy of Christian mistreatment of Jews is inevitably perpetuated and their contribution to liberation threatened. I argue, therefore, that both historical Jesus research and theologies grounded in the option for the poor have important, complementary, and sometimes mutually corrective roles to play in seeking a solution to this dilemma.

Biblical scholarship has identified sections where the Gospels retroject conflicts between nascent Christianity and Judaism into the time of Jesus, and literary and archeological sources continue to deepen our understanding of the religious, cultural, and political character of the Galilean region where Jesus spent most of his life. At the same time, the transhistorical problem of Christian anti-Judaism increasingly demands a hermeneutic to assist in the reception of these biblical accounts among Christian faith communities in a post-Holocaust environment. In what follows, I argue that Elizondo's theology and the U.S. Latino/a theologies his work has helped to initiate (1) offer important insights on questions of marginalization, alienation, and power, and (2) provide valuable hermeneutical resources for the ongoing reception of Gospel accounts of Jesus' ministry and its attendant conflicts.[4] I also suggest that Elizondo's principles be turned around to assist in the interpretation his own work, so that its ongoing reception remains true to its liberative spirit.

Elizondo frames his analysis of the Galilean Jesus in his account of the dynamics of *mestizaje*, that often-violent encounter of cultures at the heart of the Mexican-American experience.[5] He recognizes the powerful forces of exclusion faced by mestizos/as in a borderland existence, including a double rejection by those on both sides of the border. Elizondo finds hope in Jesus the Galilean who himself experiences this double rejection, and whose ministry, as narrated in the Gospels, incarnates three principles that serve to overcome such exclusion: (1) the Galilee principle: God loves what human beings reject;[6] (2) the Jerusalem principle: God calls and empowers the marginalized to resist the powers of exclusion and domination;[7] and (3) the Resurrection principle: only the power of love can conquer evil.[8]

This article argues that, viewed within the larger context of the mestizo/a's double rejection and the aforementioned principles, the basic insights of *Galilean Journey* work against anti-Jewish readings by interpreting Jesus' conflict with Jewish authorities as the prophetic battle against exclusion of a Galilean firmly rooted within the Jewish tradition. Drawing from his experience of traditional Mexican-American fidelity to ecclesial and social bodies despite marginalization, Elizondo ultimately envisions Jesus as a faithful dissenter. In this way, Jesus offers a path to resist all forms of exclusion, epitomizing Elizondo's view that resistance springs from fidelity and love of one's own tradition.

The essay begins by analyzing the structure and content of *Galilean Journey* as a constructive theological project, which draws a mutually critical correlation between Elizondo's interpretation of the contemporary situation of Mexican-American *mestizaje* and his understanding of the significance of the Galilean dimension of the identity of Jesus. My second part considers critiques that *Galilean Journey* evidences anti-intellectual romanticism, anti-Jewish rhetoric, and/or anti-historical anachronisms. My third part examines how Elizondo's distinctive hermeneutical location shapes the aforementioned principles, which, I argue, serves to adjudicate the claims made against the text. Elizondo's principles, I will propose, draw our attention to traces of the logic of exclusion in the accusations themselves. Overall, my goal is to revisit the portrait developed in *Galilean Journey* of Jesus as a faithful dissenter who speaks and acts against the dynamics of exclusion suffered by marginalized Jews and certain others in first-century Palestine and to demonstrate its ongoing significance for people of diverse races, cultures, and religions today.

Galilean Journey: Rejection of the Mestizo Transformed into Principles of Hope

The power of Virgilio Elizondo's *Galilean Journey* is rooted in its creative correlation of the Gospel Jesus with Elizondo's own Mexican-American experience.[9] Following David Tracy's understanding of theology as the mutually critical correlation between an interpretation of the faith tradition and an interpretation of a contemporary situation, I would characterize *Galilean Journey* not as a work of historical Jesus research but as a foundational correlational text of Latino/a systematic theology with important christological implications in its own right.[10]

Elizondo explicitly identifies the Mexican-American experience as the setting for his theological reflection. Methodologically, the historical influence of Latin American colleagues on Elizondo draws our attention to the see-judge-act method inherited from Catholic Action and powerfully used in the episcopal documents of Medellín and a number of liberation theologians.[11] In Elizondo's work, this method first yields a "seeing" of the basic sociocultural reality of Mexican-Americans: the situation he calls *mestizaje*. Second, Elizondo interprets this situation in light of the Gospels, and, true to his correlational approach, highlights corresponding aspects in the sociocultural situation of the Gospels and of Jesus himself.[12] And third, Elizondo formulates the aforementioned principles as implications of God's work in Jesus of Galilee for Christian action and discipleship today.[13] In what follows I summarize each of these themes and suggest their significance for theology today.

Seeing the Reality of the Mexican-American Experience: Mestizaje

Without question, Elizondo's focus on *mestizaje* as a reality demanding theological reflection represents one of the most significant and enduring contributions of *Galilean Journey*.¹⁴ For Elizondo *mestizaje* involves the (often violent) meeting of two cultures and possesses a dual nature. The term connotes both the suffering inherent in conquest and marginalization, and the positive potential linked to the creation of new identities. Elizondo asserts that Mexican-American identity is a product of two *mestizajes*: (1) the Spanish-Indigenous encounter that originated in the European conquest of Mexico and helped produce the Mexican people and their culture, and (2) the Nordic-Protestant wresting of Northern Mexico into U.S. hands and the creation of the Mexican-American reality. The genius of Elizondo's approach lies in his recognition of both the deplorable nature of the conquests and the painful struggles that have produced *mestizaje*, and his illumination of the resilient beauty of the Mexican and Mexican-American peoples and cultures that have appeared in their wake.

Elizondo outlines the cruel power dynamics that often attend *mestizaje* in three "anthropological" laws: group inclusion/exclusion, social distance, and elimination of opposition.¹⁵ The first law specifies the dangerous tendency of human beings to separate and classify each other, creating polarities of "us" versus "them" in the name of group purity.¹⁶ The second law indicates that these insider-outsider, superior-inferior polarities, when reified in social structures of domination, create social distances that order and condition even genuinely positive interpersonal relationships—witness how acts by the dominant group may, even unconsciously, involve paternalism or an implicit call to assimilation. The third law says that "anyone who threatens to diminish or destroy the barriers of group separation must be eliminated."¹⁷ Grounded as they are in the commitment to group purity, Elizondo's laws capture the fear and animosity that too often result from *mestizaje*.

Elizondo asserts that the mestizo/a blurs codes of group purity, and that this leads to a pattern of double rejection. He evocatively describes the situation of Mexican Americans who are not "Mexican" enough to achieve full acceptance by relatives and friends in Mexico, and are not "American" enough for U.S. citizens. This rejection manifests itself economically, politically, culturally, psychologically, and religiously, so that even the overcoming of oppressive obstacles is fraught with ambiguity. Despite these problems, however, Elizondo identifies creative possibilities in *mestizaje*, especially in the powerful religious symbols of Mexican-American culture.

Surprisingly perhaps, Elizondo does not attempt to excavate or construct an aboriginal or autochthonous religiosity in opposition to colonially imposed Christianity, a move that might reify the very barriers he denounces. Instead, he exalts the beauty of Mexican-American religiosity and specifically that of his own Roman Catholic tradition as a rich resource and site of resistance and survival. For Elizondo, "Christianity was not so much superimposed upon as implanted and 'naturalized' in the Mexican-American way of life."[18] Having detailed the cruel dimensions of the double *mestizaje* of Mexican Americans, Elizondo abjures benign views of the conquest. However, rather than reject the religiosity that emerges from the conquest, he extols its beauty and creative possibilities. Accordingly, he identifies elements in Mexican-American religiosity—its images, rituals, devotions, saintly figures, etc.—that serve not only as symbols of struggle, suffering, and death, but also as symbols of a new creation.[19] These popular traditions mediate a sense of ultimate belonging. Since Mexican-American religiosity is profoundly Christian, Elizondo turns to the figure of Jesus, particularly Jesus the Galilean Jew, to both articulate the characteristics of this new creation and to elicit new understandings of Christian sacred texts concerning Jesus Christ.

The Galilean Jesus and Judgment: Reading Culture and a Cultural Rereading of the Gospels

Elizondo's exploration of *mestizaje* and the value he places on Mexican-American religiosity establishes *Galilean Journey* as an important and creative theological work. How he uses these insights to carry out a cultural rereading of Jesus as a Galilean, however, defines his contribution to Christology, a contribution that must be situated correctly so that it is not confused with historical Jesus research. For, while his work explores the historical world, actions, and words of the first-century Jesus of Nazareth, *Galilean Journey* is neither a work of biblical scholarship nor a part of "third quest" historical Jesus research.[20] Elizondo clearly states that he views his work as pastoral theology,[21] a culturally-conditioned reading of the Gospels that turns to the Second Testament to shed light on the contemporary situation of Mexican Americans, but that also draws from the Mexican-American experience to "turn up previously hidden aspects of the gospel message."[22]

Elizondo's description of his correlational method places him in what Elizabeth Johnson identifies as the "second wave of renewal in Catholic Christology."[23] Rather than using the Chalcedonic formula of Jesus Christ's full divinity and full humanity as a starting point, theologians of this post-Vatican II generation turn to the scriptural narratives about Jesus' historical ministry.[24] What results is a reading of Jesus that is not less faithful or traditional, but one that, in light of modern historical consciousness, is focused on the "history of Jesus" so as to render a more faithful discipleship among believers today. Johnson writes:

> If Jesus is the revelation of God and stood for definite purposes and upheld certain values, then the significance of that for believers is inestimable. What he does in the concrete, matters; it embodies the way of God in this world which patterns our way as disciples today. . . . Jesus does not just have a human nature in the abstract, but a very concrete human history. We need to put that story into dialogue with our own lives today.[25]

Although Elizondo makes assertions regarding the historical reality of Jesus of Nazareth, *Galilean Journey* does not attempt to reconstruct the life of the "historical Jesus," and does not try to discern the intentions of the biblical authors. Instead, it rereads the Gospel narratives concerning Jesus' cultural reality in the borderland area of Galilee from the perspective of today's borderland dwellers. When Elizondo develops the notion of Galilee as a symbol of multiple rejection, he draws not just from the biblical texts and the work of biblical archeology and history, but from the very experience of multiple rejection that is part of the contemporary Mexican-American *mestizaje*. Thus Elizondo's provocative image of Jesus the Galilean as a "borderland reject"[26] correlates: (1) the Christian confession of Jesus Christ as a fully-human being—incarnated in the specific body, time, place, and culture of a first-century Galilean; (2) the biblical account of Jesus' ministry occurring primarily in the marginal area of Galilee; and (3) the Mexican-American experience of borderland marginalization.

For Elizondo, taking Jesus' humanity seriously demands attention to his cultural reality as a Galilean. Theologically, the incarnation is not abstract, but involves God becoming a human being with a cultural reality, and that is crucial for understanding what God reveals to humanity in Jesus Christ. One aspect of this revelation is that the cultural reality of the Galilean Jesus is marked by the kind of double rejection experienced by mestizo/as today. Elizondo draws this comparison:

> The image of the Galileans to the Jerusalem Jews is comparable to the image of the Mexican-Americans to the Mexicans of Mexico. On the other hand, the image of the Galileans to the Greco-Romans is comparable to the image of the Mexican-American to the Anglo population of the United States. They were part of and despised by both [Mexicans and U.S. Anglos].[27]

We have already seen that Elizondo emphasizes not only the destructive potential of *mestizaje* in the "anthropological" laws of group inclusion/exclusion, social distance, and elimination, but also its creative potential for bringing about new life. Jesus' ministry epitomizes the latter, inasmuch as he manifests the scandalous, transgressive nature of *mestizaje* by valorizing as most beloved by God what has been rejected by human beings. Elizondo asserts that the Galilean ministry of Jesus announces good news that subverts the polarizing barriers of human exclusion and, in doing so, directly confronts the powers that most benefit from the entrenched status quo.[28] If Galilee represents the margins, then Jerusalem, and specifically the rejection of Jesus and his message by some of the Temple authorities, represents the oppressive center. Accordingly, it is the movement of the Gospel narratives themselves from Galilee to Jerusalem and their ultimate culmination in the resurrection that provides the pattern for Elizondo's constructive theological statement in the Galilee principle, the Jerusalem principle, and the Resurrection principle.[29]

The Galilean Journey as Action: Three Principles and the Legacy of Latino/a Theology

Elizondo's three principles signal the engagement of his christological reflection with the "preferential option for the poor" and Christian discipleship as prophetic praxis.[30] The Galilee principle—"what human beings reject, God chooses as his very own"—succinctly summarizes the preferential option for the poor,[31] and functions as a fundamental guide for Christian discipleship.[32] The Jerusalem principle lifts up the agency of oppressed people as a way to avoid fatalism and paternalism in their confrontation with structural evils, including racism and the abuses of liberal capitalism. And the Resurrection principle—"only love can triumph over evil, and no human power can prevail against the power of unlimited love"[33]—crowns Elizondo's theological correlation, marking out parameters for Christian discipleship grounded in the disciples' encounter with the risen Jesus of Galilee.

Galilean Journey has fueled the development of U.S. Latino/a theologies for 30 years, particularly in the study of popular religiosity, mestizaje, and the everyday reflection of Latino/a communities on Jesus Christ.[34] Latino/a theological reflection on Jesus has focused on the Galilee principle of valorizing the marginalized, the Jerusalem principle of prophetic resistance, and the Resurrection principle of new creation.[35] Latino/a authors have made some of their most distinctive contributions elaborating the notion that Jesus dignifies the marginalized and shares an identity with them. In *Jesus Is My Uncle*, Luis Pedraja portrays a Jesus who responds to the cultural alienation felt by U.S. Latino/as.[36] Locating marginalization in culture and language, as well as in economics, U.S. Latino/a theologians complement Latin American liberation theology as a genuine reflection on the particularity of the U.S. Latino/a situation. This comes through in the work of Miguel De La Torre, who explores the *Ajiaco* Christ of Cuban christological reflection, devotion, and artistic depiction.[37] Such portrayals capture how Latino/a theology interprets the preferential option for the poor through what Elizondo calls the "Galilee principle," the identification of God with the marginalized person as embodied in both the person and ministry of Jesus Christ.

The Jerusalem principle asserts that God's love for the rejected should not pacify but rather empower the marginalized to transform the structures of rejection. Accordingly, U.S. Latino/a theology has always had a strong prophetic critique and a vision of Jesus as liberator, emphasizing active Christian discipleship expressed in communal and social resistance to oppressive structures. Though the legacy of Iberian colonial Christian devotion can seem to some a profoundly interiorized, emotional, and fatalistic spirituality, U.S. Latino/as have transformed this devotional background into the material for social resistance. Even a cursory glance at the many *Via Crucis* devotions around the United States demonstrates how Latino/a communities wed profound Christian religiosity with protest of social evils and exploitation.[38] Jesus is not just the victim with whom one identifies, but the liberator whose mission the disciple carries forward. For many U.S. Latino/as, Jesus' prophetic critique also empowers women, struggling for liberation from oppression as sub-alterns within a marginalized population.[39]

As seen in this reference to the *Via Crucis*, U.S. Latino/a reflection on Christ highlights the liberative dimensions of esthetic-transformative practice. Themes such as beauty, celebration, and a relational anthropology give witness to the Resurrection principle of love that triumphs over evil.[40] Despite deep and lingering marginalization and exclusion, U.S. Latino/a theology resonates with the language of new hope, new creation, and reconciliation. Though much work remains, the richness and variety of Latino/a theologies reflect and expand upon the important legacy of Elizondo's *Galilean Journey*. The future reception of this classic, however, is threatened by serious allegations that require honest scrutiny if *Galilean Journey* is to continue to bear fruit.

Journey in the Wrong Direction?
Galilean Journey *and Anti-Judaism*

Critics of *Galilean Journey* invariably focus their most vehement opposition on two short sections—"Galilee: Symbol of Multiple Rejection" and "Jerusalem: Symbol of Established Power"[41]—built around geographical and metaphorical polarities that Elizondo seeks to overcome, and to which his constructive theological-pastoral proposals respond. Though brief, detractors argue that the errors found in these sections overshadow the work as a whole.

Critics find fault particularly with the manner in which *Galilean Journey* construes Jesus' Galilee against what appears to be its polar opposite, the oppressive center of Jerusalem. Some accuse Elizondo of anti-intellectual romanticization of Galilee, an anti-Jewish juxtaposition of Jesus and the Jewish authorities of Jerusalem, and/or nonhistorical and ideologically driven eisegesis, reading his contemporary theory of *mestizaje* into the ancient world of Galilee. Any ongoing reception of Elizondo's text must take these critiques seriously. Ironically, their implications lead to the very types of exclusion that Elizondo ostensibly condemns. Among the various critics of *Galilean Journey*, the most pertinent voice for its future reception in Latino/a circles has to be that of Jean-Pierre Ruiz.[42]

Ruiz briefly analyzes *Galilean Journey* in the context of a larger conversation among biblical scholars and systematic theologians. Lamenting the fragmentation and isolation of work in these areas, Ruiz, citing Stephen Fowl, notes sadly how historical criticism of the Bible has "largely become separated from the theological ends it was initially meant to serve. While most biblical scholars of both Testaments still continue to identify themselves as Christians, they generally are required to check their theological convictions at the door when they enter the profession of biblical studies." Furthermore, Ruiz asserts that historical-critical approaches have been challenged by feminist and other explicitly contextual interpretations of the Bible "that have unmasked it as a set of contextual discourses that reflect the interests and the presuppositions of economically privileged western European Christian male readers." While *Galilean Journey* would seem a salutary example of both biblical-theological cooperation and the unmasking biased discourses, to Ruiz it represents the unconscious reinforcement of deleterious and hegemonic discourses due to its naïve use of source material.

Ruiz levies two central accusations against Elizondo's work in *Galilean Journey*: (1) anti-intellectualism in its construction of Galilean Judaism and, more perniciously, (2) unexamined anti-Judaism flowing from sources in German biblical scholarship, promoting a stark distinction between Jesus and Galilean Judaism on the one hand, and Jerusalem and the Jewish authorities on the other.[43] In light of these accusations, Ruiz calls for a reexamination of *Galilean Journey*'s "hidden assumptions" and the "unexamined implications of its discourse about mestizaje."

In what he terms, "a rare and unfortunate combination for a volume that began as a doctoral dissertation," Ruiz detects a "ruralist romanticism verging on anti-intellectualism" in Elizondo's description of the Galilean Judaism that nurtures Jesus' worldview. He says Elizondo contrasts the "refreshing originality" of Galilean Judaism characterized by "the commonsense, grass-roots wisdom of practical expertise," with the "intellectual preoccupation" of Jerusalem. And he attacks Elizondo's assertion that "Galilean faith in the God of the fathers was thus more personal, purer, simpler, and more spontaneous. It was not encumbered or suffocated by the religious scrupulosities of the Jewish intelligentsia."[44] Ruiz, however, discerns another much deeper problem in *Galilean Journey*. He argues that some of the biblical scholarship supporting Elizondo's overstatement of the tensions between Galilee and Jerusalem evidences the specter of an unexamined anti-Judaism.[45]

Ruiz's central indictment on this score is that, "At the heart of Elizondo's inadvertent anti-Judaism is his uncritical embrace of Western

European exegetical discourses that were themselves irreparably racialized."[46] The key piece of evidence is the fact that Ernst Lohmeyer's *Galiläa und Jerusalem* (1936) appears in Elizondo's bibliography.[47] In this work, Lohmeyer sets Galilee against Jerusalem as part of a two-site origin theory of Christianity,[48] contrasting a universalistic, Son of Man eschatology associated with Galilee, with a nationalistic, Jewish eschatology emerging from Jerusalem. Once the two sites are thus juxtaposed, Ruiz asserts that a supersessionist and ultimately anti-Jewish/anti-Semitic view of Christianity as triumphing over Judaism follows. This leads Ruiz to the startling claim that "here then, are the twisted roots of Elizondo's 'Galilee principle' and his 'Jerusalem principle.'"[49]

Ruiz views *Galilean Journey* as a tragic instance of irresponsible theological research, a negative example that underscores his call for greater cooperation between systematic theologians and biblical scholars. To be clear, Ruiz does not accuse Elizondo of being anti-Semitic, but rather criticizes what he sees as an inadvertent anti-Judaism in *Galilean Journey* owing to its naïve or ignorant use of sources. Thus, Ruiz concludes his essay by admonishing systematic theologians to bear in mind the contextuality of exegetical discourses, which by implication is a standard met by neither Elizondo nor the many theologians who have drawn upon *Galilean Journey* for inspiration.

Though the charge of anti-Judaism (latent or otherwise) represents the most serious criticism of *Galilean Journey*, it is sometimes accompanied by questions of hermeneutical method. Jeffrey Siker seconds Ruiz's criticism that *Galilean Journey* enacts an underlying anti-Judaism in its portrayal of Jerusalem's Judaism as an ossified, legalistic religiosity.[50] He goes beyond Ruiz's charge of ruralist romanticism, however, arguing that Elizondo simply makes claims without foundation. The problem is a hermeneutical one for Siker. He views Elizondo as reversing the "proper" interpretive strategy of "moving from the historical Jesus to a theological appropriation of Jesus," charging that "it appears that Elizondo is really working the other way around, applying the reality of modern mestizo culture in an anachronistic manner onto the map of first-century Galilee and claiming it as an historic reality."[51] Thus, he portrays Elizondo's hermeneutical strategy as an ideological effort to provide a scriptural basis for a theological interpretation of *mestizaje*.

Siker believes that Elizondo does not rely on historical Jesus research in his reconstruction of Galilee and so questions the entire notion of a mestizo Jesus. For Siker, "this anachronistic rendering of first-century Galilee in the image of the borderlands of the American Southwest can undergird Elizondo's theological project only if he is willing to advocate what increasingly appears to be an historical fiction, Galilee as the land of *mestizaje*."[52] What further complicates the scenario is Siker's understanding of *mestizaje*. He states that "Elizondo poses the idea of *mestizaje* in Hegelian terms as the transcendent synthesis of what appear now to be two lesser realities."[53] The implications of Siker's diagnosis leads to a conclusion similar to Ruiz's: not only is *Galilean Journey* bereft of support from biblical research, but given the nefarious nature of its latent anti-Judaism, both the text and the theological enterprise of relating the Galilean Jesus to the notion of *mestizaje* are called into question.

Guide for the Journey:
Jesus, Galilean Jew and Faithful Dissenter

Elizondo's critics, then, not only raise substantive questions about *Galilean Journey* but also pose broader questions regarding the relationship between biblical-historical research and the contemporary appropriation of sacred texts by theologians and communities of faith. Though voicing a relative sympathy for his wider theological program, the basis of their concerns resides in what they perceive to be misguided or erroneous claims about the historical Jesus and the Galilee he inhabited. Thus, historical Jesus research is assumed to provide constructive counterevidence and much needed norms for what can and cannot be said about Jesus.[54] Of course, historical Jesus scholarship is not without its own problems. From ongoing debates among scholars who study Jesus and first-century Galilee, to critics of the entire enterprise who view the historical Jesus as the wrong object of study, historical research on Jesus must not be seen monolithically or simplistically as a clear standard against which all claims about Jesus can be judged. Moreover, as contemporary hermeneutics has demonstrated, the reader's own "horizon of understanding" must be factored in as a crucial component in the process of interpretation. Indeed, I believe this has been the area of Elizondo's primary contribution to theological discourse.[55]

Accordingly, while the final section of this article addresses the aforementioned criticisms of *Galilean Journey*, it also outlines what I see as fundamental hermeneutical and methodological parameters for the proper use of historical Jesus (and Galilee) research, and suggests how these may correct problematic aspects Elizondo's thought. My claim is that, on the one hand, both Elizondo's critics and more recent historical research on Jesus and Galilee provide important correctives to aspects of *Galilean Journey*. On the other hand, however, I will maintain and use Elizondo's three "principles," which undermine the logic of exclusion, to address some of the concerns raised above, and to highlight certain problematic aspects of the critiques themselves.

Reading Jesus: Historical, Historic, and Historicized

Historical research on Galilee and Jesus helps to clarify two shortcomings identified by the aforementioned critics of *Galilean Journey*. First, recent studies undermine the polarities embodied in two outdated and extreme portraits of Galilee at the time of Jesus.[56] It appears that the region conformed neither to the portrait of a staunchly Jewish enclave with no outside cultural exchange or influence favored by some commentators, nor to the portrait of a cosmopolitan, pluralistic region with a limited or non-Jewish identity promoted by others.[57] The more likely scenario is of a Galilee that, though possessing a diverse population and including the imperial cities of Tiberias and Sepphoris, remains profoundly Jewish in identity and rooted in the symbol system of Jerusalem.[58] And for all the cultural interaction that may have occurred, Galilee seems to have been a tense and conflictual setting, not a sunny cosmopolitan land. Thus, to the degree that Elizondo sees Galilee in the latter terms, this scholarship represents a helpful corrective.

Second, recent studies have provided valuable information about Galilean tensions with Judea and the Temple authorities of Jerusalem. Recognizing that these tensions have been exploited by anti-Jewish theologies, most contemporary scholarship insists that they must be interpreted in the context of intracommunity struggles typical of a vibrant and complex first-century Judaism. How to do so remains a debated topic. Richard Horsley situates Jesus and the early Jesus movement within a stream of Galilean resistance movements in the Late Second Temple period.[59] Arguing that Galilee's development is historically distinct from that of Judea, Horsley stresses traditions of Galilean independence within Israel and resentment of the Jerusalem establishment, while emphasizing its profound Jewish identity. Sean Freyne envisions much closer relations between Galilean Jews and their counterparts in Judea, arguing for an orthogenetic relationship with Jerusalem grounded in a shared worldview and symbol system.[60] He insists that this shared worldview implies a Jesus deeply familiar with the Jewish Scriptures of his day.[61] From stories of conquest and settlement to the universalizing vision of the Isaian corpus, Jewish tradition nurtures creative and critical elements in Jesus' ministry and preaching. In this way, Jesus' conflicts with the Temple authorities find their proper context in his synthesis of various strands of Jewish thought.[62]

Though disagreements abound regarding the particulars, contemporary historical scholars studying Jesus and Galilee generally agree that Jesus' conflicts with the Jerusalem authorities do not lead to the conclusion that he is condemning or moving beyond Judaism. This consensus serves as an important corrective to the tenor of some of Elizondo's comments about the novelty of Jesus' preaching or message,[63] which can sound as if Jesus is breaking with Judaism itself. Historical research on Jesus allows us to frame his position as that of a critical and prophetic "insider" who is faithful to Judaism—a position, as will be demonstrated, analogous to what Elizondo himself ultimately assumes.

Thus I would agree, on the one hand, that historical research on Jesus and Galilee provides an important corrective to contemporary formulations about Jesus, including those of Elizondo. At its best, this research enacts a negative function, guiding what cannot said about Jesus without dictating what can be said,[64] and providing leads for new theological ideas. On the other hand, I would argue that this important function does not diminish serious difficulties with both the nature and the object of these studies themselves. As Terrence Tilley notes, several critics of the so-called Third Quest seem to highlight the need for new approaches.[65] Seen in authors as varied as Elisabeth Schüssler Fiorenza, James D. G. Dunn, and Larry Hurtado, these new approaches shift the focus from the historical Jesus to what Tilley calls the "historic Jesus," the person remembered by his followers who enact that memory in story, worship, ritual, and action.[66] Tilley summarizes the methodological significance of this shift:

> The fundamental methodological point we can take from their work is crucial: practices like living in and living out the *basileia tou theou*, worship, and remembering in the community do not merely count in understanding the significance of Christological claims, but in fact

constitute the context of discipleship, the context in which the imaginative and faithful Christological claims in the developing tradition can even have significance.[67]

If Tilley's thesis is correct, Elizondo's claims as articulated in the principles he espouses, are better tested by examining how they are lived out in believing Latino/a communities; and by comparing this with the practical manner in which Jesus' followers enact his memory—be it through worship, the transmission of stories through oral tradition, or actions motivated by the confession of Jesus as Christ. While this comparison to the "historic" Jesus enacted by his followers in story, worship, ritual, and action does not replace "historical" Jesus and Galilee research, it does offer a more nuanced and, I would argue, appropriate standard for judging Elizondo's claims than what critics of *Galilean Journey* have offered to date.

New programs of "historic" Jesus research may indeed open up fruitful avenues of analysis. They nonetheless require a hermeneutics committed both to reading "behind" the text, which characterizes the critics of *Galilean Journey* cited above, and to reading "in front of" the text,[68] which I would argue more properly characterizes Elizondo's approach. My point is that in *Galilean Journey* Elizondo does not seek to describe the historical Jesus but rather focuses on the theological import for the reader of the Gospels' portrayal of Jesus as a Galilean. Elizondo reminds us that Galilee, as it is theologically and symbolically evoked in the Gospels, represents a marginality that resonates with the marginal location of U.S. Latino/as who read the Gospels today. This perspective constitutes the particular hermeneutic of *Galilean Journey* and demarcates its unique contribution. Thus, while historical research may provide cautionary or regulative principles of interpretation or be used to suggest new theological connections, it must be employed cautiously, always explicitly acknowledging the historian's own interpretive horizon.[69]

In this connection, the interpretive locus of marginalized peoples adds an important dimension to the "historical" vs. "historic" Jesus debate. I would argue, in fact, that Elizondo's three principles "historicize" the Jesus found in the Gospels[70] (to borrow the term from Ignacio Ellacuría) and play a crucial role in his correlational interpretive framework. For it is through the mediation of such interpretive devices that the experience of marginalization typical of South-Texas Mexican-Americans of Elizondo's generation is able to illuminate and to actualize the untapped semantic potential of the marginalization of Jesus portrayed in the Gospels. Just as the Gospels historicize in their own narrative and historical worlds the good news announced by Jesus through portraits that highlight the way he resists and overcomes marginalization, so Elizondo's interpretation illumines and historicizes the untapped semantic potential of those portraits for faithful discipleship today. Therefore, while discussions about the "historical" and "historic" Jesus serve to draw our attention to the relationship between the world "behind" the text and the reader "in front of" it, they are enriched when we ask how the Jesus found in each location is "historicized." With this principle in mind, I return to the criticisms of *Galilean Journey*, noting that, while they point to important issues in Elizondo's work, if taken too far, they enact the very logic of exclusion against which they protest.

Faithful Dissent: Speaking against One's Own

Jean-Pierre Ruiz correctly criticizes *Galilean Journey* for espousing a kind of ruralist romanticization in its portrayal of first century Galilee. Given the sad history linking negative portrayals of the Jerusalem/Jewish intelligentsia to anti-Semitic scholarship, he is right to address this issue. Sweeping statements contrasting the fresh originality of Galilean faith with the hypocrisy of the Jerusalemite religious rulers do not belong in a scholarly treatment of Jesus and contribute little to our understanding. On the other hand, Ruiz's accusation that the text is anti-intellectual seems to suggest that Elizondo demeans the intellectual task itself. Similarly, he appears to suggest that Elizondo's portrayal of Jesus as critical of Jewish religious leaders places Jesus outside the circle of Judaism itself.

I would argue, instead, that Elizondo's "rural romanticism" constitutes an extension of the Galilee principle, his theological articulation of the preferential option for the poor. *Galilean Journey* attacks the exclusionary anthropological laws of *mestizaje*, finding beauty and dignity in the mestizo who has been marginalized and excluded. The fact that Elizondo lifts up the dignity of the rural peasant is an important trope, representing a point of view found among those who have been marginalized, the self-defense of those who have been told that they do not have the intellectual capacity to match wits with their oppressors. A wealth of examples from Latino/a culture provides a trajectory within which to situate Elizondo's statements.[71] In this world, as St. Paul would suggest to his mainly non-Jewish followers from the middle and lower classes, the fool confounds the wise and, in doing so, ironically shows where true wisdom abides, which is crucial. Thus, what may seem to some like anti-intellectualism, turns out from another perspective to be a faithful reliance on a God who confounds the wise and unites learning with true wisdom. While I will grant that Elizondo's portrayal requires pruning, I would argue that it captures something real and prophetic in the perspective of the peasant at the margins.

Correspondingly, Elizondo's critique of part of the Jerusalem intelligentsia of first-century Palestine is not a deprecation of the intellect itself but a statement about its proper use. The seemingly contradictory trajectories of Elizondo's own biography make the point: he criticizes an exclusivist intelligentsia while writing his own doctoral dissertation; he is a parish priest from San Antonio on a one-year sojourn in Paris, one of the great intellectual centers of the last 800 years, and funded mainly by the meager savings of his working class mother. In the end, I would argue, Elizondo's critique of the Jewish intelligentsia in Jerusalem is no more "anti-intellectual" than that of Ruiz, when the latter (rightfully) questions the "centrist" bias of much contemporary biblical criticism. Both highlight how "intelligentsia" can lose touch with and marginalize others. What remains to be seen, however, is whether Elizondo's criticism of the Jewish intelligentsia of Jesus' time evidences an anti-Jewish bias.

Nineteenth-century anti-Jewish readings of the Gospels divorce Jesus from his Jewish heritage and Hellenize the early Jesus movement in making the case for a supersessionist Christianity. Elizondo, however, makes no argument for the superior origins of Christianity over against Judaism. He does not advocate Lohmeyer's two-site origin theory, much less Grundmann's notion of a pagan or Aryan Jesus. *Galilean Journey* falls into danger when it amplifies aspects of the conflict between Jesus and the Jerusalem authorities. And vague statements about the Jewish law becoming a burden or about the legalistic scrupulosity of Pharisees not only beg verification but also evoke harmful stereotypes. Despite these shortcomings, however, Elizondo does not divorce Jesus from his Jewish identity. Rather, he emphasizes Jesus' identity as a Jew who, while remaining firmly rooted in his tradition, must face the double marginalization of a mestizo:

As a Galilean confronting Jerusalem, Jesus confronted a structured system to which at the same time he did and he did not belong: he was not one of the in-group, but neither was he a total outsider. In his Galilean identity, he questioned the official structures. *But still, he was a Jew; he questioned the system from within.* . . . As a Galilean he demonstrates the role of a marginal person who by reason of being marginal is both an insider and an outsider—partly both, yet fully neither.[72]

Rejection by one's own constitutes a central theme in Elizondo's treatment of *mestizaje*. Accordingly, I would argue that scholarly evaluation of Elizondo's treatment of the Jewishness of Jesus and his Galilean context must move beyond its present, somewhat narrow, focus on the self-identity of Jesus to include the perception by others of the Jewishness of Jesus—specifically, the views of the first century Jewish intelligentsia and leadership in Jerusalem. The claim that Jesus was critical of the authorities in Jerusalem does not make Jesus any less Jewish.[73] Baldly stated, the claim that it does can be said to echo the logic of first-century and contemporary elites who interpret such protests as heretical. On the other hand, Elizondo brings the insight from the borderland that, while those on the border may identify with the center, those living at the center(s) often reject people from the border in the name of purity. Elizondo's Jerusalem principle, then, provides a model for critical fidelity grounded in the prophetic ministry of the Galilean Jesus and its historical rejection by the Jerusalemite authorities. In fact, neither the Jerusalem principle nor its sources lead inevitably to an anti-Jewish or an anti-intellectual Jesus.

In light of this discussion on "historicizing" Jesus, the final charge that Elizondo's theological ruminations on *mestizaje* reverse the "proper" strategy of assessment seems unfounded. First-century Galilee, like all places, is a constructed and contested space, and Jesus' own ministry has been examined fruitfully using that notion.[74] Though historical research has much to offer, it is subject to the same problems of construction as contemporary theology and offers no more an "objective" place on which to base its conclusions.[75] Elizondo does not superimpose *mestizaje* on Galilee but rather rereads the Gospel narratives from the perspective of *mestizaje*, bringing a fresh perspective that actualizes the untapped semantic potential of the marginalized Galilee portrayed in the Gospels. Elizondo's work, like that of other explicitly contextual theologies of marginalized peoples, offers distinctive insights into issues of power and exclusion particularly from a location of marginalization that has too often been overlooked by elite interpreters.[76]

Finally, the accusation that Elizondo's understanding of *mestizaje* involves a Hegelian sublation of inferior races is an unfortunate example of a dangerous logic of exclusion, particularly the mistaken assertion that Elizondo's focus on raising up the dignity of those facing double rejection is based on the exclusion of others. Elizondo argues that a society is enriched when it embraces the "mixture" of the mestizo/a, but he never suggests that this should happen at the expense of the other. Ultimately, Elizondo's view of *mestizaje* corresponds to the Resurrection principle that "only love can triumph over evil," and that love rejects all forms of exclusion.

Conclusion

Christian claims that Jesus opposed the Jewish authorities have too often tragically focused on the term *Jewish*, whereas they should emphasize *authorities*. Jesus was a faithful Jew whose prophetic critique springs precisely from fidelity to his own religious tradition. The Gospels attest that Jesus assumed a critical prophetic stance toward the excesses of some of the authorities of his day, a stance similar to that of Jesus' prophetic predecessors, Isaiah, Jeremiah, and Amos. This is the tradition of Paul's confrontation with Peter, Catherine of Siena's admonishment of the Avignon papacy, and Martin Luther King Jr.'s scolding of clergymen who sided with the segregationists. The assertion that Jesus criticizes the religious authorities of his own tradition need not, indeed must not, be understood to imply that Jesus is moving outside his tradition. Ironically, claiming so enacts the logic of his adversaries among the elite. Equating faithful dissent with the betrayal of one's tradition perpetuates the age-old strategy of exclusion directed against the mestizo/a, the borderland figure abandoned by both sides.

The deepest pain of the mestizo/a, so powerfully articulated by Elizondo, consists in feeling loyalty and a sense of identification with two groups, yet being rejected by both. For some, rejection flows from characteristics not voluntarily possessed—one's culture, race, gender, etc. For others, exclusion follows from a stance: called a traitor for protesting a nation's unjust war, or a heretic for excoriating the church's injustice and scandal. Purity codes, be they racial/ethnic or ideological, enact logics of exclusion grounded in one-dimensional portraits of those who protest as "the other."

In this article, I have argued that scholars of the historical Jesus and Galilee offer important correctives to aspects of the views of Virgilio Elizondo and other contemporary theologians. On the other hand, I have insisted that theology has an important, sometimes corrective, role to play as well. While John Meier describes Jesus as a "marginal Jew in a marginal province at the eastern end of the Roman empire,"[77] Elizondo offers insight into the significance of that marginality from the margin itself. He reminds us that "marginal" is not an innocent term; it means marginalized. He correlates the double rejection of U.S. Latino/as with the situation of the Jewish Jesus of Galilee, whom the Gospels portray as the object of a double rejection that leads to his execution.

I hope that scholars of both the historical Jesus and the preferential option for the poor will continue to enrich each other's work and end the scourge of anti-Judaism in Christian theology. In this article, I have, on the one hand, argued that biblical scholarship offers a helpful corrective to certain aspects of *Galilean Journey*. On the other hand, I have tried to show how, by lifting the veil on the logic of exclusion, Virgilio Elizondo amplifies the words and illumines the lives of contemporary prophets, authentic disciples of the Galilean Jesus carrying on his ministry in the marginalized Galilees of the world today.[78]

MICHAEL E. LEE received his Ph.D. degree from the University of Notre Dame and is assistant professor in the Theology Department and Institute of Latin American and Latino Studies at Fordham University, New York. His areas of special competency include Christology, soteriology, Latin American theology, and U.S. Latino/a theology. Having recently published *Bearing the Weight of Salvation: The Soteriology of Ignacio Ellacuría* (2008), two works are in progress: a translation of essays by Ellacuría, tentatively titled *Liberation: The Task of History* (Orbis); and a monograph on the theology of Archbishop Oscar Romero.

Notes

1. See, for example, the critique of Jon Sobrino in John P. Meier, "The Bible as a Source for Theology," in *Catholic Theological Society of America, Proceedings*

of the Forty-Third Annual Convention, ed. George Kilcourse, Toronto 43 (June 15–19, 1988) 1–14, at 3.
2. Virgilio Elizondo, *Galilean Journey: The Mexican-American Promise*, 2nd ed. (Maryknoll, N.Y.: Orbis, 1983, 2000).
3. Mary C. Boys, *Has God Only One Blessing? Judaism as a Source of Christian Self-Understanding* (New York: Paulist, 2000) 314 n. 19.
4. Here, the work of feminist theologians, in its self-criticism and (re-)constructive vision, illustrates analogous possibilities. See, for example, Judith Plaskow, "Anti-Judaism in Feminist Christian Interpretation," in *Searching the Scriptures: A Feminist Introduction*, ed. Elisabeth Schüssler Fiorenza (New York: Crossroad, 1993) 116–29; Elisabeth Schüssler Fiorenza, *Jesus, Miriam's Child, Sophia's Prophet: Critical Issues in Feminist Christology* (New York: Continuum, 1994).
5. Noting this violence helps to overcome a romanticization of the term. On its limits, see Roberto Goizueta, "¿La Raza Cósmica? The Vision of José Vasconcelos," *Journal of Hispanic/Latino Theology* 1 2 (1994) 5–27.
6. Elizondo writes, "What human beings reject, God chooses as God's very own" (*Galilean Journey* 91).
7. Elizondo asserts, "God chooses an oppressed people, not to bring them comfort in their oppression, but to enable them to confront, transcend, and transform whatever in the oppressor society diminishes and destroys the fundamental dignity of human nature" (ibid. 103).
8. Elizondo writes, "Only love can triumph over evil, and no human power can prevail against the power of unlimited love" (ibid. 115).
9. Throughout this analysis of the text proper, I prefer to use Elizondo's own phrase "Mexican-American" rather than "Hispanic" or "Latino/a."
10. For a succinct elucidation of the method, see David Tracy, "Theological Method," in *Christian Theology*, ed. Peter C. Hodgson and Robert H. King (Philadelphia: Fortress, 1985) 35–60.
11. Clodovis Boff articulates this method as a triad of "mediations." So, see-judge-act translates into the use of socioanalytical, hermeneutic, and practical mediations. "Epistemology and Method of the Theology of Liberation," in *Mysterium Liberationis: Fundamental Concepts of Liberation Theology*, ed. Jon Sobrino and Ignacio Ellacuría (Maryknoll, N.Y.: Orbis, 1990) 57–85. For an ecclesiastical example of the method, see Oscar Romero, *Voice of the Voiceless: The Four Pastoral Letters and Other Statements*, trans. Michael J. Walsh (Maryknoll, N.Y.: Orbis, 1985).
12. Here Elizondo's innovative work fulfills the 1965 mandate of Vatican II stated in the *Pastoral Constitution on the Church in the Modern World*: "In every age, the church carries the responsibility of reading the signs of the times and of interpreting them in light of the Gospel, if it to carry out its task" (*Gaudium et spes* no. 4, in *The Documents of Vatican II*, ed. Walter M. Abbott [New York: America, 1966], 202).

13. Elizondo never explicitly refers to the see-judge-act model, but I believe it a fruitful way to interpret the three major parts of the text: "The Mexican-American Experience" (see), "The Gospel Matrix" (judge), and "From Margination to New Creation" (act). See Elizondo's essay in this issue for his indebtedness to this pastoral model.
14. Elizondo develops this category more fully in his *The Future is Mestizo: Life Where Cultures Meet*, 2nd ed. (Boulder, Colo.: University of Colorado, 2000).
15. Elizondo, *Galilean Journey* 17–18.
16. It is interesting to note how Elizondo's first "law" resonates with the basic insight of Edward Said's highly influential *Orientalism* (New York: Pantheon, 1978). This is not to imply any overt relationship, but rather to signal how subsequent Latino/a theologians will read *Galilean Journey* in relation to postcolonial theory.
17. Elizondo, *Galilean Journey* 18.
18. Ibid. 32, emphasis original.
19. Certainly, foremost among these is La Morenita, Our Lady of Guadalupe, whom Elizondo has named elsewhere as "mother of the new creation"; see Virgilio Elizondo, *Guadalupe: Mother of the New Creation* (Maryknoll, N.Y.: Orbis, 1997).
20. Outstanding examples include the multivolume project that began with John P. Meier, *A Marginal Jew: Rethinking the Historical Jesus*, 3 vols. (New York: Doubleday, 1991); and the work of John Dominic Crossan, a leading member of the Jesus Seminar:. e.g., *The Historical Jesus: The Life of a Mediterranean Jewish Peasant* (San Francisco: HarperSanFrancisco, 1991).
21. Elizondo, *Galilean Journey* 47.
22. Ibid.
23. Elizabeth A. Johnson, *Consider Jesus: Waves of Renewal in Christology* (New York: Crossroad, 1990) 49. Johnson describes the "first wave" as occurring in the 1950s and 1960s "when theologians pondered the dogmatic confession of Jesus Christ's identity" that yielded a "deeper appreciation of the genuine humanity of the Word made flesh, and of the dignity and value of every human being" (ibid.).
24. Examples cited by Johnson include Karl Rahner (in his later years), Edward Schillebeeckx, Hans Küng, Walter Kasper, Gerald O'Collins, James Mackey, Monica Hellwig, and William Thompson.
25. Johnson, *Consider Jesus* 50.
26. Elizondo, *Galilean Journey*, 54. Methodologically, Elizondo's openness to biblical explanatory methods moves away from Gadamer's comprehensive rejection of method and more closely to the "arc of understanding" found in the work of Paul Ricoeur.
27. Ibid. 52.
28. Specifically, Elizondo argues that the Galilean ministry of Jesus—preaching, healing, and table fellowship with powerful and marginal persons

alike—was the result of his rejecting the rejection he faced as a Galilean and announcing the universal love of God-Abba to other "rejects" of this time and place. This led to his confrontation with systems carrying out that rejection and eventually the cross. Ibid 50–78.

29. For a clarification of Elizondo's treatment of Jerusalem, see his essay in this issue.
30. In identifying these categories as important developments of the 20th century, I do not wish to imply that they are innovations, but rather that this nomenclature identifies important motifs throughout the Christian tradition.
31. Elizondo, *Galilean Journey* 91. Perhaps the theologian who has developed this notion the most in the past few decades is Elizondo's good friend, Gustavo Gutiérrez. In addition to his landmark work, *A Theology of Liberation* (Maryknoll, N.Y.: Orbis, 1973, 1988), see Gutiérrez's concise explanation in "Option for the Poor," in *Mysterium Liberationis* 235–50.
32. Elizondo, *Galilean Journey* 103.
33. Ibid. 115.
34. The following is indebted to the summary of Michelle A. Gonzalez's Hispanic Christology, "Jesus," in *Handbook of Latina/o Theologies*, ed. Edwin David Aponte and Miguel A. De La Torre (St. Louis: Chalice, 2006) 17–24. Her tripartite division of this work is: mestizo Jesus, liberating Jesus, and accompanying Jesus.
35. Of course, this designation is merely heuristic. In fact, most authors combine all three themes in some way. Another dimension of Hispanic research has focused on the reception of Jesus as expressed in symbols of popular religiosity. See, e.g., Orlando Espín, *The Faith of the People: Theological Reflections on Popular Catholicism* (Maryknoll, N.Y.: Orbis, 1997) 77–82.
36. Luis G. Pedraja, *Jesus Is My Uncle: Christology from a Hispanic Perspective* (Nashville: Abingdon, 1999).
37. Miguel A. De La Torre, *The Quest for the Cuban Christ: A Historical Search* (Gainesville: University of Florida, 2002).
38. Karen May Davalos, "'The Real Way of Praying': The *Via Crucis*, Mexicano Sacred Space, and the Architecture of Domination," in *Horizons of the Sacred: Mexican Traditions in U.S. Catholicism*, ed. Timothy Matovina and Gary Riebe-Estrella (Ithaca, N.Y.: Cornell University, 2002) 41–68.
39. Ada María Isasi-Díaz, "Christ in Mujerista Theology," in *Thinking of Christ: Proclamation, Explanation, Meaning*, ed. Tatha Wiley (New York: Continuum, 2003).
40. Perhaps the most powerful example of this theme, and indeed a theological synthesis of all of the above-mentioned themes, can be found in Roberto Goizueta, *Caminemos con Jesús: Toward a Hispanic/Latino Theology of Accompaniment* (Maryknoll, N.Y.: Orbis, 1995).
41. Elizondo, *Galilean Journey*, 51–53 and 68–70, respectively.
42. Jean-Pierre Ruiz, "Good Fences and Good Neighbors? Biblical Scholars and Theologians," *Journal of Hispanic/Latino Theology* 14 (May, 2007),

http://www.latinotheology.org/2007/fences_neighbors (accessed March 16, 2009; site requires subscription). Because this is now an electronic journal, citations of the article will not contain page references.
43. For this second accusation, Ruiz follows much of the argument laid out in Boys, *Has God Only One Blessing?*
44. Elizondo, *Galilean Journey* 51–52.
45. Indeed, it leads Ruiz to assert that "odd anti-intellectualism cum anti-Judaism is a persistent motif in *Galilean Journey*."
46. Ruiz, "Good Fences and Good Neighbors?" Here Ruiz is indebted to the broader analysis of Shawn Kelley, *Racializing Jesus: Race, Ideology, and the Formation of Modern Biblical Scholarship* (New York: Routledge, 2002).
47. Elizondo elsewhere cites Lohmeyer in the text as part of a triad of recent scholars (along with R. H. Lightfoot and Willi Marxsen) who have pointed to Galilee as a significant theological motif in the Gospels. Elizondo, *Galilean Journey* 50.
48. Here Ruiz refers to the work of Susannah Heschel, *Abraham Geiger and the Jewish Jesus* (Chicago: University of Chicago, 1998).
49. Lest there be any doubts about the implications of this tie, Ruiz adds that shortly after Lohmeyer's work appeared, Walter Grundmann (who does not appear in Elizondo's bibliography) suggested that Jesus' taking of the title, "Son of Man," "proved his Galilean, and thus his Aryan, origin."
50. As with Ruiz, Siker understands the Galilee-Jerusalem distinction as ultimately supersessionist. "Elizondo's image of a decrepit and ossified Judaism in Jerusalem buys into a now discredited Christian caricature of Judaism as the dying religion that gave way to nascent Christianity" (Jeffrey S. Siker, "Historicizing a Racialized Jesus: Case Studies in the 'Black Christ,' the 'Mestizo Christ,' and White Critique," *Biblical Interpretation* 15 [2007] 43).
51. Ibid. 40.
52. Ibid. 41.
53. Ibid. 46.
54. This is true particularly in the case of Boys and Siker. And while Ruiz warns against the naïve appropriation of historical research and its underlying racialized discourses, he offers neither constructive counterevidence nor an alternative construction.
55. For a concise summary of the relevant developments in hermeneutics, see Richard E. Palmer, *Hermeneutics: Interpretation Theory in Schleiermacher, Dilthey, Heidegger, and Gadamer* (Evanston, Ill.: Northwestern University, 1969).
56. For a helpful summary of current research on Galilee, see Mark Rapinchuk, "The Galilee and Jesus in Recent Research," *Currents in Biblical Research* 2 (2004) 197–222.
57. There are differing ways to portray this reality. For example, Douglas Edwards argues that the villages of Galilee had access to urban markets and engaged in intra- and interregional trade, while Richard Horsley envisions

a more traditional agrarian society, but with a greater population diversity than Judea's. Douglas Edwards, "The Socio-Economic and Cultural Ethos of the Lower Galilee in the First Century: Implications for the Nascent Jesus Movement," in *The Galilee in Late Antiquity*, ed. Lee I. Levine (New York: Jewish Theological Seminary of America, 1992) 53. Richard A. Horsley, *Galilee: History, Politics, People* (Valley Forge, Penn.: Trinity Press International, 1995) 243.

58. Debate continues over whether to characterize Sepphoris and Tiberias as predominantly Jewish or Gentile. Richard Batey argues for a reevaluation of Jesus' sayings because of Nazareth's proximity to a Greco-Roman city like Sepphoris, while Eric Myers and Mark Chancey see little evidence of its Hellenized character in the first century. See Richard Batey, "Sepphoris and the Jesus Movement," *New Testament Studies* 46 (2001) 402–409; Eric M. Myers and Mark Chancey, "How Jewish was Sepphoris in Jesus' Time?" *Biblical Archaeology Review* 26.4 (July–August 2000) 18–33, 61.

59. See Richard A. Horsley, "Popular Messianic Movements around the Time of Jesus," *Catholic Biblical Quarterly* 46 (1984) 471–95; and Horsley, "'Like One of the Prophets of Old': Two Types of Popular Prophets at the Time of Jesus," *Catholic Biblical Quarterly* 47 (1985) 435–63.

60. Sean Freyne, "Urban-Rural Relations in First-Century Galilee: Some Suggestions from the Literary Sources," in *Galilee in Late Antiquity* 75–91; and Freyne, "Behind the Names: Galileans, Samaritans, *Ioudaioi*," in *Galilee through the Centuries: Confluence of Cultures*, ed. Eric M. Meyers (Winona Lake, Ind.: Eisenbrauns, 1999) 39–56.

61. In making this claim, Freyne intones Gerd Theissen's criteria of historical plausibility, relying on influence and context, as superior to the older principle of dissimilarity that stressed the uniqueness of Jesus over against his Jewish traditions. Sean Freyne, *Jesus, A Jewish Galilean* (New York: T. & T. Clark, 2004) 11–12.

62. As Freyne avers, "These various strands provide a broader and richer set of associations for Jesus' word and deed against the temple, without in any sense removing him from his own tradition as this had been articulated by prophetic voices. . . . It was a potent mix of wisdom and apocalyptic, creation and restoration, and Jesus' particular synthesis of the various stands, allied to his passionate concern for the poor, who had been marginalized by the temple system, help to make the incident both predictable and intelligible" (*Jesus, A Jewish Galilean*, 162–63).

63. E.g., Elizondo states, "It is equally evident that from the very beginning [Jesus' followers] had difficulty accepting and understanding his ways, especially in the light of their laws, customs, and tradition." He then claims, "Yet from the very beginning he begins to break with many of their traditions. Every 'tradition' that was supposed to be a way of forcing the kingdom to come is questioned or transgressed by Jesus—the purity laws, the pious practices, the religious observances" (*Galilean Journey* 65).

64. For example, Meier identifies four ways that the appropriation of historical Jesus research may serve the interests of theology by working against attempts to reduce faith in Christ to a content-less cipher, to swallow up the real humanity of Jesus in a Docetic manner, to domesticate Jesus, or to co-opt Jesus for political programs. Meier, *A Marginal Jew* 1:199.
65. See Terrence W. Tilley, "Remembering the Historic Jesus—A New Research Program?" *Theological Studies* 68 (2007) 3–35.
66. Significant works by these authors include: Elisabeth Schüssler Fiorenza, *Jesus and the Politics of Interpretation* (New York: Continuum, 2000); James G. D. Dunn, *Jesus Remembered*, Christianity in the Making 1 (Grand Rapids, Mich.: Eerdmans, 2003); Larry Hurtado, *Lord Jesus Christ: Devotion to Jesus in Earliest Christianity* (Grand Rapids, Mich.: Eerdmans, 2003).
67. Tilley, "Remembering the Historic Jesus" 34.
68. The nomenclature here comes from Hans Georg Gadamer's landmark work of hermeneutics, *Truth and Method*, 2nd rev. ed. (New York: Continuum, 1999).
69. Thus, rather than adopt Gadamer's more thoroughgoing rejection of interpretive methods (after all, for Gadamer, Truth *and* Method really means Truth *or* Method), I would subscribe to the manner that Paul Ricoeur's arc of understanding-interpretation-understanding both allows for the contribution of critical-interpretive methods in dealing with our distance from texts and recognizes the reader's or community's interpretive horizon. See, e.g., Paul Ricoeur, *Interpretation Theory: Discourse and the Surplus of Meaning* (Fort Worth, Tex.: Texas Christian University, 1976).
70. Ellacuría defines this neologism: "Demonstrating the impact of certain concepts within a specific reality is what is understood here as their historicization. Hence, historicization is a principle of de-ideologization" ("La historización del concepto de propiedad como principio de desideologización") (*Veinte años de historia en El Salvador (1969–1989): Escritos políticos* (San Salvador: UCA, 1993) 591. For a further explanation of this term in Ellacuría's complex philosophy, see Kevin F. Burke, *The Ground Beneath the Cross: The Theology of Ignacio Ellacuría* (Washington: Georgetown University, 2000); and Michael E. Lee, *Bearing the Weight of Salvation* (New York: Crossroad, 2007).
71. Consider the Puerto Rican rhapsodizing of the *jíbaro* figure, or comedic tales of Juan Bobo (a synonym for fool), the cinematic portrayals by the Mexican icon Cantinflas, or even the retelling of Juan Diego's confrontation of episcopal authority.
72. Elizondo, *Galilean Journey* 107, emphasis added.
73. Meier's summary is instructive: "Jesus, the poor layman turned prophet and teacher, the religious figure from rural Galilee without credentials, met his death in Jerusalem at least in part because of his clash with the rich aristocratic urban priesthood. To the latter, a poor layman from the Galilean countryside with disturbing doctrines and claims was marginal

both in the sense of being dangerously antiestablishment in the sense of lacking a power base in the capital. He could be easily brushed aside into the dustbin of death" (*A Marginal Jew* 1:9).

74. See Halvor Moxnes, *Putting Jesus in His Place: A Radical Vision of Household and Kingdom* (Louisville: Westminster John Knox, 2003).
75. Even archeology is ambiguous in this respect. See Marianne Sawicki, *Crossing Galilee: Architectures of Contact in the Occupied Land of Jesus* (Harrisburg, Penn: Trinity Press International, 1998).
76. For a feminist correlate to this principle, see Mary McClintock Fulkerson, *Changing the Subject: Women's Discourses and Feminist Theology* (Minneapolis: Fortress, 1994). Elizondo himself, through his work as founder of the Mexican American Cultural Center and pastor of San Fernando Cathedral in San Antonio, has been profoundly affected by the insights of "ordinary" Latino/as.
77. Meier, *A Marginal Jew* 1:25.
78. I wish to acknowledge Fordham University's Ames Fund for Junior Faculty for providing support of research leading to this article.

Jesus and the Samaritan Woman
(John 4:1–42) in Africa

Teresa Okure, SHCJ
Catholic Institute of West Africa (CIWA)
Port Harcourt

A STUDY IN AFRICA of the Johannine Jesus and the Samaritan woman could take a number of directions. One might be a reader response approach in which different aspects of the story could be matched with situations of marginalization and exploitation on the Continent.[1] Another could explore the specifically "feminist" dimensions and their implications for the Church in Africa and beyond.[2] In my first major work on the episode, given the dominance of the historical critical method at the time, the nearest I could get to contextualizing my reading of the passage was to relate it to the possible contexts of the Evangelist and his immediate audience.[3] Even that seemed a major departure from the beaten track at the time.[4] Since then the situation has changed, and the scholarship is more open to "other ways of reading" the biblical text both in Africa and beyond.[5]

The current volume of *Theological Studies* marks the 30th anniversary of Virgilio Elizondo's "groundbreaking dissertation, which addressed the significance of the Galilean Jesus for U.S. Latinos . . . and the 40th anniversary of the option for the poor of the Latin American Bishops at Medellín" (1968).[6] Such an event celebrating the Galilean Jesus and the option for the poor calls for yet another contextual approach. To better situate this study of Jesus and the Samaritan woman from an African perspective shaped by this double axis, my contribution invites Jesus and the woman to the Continent where they share certain elements with Africans – thus the title: "Jesus and the Samaritan Woman (John 4:1–42) in Africa".

The contours of the story are very simple. Rejected in Judea, Jesus left for Galilee through Samaria in obedience to the divine imperative of his mission. Sitting there exhausted at a well, he enters into dialogue with a Samaritan woman who has come to fetch water, and leads her to faith in him as her long expected Messiah. She abandons her water pot, symbol of her daily and society-gendered chores, goes to the city, and invites her people to come and encounter Jesus, discovering him for themselves as she had done. While she is gone, Jesus prepares his disciples to enter into the harvest of his work in Samaria, and to reap a fruit that would overcome their inherited prejudices on race, class and gender. At the end of the encounter, Jesus, the disciples, the woman, and the Samaritans enter into a communion fellowship, transcending a complex variety of socio-cultural, gender, and religious barriers that would otherwise keep them apart. Of their own accord, the Samaritans confess Jesus not simply as their expected Jewish Messiah, but as the "Savoir of the world."

The proposed invitation of Jesus and the Samaritan woman to Africa raises certain questions. Who are they in their own contexts before they take the trip? Under what circumstances will they visit Africa, a continent of over 52 countries, each with a multiplicity of cultures and languages, and of a size that cannot be traversed in a day? And what of the fact that both Samaria and Galilee, taken together, are far smaller in size and population than some of Africa's largest cities? Who would they meet; on what subjects would they dialogue? Are there situations in Africa with which they would readily identify? What Messianic expectations would Jesus address in the people of Africa so as to lead them to faith? Would they listen to the woman's gospel invitation to come and see a person who told her all that she ever did, and would they consider him a possible Messiah on that basis? Would they call him the "Savior of the world," not on the woman's word, but after meeting him personally as the Samaritans did? These are some questions that might guide this study. Interesting as they are, however, I will focus on the question most salient for this special issue of *Theological Studies*. Namely, what do Jesus of Nazareth in Galilee and the woman of Samaria share in common from their own contexts with those they would likely meet in their "homecoming" visit to Africa?[7]

The method I will use is narrative and inter-textual. First, I will situate Jesus and the woman in their context, and then examine their encounter in Samaria before taking them to Africa, where they will feel very much at home. The Gospel narrative sets the terms of their encounter with the African audience, helping them break through inherited and imposed socio-cultural and religious barriers that tear Africans apart. These are barriers that Africans have internalized and imposed on one another; barriers that hinder them from knowing and receiving God's free and humanizing gift of community; barriers that keep them from meeting Jesus on their own terms as Savior of the world. The encounter also challenges the privileged who are equally enslaved to inherited racism and prejudice, which prevents them from seeking God in true worship, from receiving God's gift of living water, Holy Spirit, and from confessing Jesus of Nazareth in Galilee as God's unmerited universal Messiah.

Jesus of Nazareth in Galilee

Both Medellín and the culturally contextualized theology of Virgilio Elizondo highlight the significance of Jesus for the poor and marginalized today. Jesus of Nazareth was himself poor and marginalized, though as God, he was rich (Phil 2:6–11; 2 Cor 8:9; Rom 11:33–36) and came to enrich all with the gift of unending life, feeding them with himself, God's life-giving bread from heaven (John 10:10). Nathanael, a Galilean from Bethsaida, articulates the prevailing view when he asks ironically, "Can anything good come from Nazareth" (John 1:46)? Could the long expected Messiah be from Nazareth? It is noteworthy that Jesus later decries Bethsaida as one of the cities that would not repent, despite having witnessed his miracles, wallowing instead in pride and boasting (Matt 11:21–24). Nathanael, however, is able to transcend his prejudice against Nazarenes when he encounters Jesus in person (John 1:49), much like the Samaritans later.

Though Jesus grows up in Nazareth, and is popularly known as "Jesus of Nazareth,"[8] Matthew and Luke place his birth in Bethlehem of Judah, thereby burnishing his geographical and family credentials by linking him to the royal house and lineage of David (Mic 5:2–3; Matt 2:1–6; Luke 2:1–7). On the other hand, his designation at the time of the triumphal entry into Jerusalem as "the prophet Jesus from Nazareth of

Galilee" directly challenges the traditional view that prophets do not arise from Galilee and justifies the turmoil it causes in the whole city (Matt 21:10-11). His mother Mary also lives in Nazareth, where angel Gabriel meets her (Luke 1:26). Her Magnificat (Luke 1:42-55) reflects an awareness of what tradition thinks of her as a woman, and celebrates God's radical reversal of that view.[9] It is perhaps because the only biological parent of Jesus is a Nazarene that the narrative makes Jesus a Nazarene as well (or Nazorean; Matt 2:23). In the post-exilic era (to prevent mixed marriages by Jewish men), mothers, not fathers, determined the nationality of Jewish children.[10] Viewed from the mother's side, Jesus' Nazarene origin has rich historical and theological significance.

The prejudice against Jesus is not limited to Nathanael's low opinion of Galileans. His very own relatives and neighbors in Nazareth do not think much of him. All four gospels are agreed on this. The Synoptics report his rejection at his homecoming after the temptations to proclaim "the good news to the poor." They reject him on the grounds that they know his parents and relatives well (Matt 13:53-58; Mark 6:1-1-6; Luke 4:16-30). In Luke, Jesus' own people make the first attempt on his life (4:16-30).[11] In Mark he is pejoratively called "the son of Mary" (6:4). John moves the rejection closer to home when fellow Galileans mock his claim to be "the bread of life that came down from heaven" with the incredulous response, "Is not this Jesus, the son of Joseph, whose father and mother we know" (6: 41-42)? Indeed, John adds that his own "brothers [αδελφοι] did not believe in him," (7:5) and urge him to go to Jerusalem and display himself, accusing him of hiding in Galilee where the ignorant could be easily fooled. On the other hand, later in the tradition, James, "the brother of the Lord", becomes a prominent disciple (Acts 15:13-21; Gal 1:18-19).

Galilee receives equal contempt from the Judeans, especially the authorities. Nicodemus cautions the Sanhedrin against condemning Jesus a priori without first listening to him and finding out what he is doing (7:51), as required by the law (which Nicodemus does in 3:1-21). They ask accusingly in reply, however, whether Nicodemus is a Galilean as well, and challenge him to "search" (with no indication of where to search!) and "you will see that no prophet is to arise from Galilee" (εραυνησον και ιδε οτι εκ της Γαλιλαιας προφητης ουκ εγειρεται) (7:52). In other words, Galilee is excluded from the very possibility of ever producing a prophet, not to mention the Messiah. Still, the leaders are not satisfied and go home disgruntled, unable to come to grips with this "Jesus, the prophet from Nazareth in Galilee," whose presence and deeds turn their perceptions of Galileans upside down. The man born blind later challenges them to revise their view of him on the basis of his deeds, but to no avail (9:30–34).

In John's narrative, however, it is not their rejection of the incontestable evidence of Jesus giving sight to the man born blind (something which has never been heard of "since the world began"; 9:32) that confirms their hardheartedness and prejudice. Rather, it is the raising of Lazarus from the dead after "four days" (11:39), and the notion that, "If we let him go on thus, every one will believe in him" (11:48). Once again unable to deny the evidence, they decide to get rid of him fast, lest the people declare and install him as king, and the Romans remove them from their posts and "destroy the nation" (11:47–52; 12:19). In this drama, the Jewish leaders feel threatened by Jesus as a Messiah because of his deeds (curing the blind, raising the dead, challenging them to reread the Mosaic Law in light of his teaching and deeds). In contrast, however, the ordinary people whom they denounce as accursed "rabble who know not the law" (7:49) are able to perceive God at work in him, and respond positively according to their own Messianic expectations (6:15; 12:12–13).

The pejorative views of Galilee running beneath this narrative go back to the time of settlement. Joseph's descendants (Ephraim and Manasseh, by his Egyptian wife, daughter of the priest of On; Gen 41:45) and Leah (the non-beloved wife of Jacob/Israel) are assigned to Galilee. In the long history of Israel, Galilee more than Judah is subject to foreign influence and occupation, sustaining the presence of heterogeneous cultural groups especially from the time of the Assyrian deportation and importation in 722 BC (2 Kings 17). In the New Testament era cities, fortresses, and garrisons dot Galilee and the Roman Decapolis is nearby; Caesarea Philippi, Sepphoris, and the Jewish friendly centurion of Capernaum (to name but a few) are all in Galilee. The Matthean designation of this region as "Galilee of the Gentiles" (Matt 4:13–16) captures the multi-ethnic reputation of this region of Israel.[12]

In sum, the Gospels suggest that the experience of Jesus of Nazareth in Galilee is colored by prejudice and rejection. For his part, Jesus chooses to identify himself with this good for nothing place. For Paul, this decision contributes to his conclusion that " . . . Christ Jesus, who though he was in the form of God . . . emptied himself, taking the form of a slave . . ." (Phil 2:6–11). In the end, rejected and abandoned, he redeems all of humanity enslaved to sin, and restores us to our God-given status as children of God (Rom 8:14–17). The choice of Jesus to embrace this status is reflected in his approach to the Samaritan woman, which we will examine below.

The Samaritan Woman in Her Context

Like Jesus of Nazareth, the Samaritan woman belongs to a people who are subject to inherited social prejudice because of their origin, and, in the case of the woman, simply because she is a woman. John's Gospel states cryptically that Jews did not co-use or share things in common (συγχρωνται, 4:9c) with Samaritans, which would mean throwing their lives together. Eating and drinking are activities that sustain life, and to eat and drink with a person would be to identify or be in solidarity with them. The narrative, however, highlights the animosity between Jews and Samaritans, which Hebrew scripture (2 Kings 17) dates back to the settlement of five nations in Samaria after the deportation of leading Israelites by the king of Assyria (Sargon II). The mutual hatred of Jews and Samarians intensifies in the post-exilic period when Zerubabel refuses to allow the Samaritans to help in rebuilding the Temple (Ezra 4). In about 300 BCE the Samaritans built their own shrine on Mount Gerizim as a rival to the Temple in Jerusalem, which is destroyed by John Hyrcanus in 128 BCE. In the New Testament era, Josephus reports a desecration of the Temple in Jerusalem by Samaritans (*Ant* Antiquities 18.29–30). And Ben Sira sums up Jewish hatred and prejudice against Samaritans when he writes, "Two nations my soul detests, and the third is not even a people: Those who live in Seir and the Philistines, the foolish people that live in Shechem" (Sir 50:25–26). The Rabbis saw Samaritan women as menstruous from birth, that is, perpetually unclean and consequently a permanent source of uncleanliness for their community.[13] The Jewish leaders in John's Gospel perceive Samaritans as demon possessed, and see Jesus as one of them: (8:48). Racial prejudice and hatred could not go any further.

On the home front, the woman is described as five times married and living with someone who is not her husband (4:17–18). Rabbinic laws allowed marriage a maximum of three times. Critics conclude from this that the woman in the story leads a loose moral life, though the text does not explicitly say this. It is enough that she is a woman and a Samaritan. In this society the five husbands could have been permitted by levirate marriage (Deut. 25:5–10), while the sixth might have refused to marry her.[14] Given the highly gendered moral standards of the time, however, it is unlikely that such a person could have persuaded the man to live with her on her own initiative (assuming they were living together). Whatever the case, in the narrative world of John's Gospel the woman is a likely outcast in own her society due to her marital history. That she comes to draw from the well at about noon, the hottest part of the day when people did not normally go fetching water, is evidence of this impression. Nothing is said about the sixth man who is not her husband, though it is worth noting that in cases of sexual immorality, the woman is always at fault (cf. John 8:1–11).

Socio-cultural prejudices against the Samaritan woman notwithstanding, her character is not ignorant of her personal worth. She has traditions and parentage, which even the sneer of a Ben Sira or one-sided community norms cannot nullify. She traces her ancestry to Jacob/Israel, the founder of the nation. She reminds Jesus that Jacob gave them the well where they sit, and drank from it with his descendants and their livestock (4:12). The Jewish reader might know that Joshua testifies that Joseph's bones are buried in Shechem, and that the land was an inheritance of his descendants (Joshua 24: 32). In Luke-Acts, Stephen extends the ancestral connections of Shechem all the way to Abraham and the Patriarchs (Acts 7:16). Thus, the woman seems convinced that despite inherited and competing claims for Gerizim and Jerusalem as the fitting place of worship, that the Messiah (God's Messiah) will put them right (4:25).

She is very much aware of the tense relationship between her people and Jews, and the complications this implies for a Jewish man who would speak with a Samaritan woman (both "you a Jew" and "me a Samaritan woman" in 4:9 are in emphatic position); indeed, she expresses surprise that Jesus seems not to know this. Yet she has her feet firmly on the ground and her wits about her, and is able to reason and reach her own conclusions in her dialogue with Jesus. Contrary to critics who view her character as dependent on the men from her town to tell her that Jesus is the Messiah, she is not afraid to engage in conversation with an enemy Jewish male.[15] Once persuaded that Jesus is the

Messiah, she wastes no time in running to the town and convincing the people to come meet Jesus for themselves. Her action looks forward to that of Mary of Magdala, who runs to call Peter and the beloved disciple to come and see the empty tomb for themselves, an action that engenders the disciples' belief (20:1-10). In short, the woman lives and is sustained by hope, which helps her transcend and overcome her socio-cultural and religious predicaments. This disposition makes her ripe for Jesus' self-revelation to her as "the Messiah" (4:26). Similarly, Mary of Magdala's love for Jesus helps her to look beyond death, making her the bearer of the resurrection message, the disciple to the disciples (20:17).

What Jesus and the Woman Have in Common

These brief analyses of Jesus and the Samaritan woman in their different contexts have revealed that they share the experience of rejection, prejudice, and isolation. Jesus is rejected in Judea by his own people and goes to Samaria either by necessity or as part of his divine mission (εδει δε αυτον διερχεσθαι δια τνs Σαμαρειας, 4:4) where he finds a hearing and hospitality. The woman, living on the fringe of her society, goes to the well as part of her daily assigned chores, and is welcomed by Jesus and placed at the center of his missionary efforts there. For Jesus, society is averse to his speaking in public with the woman (rabbinic laws forbade a man to speak in public to a woman even if she were his own wife). Indeed, the Evangelist also intimates that the absence of the disciples to buy food is a liberating opportunity for Jesus to engage the woman in conversation (4:8). The disciples confirm the reader's impression when they return and are dumbfounded (εθαυμαζον, 4:27) to see Jesus speaking with a woman. They are amazed not so much because Jesus is speaking with a Samaritan, but because he is speaking with a woman (οτι μετα γυναικοs ελαλει, 4, 27). Yet Jesus' divine mission is not subject to and cannot be vetoed by such considerations. While the woman leads her townspeople to come and encounter Jesus for themselves, Jesus himself spends his time working on the disciples, enabling them to overcome their inbred aversion to public contact with women, and more widely with Samaritans, by explaining to them their part in his mission there.

Through their dialogue Jesus gradually leads the woman to transcend the barriers of prejudice and the stigmas of racism and sexism, and to know and accept God's free gift in Jesus who offers to all who believe in him salvation, "living water," and the Holy Spirit (4:7–10; 7:37–39). In the scheme of values portrayed here, human traditions of worship cede place to God's action in the individual's life. It is no longer a question of worshippers seeking God, but of God seeking followers who will worship him in the way God wants, "in spirit and in truth" (4:24). Such worshippers surrender their lives to God, making him the organizing principle of their lives and receiving the salvation that comes with the divinizing gift of the Holy Spirit that God gives free of charge to all who follow Jesus (1:12–13). This worship, neither in Jerusalem nor on the Gerizim mountain, transcends race, class, and gender (Gal 3:28). Receiving this message, the woman is freed from the socio-cultural shackles that bind her (cf. Gal 5:1–2), and is able to lead her own townspeople to do the same.

The consistent New Testament message embodied in this narrative, which we seemed to have lost sight of in the course of the centuries, is that God does the seeking and saving of humans, not the reverse. We can trace this theme back to the fall and the proto-evangelium of Genesis (3:15) where God indicates that the trajectory of salvation will run through the seed of the woman. What human beings must do is to allow themselves to be sought and found by God,[16] to open themselves to God's free and unconditional gift of salvation and redemption. In this divine enterprise no human being has the advantage or edge over others, since all may receive this gift, and God's gift is not based on partiality or any human considerations. The Samaritans demonstrate the truth of this statement by exercising their freedom and God given right to recognize and proclaim Jesus as the Savior of the world (4:42).

Jesus and the Woman Visit Africa

Before going further we will take a brief look at the African scene where Jesus and the woman will feel very much at home. My aim is simply to highlight the reality that Jesus and the woman would encounter, and with which they would readily identify in their visit to Africa. Samaria was a city, and the encounter takes place at a well in the course of Jesus' tired journey from Judea to Galilee. As was said earlier, Africa is a vast continent of some 52 countries, each with its multiplicity of languages, cultures and practices. By size and population, all of Palestine could fit into one large African city, such as Lagos in Nigeria, with over twelve million inhabitants. Where, then, might Jesus and the woman travel, and with whom would they meet? Would they journey to South Africa or Zimbabwe with their post-apartheid problems; to one of the many African countries with ethnic conflicts; or would they visit the boardrooms of global power where Africa, even at home, remains marginalized? They could visit the slums of Nairobi where millions of people are reduced into a kind of West Bank refugee situation in their own country, or simply look around the airports where women and children are being smuggled out for trafficking, prostitution, and cheap labor overseas. Were they to visit the churches, Jesus would hear (perhaps to his surprise) that he had decreed that women are to be seen not heard; that their role is to labor cleaning the church and then disappear into the background when the liturgical functions begin; that they are called to teach seminarians the "sacred" disciplines and then to become their pupils when the latter are ordained because Jesus was a male.

Interesting questions emerge from this picture, well worth pursuing, though not here. Instead we focus on the realities of prejudice and rejection that Africans experience from the world community on the basis of their God given color, and which we unfortunately assimilate and apply to one another. Jesus and the Samaritan woman would encounter and readily identify with this prejudice. Africa is richly blessed by God in human, land, animal, mineral, and other natural resources. Africans helped build and continue to build the economy of the West, in the past through the slave labor, and today through the "brain drain" of intellectuals and professional in all fields, a practice akin to what the Assyria did to Samaria and other conquered peoples in ancient times. Africa's resources have been looted and exploited by colonial masters and would-be messiahs, both in the past and the present. For centuries Western countries have carted out the wealth of Africa, and now the Chinese and the Indians are following suit under the guise of helping Africa to develop. Scholars are also beginning to include new messianic figures, or "husbands" as Dube tags them,[17] in their studies of colonialism in Africa.

Many Africans believe that the decades of economic aid given to Africa have weakened their economies, like the auto-immune disease brought on by HIV/AIDS, imported from the West, which attacks not just the economy but the very life and survival of the nation.[18] On the global scene, both in the church and in society, Africans have only to appear and their color disqualifies—"Can anything good come from Africa?" Discriminations based on sex and class, though not peculiar to Africans, take a distinctive twist where Africans are concerned. These discriminations are both internal and external. Fortunately these attitudes are gradually changing. The recent election of Barack Obama as President of the United States is a significant example. This history making event is a realization of the dream of Martin Luther King Jr., and all well meaning Americans (black, colored or white). Two successive Secretaries of State in the administration of George W. Bush, Colin Powel and Condoleezza Rice, have been African Americans. Kofi Annan, an illustrious son of Africa, was Secretary General of the United Nations for two consecutive terms, and Francis Cardinal Arinze of Nigeria was a *"papabile"* (a possible papal candidate) in the last election. But racial prejudice is by no means gone. One recalls the breathless coverage in the Western press of the Williams sisters, Serena and Venus, as though their debut in the world of tennis was a crime of trespass, where blacks had no right to intrude. Here too, the press grudgingly changed its mind thanks to the sisters' sustained excellence.

Here in Africa, Jesus and the woman would discover that they too would be subjected to all kinds of racial, ethnic, class, and gendered prejudice. Arguably this is one of the most debilitating forces impeding development on the Continent. Rwanda, Burundi, Darfur, Democratic Republic of Congo, South Africa, Zimbabwe, Sierra Leone, Liberia, Côte d'Ivoire, even Nigeria with its "son of the soil" syndrome, all suffer from the debilitating effects of ethnic prejudice largely inherited from the legacy of "divide and rule" promoted by the colonial and neo-colonial masters, and internalized by Africans. Like Jesus in Nazareth, Africans are rejected by their own neighbors, their talents ignored because people know their parents. "Is this not the son or daughter of . . . ? Did I not teach him or her in primary school? Who does s/he think s/he is? Where did s/he get this knowledge?" After all, she is only a woman!" So many Africans will not believe in their own people. Worse still, some try (and some succeed as happened to Jesus in Nazareth in Jerusalem) to kill them because they feel such talented daughters and sons threaten their political or religious position.

While these reflections could continue, my point is that prejudice in all its forms kills and destroys the opportunities and talents that God gives to individuals and communities in Africa and around the globe to improve themselves and to promote their growth in all spheres of life. It is self-defeating to reject that talent or to dismiss people on the basis of race, color, or gender. No human being, male or female; black, colored, or white; gives life to themselves, or has any say over the circumstances in which they come into existence. Life in all its ontological and socio-cultural circumstances is a pure gift to every human being. Awareness of this truth is freeing and should lead all people to respect others equally. The dialogue of Jesus with the disciples on their mission (4:35–38) to complete the work of God that he has begun (4:31–34) highlights this point. Theirs is essentially a harvesting mission (like all disciples), a harvesting of the fruit that Jesus and the Father have sown (v. 38).[19]

The fulcrum, then, of the entire episode between Jesus and the Samaritan woman is her discovery of "who Jesus is," of his true identity, which constitutes "God's gift" given freely to her and to all who accept this truth (4:10). This exchange constitutes the foundational text on mission in the Gospel of John, embodying the proper response to its message that "God so loved the world that he gave his only Son, that whoever believes in him should not perish but have eternal life" (3:16 and 1:12–13). All who are able to go beyond ethnic and religious prejudice to encounter the true identity of Jesus are given the enabling power to truly become children of God, a gift offered on God's own terms, not on the basis of human considerations.[20]

Jesus, the Woman, the Samaritans, Africans and All Jesus' Disciples

This brings us to the final part of our study, the encounter and dialogue between Jesus, the Samaritan woman, his immediate disciples, Africans, and disciples of Jesus the world over. The contours of this imaginative meeting are taken from the encounters described in the Gospel. How does Jesus, the Messiah and Savior of the world, elicit transformative responses from the woman, the Samaritans, and his accompanying disciples, and what might this tell us about future encounters with Africans and other disciples around the globe (sheep who do not belong to his immediate fold, but who he wishes to bring into the one flock under his shepherding, 10:16)?

Jesus' proclamation of God's good news to the poor has two essential components that free their voices, and elicit a personal, liberating option for God's free gift of salvation. First is his humble self-emptying attitude, and second, his respect for dialogue partners as persons with concerns deserving full attention. Much has been written about the self-emptying of Jesus and its role as a model for Christians, especially consecrated persons. Yet one cannot empty a self that one does not have. Self-emptying makes sense in the context of mission where the missionary decreases by choice so that the other may increase and have life to the full. This is the rationale for Jesus' self-emptying: to make room in himself for humanity, thereby uniting them inseparably with God. Phil 2:6–11 underscores this notion with its claim that "Christ Jesus, who though he was in the form of God, did not count equality with God a thing to be grasped, but emptied himself, taking the form of a servant, being born in the likeness of man." In John's pericope Jesus presents himself as an exhausted needy beggar in enemy territory, so desperate for a drink that he does not hesitate to ask a Samaritan woman for water, though he has a gift to give that cannot be measured in human terms.[21] This approach (in which he stoops to conquer) gives the woman the advantage: she is a daughter of the soil, with a bucket to draw from a deep well of long-standing ancestral history.

Once he begins the dialogue, the woman takes the lead and at each point Jesus uses her concerns (of water fetching, marital life, and the right place to worship) in order to reveal to her his true identity and convey to her the gift he offers. With the disciples, Jesus uses their concern for food. Water and food are indispensable for all human life; they are thus fundamental symbols of his life-giving mission. Secondly, what Jesus offers is truly a gift. Once given, it becomes the unique property of the receiver ("living water within the person welling up to eternal life"). The gift is not dependent on superior status, good will, or benevolence. All receive the same gift and on equal terms because God, the giver, makes no distinction between persons in this regard (Rom 2:11; Gal 2:6; Acts 10:34; 1 Pet 1:17). This manner of giving truly liberates the receiver (cf. Rom 5:1–2), and imparts enabling power to be and to act as a full human being destined for the fullness of life (10:10).

The woman's excitement over her personal discovery of Jesus moves the Samaritans (themselves an estranged and belittled outcast people) to look beyond traditional practices whereby women do not lead men (Sir 9:1–9), and to accompany her to meet Jesus "on account of the woman's word" (4:30). Later, setting aside the lack of communion fellowship between them and the Jews (" . . . For Jews have no dealings with Samaritans" 4:9c), they invite him to their city. Jesus graciously accepts and stays there two days, the maximum allowed by the *Didache* for a missionary in any given place. Jesus' humble acceptance of their invitation leads the Samaritans to confess him as the Savior of the world, not only because of the woman's word (4:30), but also because they have seen and heard him for themselves (4:42). If Jesus can be this gracious to Samaritans, whom fellow Jews treat not as a people, but as dogs, then they conclude he must be "the Savior of the world."

The passage says nothing about the response of the disciples (4:31-38). Perhaps a reply is unnecessary. The narrative indicates what the response is or should be. Beyond the Samaritan woman and her people, the Evangelist wants to lead his own generation of disciples to embrace both the content and methods[22] of the mission of Jesus. This is where the Church must pay heed in order to be relevant in Africa and elsewhere today.

Like his visit to Samaria, a visit from Jesus would challenge Africans to a number of steps. First, his visit would call us to become aware of and to accept God's gift of eternal life and salvation, which is uniquely ours, regardless of who may have brought it. Second, he would invite us to get to know him personally and to open the reality of our lives intimately to him. Third, it would challenge us to articulate belief in Jesus based on our own experiences of him in the concrete settings of our real lives. This is the task of inculturation to which African and universal church leaders continue to pay lip-service, but which the Second Vatican Council deemed indispensable over 40 years ago when it said the proclamation the Gospel must take into substantial consideration people's own cultures (*Gaudium et Spes* 22). Fourth, African church leaders and those to whom they proclaim the gospel must stand as equal, harvesters of the work of salvation, reaping what was sown by God alone in/and through Jesus (4:34; 17:4). Fifth, his visit would call women in Africa and worldwide to recognize and claim the Christological grounds for their right to participate along with men in all aspects of the church's life.

On a broader scale, the African encounter with Jesus would no doubt challenge the male clerical church to be open to, and to let go of their scandal at "what Jesus wants with woman." The Fourth Gospel seems to emphasize the importance of women in the story of Jesus.

He calls his mother, "Woman" (2:4), and the text tells us "the mother of Jesus" not only gives him birth, but mothers the launch of his missionary career and his revelatory *alpha* sign (αρχην των σεμειων, 2:11). She accompanies him throughout his life to its completion in the *ōmega* sign of his death and resurrection, where she receives the mission to mother his newborn child, the church (19:25–26, 30), into full maturity (Acts 1:14). The Samaritan woman is instrumental in effecting the conversion of her townspeople and, by implication, the disciples who would have accompanied Jesus into the city for the two-day stay, despite their mutual animosity with its inhabitants. Martha first articulates the confession that is the entire aim and purpose of the Gospel: that Jesus is "the Christ, the Son of God, the one who is coming into the world" (11:27; 20:31). Mary of Bethany performs the last liturgical rites for Jesus, "the lamb of God," by anointing him for burial (12:7; cf. 14:8). And Mary of Magdala loves and follows Jesus beyond death (20:1–2, 11–18), receiving from him the commission to proclaim the resurrection message that all believers are henceforth brothers and sisters, children of the same God, who is father/mother of us all (20:17). If the church in Africa today wants to participate in what God and Jesus want with women for the redemption and transformation of humanity, both genders will need to revisit long-held derogatory attitudes towards women, and learn to celebrate the gifts that God gives to them for their good as persons, and for the good of all.[23]

Furthermore, the visit would challenge all disciples to eschew traditions of racism, ethnocentrism, and sexism that sicken Christian life and witness like a virus that renders its victims incapable of recognizing who Jesus really is, especially in his brothers and sisters (Matt 25:40; 45). His presence would reveal in full God's gift of salvation that beckons all Africans to reconciliation, drawing us to cross boundaries (socio-cultural, religious and political) in forming communion fellowship with the Trinity and all believers (1 John 1:1–4). Jesus would challenge the church in Africa and elsewhere to look to the what the Gospels tell us of Jesus of Nazareth in Galilee in searching for solutions in ecclesiology (who is or is not church), ecumenism (who has the last word concerning the right place to worship, how and when), missiology (who should evangelize who and where), and dialogue (a readiness to rethink traditional practices, positions, and views through a genuine and respectful exchange that leads to insights inspired by the example of

Christ). All this is possible when our way of being Church is rooted in what God does and will continue to do in individuals and communities, irrespective of who they are or from whence they come.

Toward a Conclusion

This study of Jesus' encounter with the Samaritan woman, then, has surfaced their shared experiences of prejudice, racism, and sexism flowing from the inherited social norms of their societies. Jesus reaches beyond these prejudices, however, leading the woman, the Samaritans, and his own disciples to do the same. Unfortunately, contemporary discourse on the option for the poor has paid little attention to the role of inherited and ingrained prejudices in regards to Africans, though changes are taking place slowly. Secondly, the discourse tends to focus on economic issues as evidenced by such expressions as "option for the poor," which is understood to include the marginalization of women, allowing them to participate, have a voice, be empowered, and so forth.

In the dialogue with the Samaritan woman, however, Jesus does not simply opt for the poor, but rather identifies himself as poor so as to make all rich (John 10:7–18; 2 Cor 8:9). His option to identify himself as poor makes Jesus accessible to all and sundry, helping them to feel they are his equal, at times even his superior, as we saw in the dialogue with the Samaritan woman. John's narrative presents this as a deliberate choice, which enables Jesus' dialogue partners to become aware of, to claim, and to celebrate their own God-given dignity, as do the woman and the Samaritans (cf. *GS* 26). Jesus respects and works within people's own concerns in leading them to where God wants them to be. He eschews the dispute over competing claims and systems of nationality and worship, leading them instead to focus on God's action in their lives and in the world, and to see worship as the celebration of what God does in believers and wants to do in all God's children everywhere.

In reality, contemporary disciples of Jesus do not have to give the poor a voice or be their voice, because God has already given each one a voice in their own right and on God's own terms. By engaging the woman in respectful conversation as an equal partner (traditions and taboos to the contrary notwithstanding), Jesus gives the woman the opportunity to use her God-given voice, thus liberating the great potential within her. The abiding challenge for those who feel that theirs is the only voice worth hearing, or who have encroached into the voice space of others in church and society, is to retreat to their own space and to listen to those they previously thought had no right to speak. Both Vatican II and John Paul II say that promoting the dignity of "the human being" is the proper route to empower the poor and evangelize the rich. Jesus takes this route first by becoming a human being (1:14; Heb 4:15); and second, in his manner of proclaiming the good news to the poor (which includes the spiritually poor, since God's general amnesty excludes none; Luke 4:18–19).

The story of Jesus and the Samaritan reveals that when this is done, individuals discover living water welling up from within that promotes life in its fullness. Satisfaction with this way of living turns them away from the accumulation of wealth which impoverishes others, and from calculating their worth as human beings by the size of their bank accounts. I have written elsewhere about the corresponding need for a "salvific option for the rich," adopting the same respectful approach towards them as Jesus adopts towards Zacchaeus.[24] In Luke's description, Zacchaeus is "a chief tax collector and rich," (19:2b), but he is moved of his own accord to redress the fraud he may have practiced and the impoverishment of others (19:8). Jesus, who notes that "the Son of man came to seek and to save the lost," declares in response, "Today salvation has come to this house," adding that Zacchaeus "is also is a son of Abraham" (19:9).

In the last analysis, the poor offer a special grace to the rich, but not because they need the accumulated or surplus wealth of the rich. The poor call the rich to become aware of their own God-given status as children of God, whose primary identity and worth is not measured by money, bank accounts, shares of stock, or whether they belong to the G8, G15, or G22 groups of wealthy nations. They call the rich to the realization that it is unbecoming of them as human beings and children of God to serve, pursue, and be pursued by money/Mammon (Jas 2:1–13; 5:1–5). This type of approach to the option for the poor also helps ensure that the poor will not simply jump onto the band wagon of the rich when they too become rich and, like the fool of the Psalmist, feel they have no need of God (Ps 14:1).

Applying to Africa this discourse on the graces that the poor offer to the rich, I have argued elsewhere that the martyrdom of Africa is hope for a new humanity. The innocent suffering of Africa is like the blood of martyrs that soaks, waters and transforms the entire earth, including the lives of those who killed them.[25] If we keep this in mind, Jesus' successful dialogue with the Samaritan woman, her people, his disciples, and with Africans and the global community, will bear lasting fruit. For the living water that Jesus gives has become in us "a spring of water welling up to eternal life" (4:14c), where both the rich and the poor can come to drink and rejoice together eternally in God's all inclusive company. Nurtured and refreshed by this living water, we are empowered to begin living this way here on earth, which Jesus teaches us is possible as we pray each day in the Lord's Prayer to the one Father of us all.

Notes

1. Musa Dube takes this approach in her "Readings for Decolonization (John 4:1–42)" *Semeia* 75 (1996) 37–59; "John 4:1–42 - The Five Husbands at the Well of Living Waters," in ed. Nyambura J. Njoroge and Musa W. Dube, *Talitha cum!: Theologies of African Women* (Pietermaritzburg: Cluster Publications, 2001) 40–65.
2. See, for instance, Chris Ukachukwu Manus, "The Samaritan Woman (Jn 4:7ff): Reflections on Female Leadership and Nation Building in Africa," *African Journal of Biblical Studies (AJBS)* 2, 1–2 (1987) 52–63; Justine Kahunga Mbwiti, "Jesus and the Samaritan Woman (John 4:1–42)" in ed. Mercy Amba Oduyoye and Musimbi R. A. Kanyoro, *"Talitha qumi!": Proceedings of the Convocation of African Women Theologians, Trinity College , Legon-Accra, Sept 24–Oct, 2, 1989* (Ibadan: Daystar, 1990) 63–75; and Musa W. Dube, "Jesus and the Samaritan Woman: A Motswana Feminist Theological Reflection on Women and Social Transformation," in *Boleswa Journal of Occasional Papers* (1992) 5-9; and Grant LeMarquand's 170-page long "Bibliography of the Bible in Africa", in ed. Gerard O. West and Musa W. Dube, *The Bible in Africa: Translations, Trajectories and Trends* (Boston/Leiden: Brill Academic Publishers, Inc. 2001) 633–800.
3. Teresa Okure, *The Johannine Approach to Mission: A Contextual Study of John 4:1–42*; WUNT 2/31 (Tübingen: JCB Mohr [Paul Siebeck], 1988). The work encountered two major objections while it was still in the making: one was the contextual approach adopted, the other and perhaps the more objectionable, the assumption that John's Gospel had something to do with mission, understood mainly as outreach to unbelievers in the third world (see on this *The Johannine Approach*, 7–22). Treating the pericope in the African context was ruled out within that view. The review of Robert Morgan (*Theology Book Review* 1/3 [1989] 13) faulted its lack of attention to the *feminist* dimensions of the episode.
4. *The Johannine Approach*, xvi–vii.

5. Examples: John S. Pobee and Barbel von Wartenberg-Potter, eds., *New Eyes for Reading: Biblical and Theological Reflections by Women from the Third World* (Quezon City, Philippines: Claretian Publications, 1986); ed. Musa Dube, *Other Ways of Reading: African Women and the Bible* (Atlanta: Society of Biblical Literature. Geneva: WCC Publications, 2001); Gerard O. West, *Biblical Hermeneutics of Liberation: Modes of Reading the Bible in South African Context;* rev. ed. (Pietermaritzburg: Cluster Publications/Maryknoll: Orbis, 1997 [1991]). The SNTS and SBL are also making appreciable efforts to incorporate these newer approaches in their continuing seminars on contextual studies as valid ways of reading within their associations.
6. From "the short précis" of the editors describing this Special Issue of *Theological Studies* (July 31, 2007).
7. Increasingly African and African American scholars are discovering the Biblical evidence which reveals that the Israelites were in fact Africans. To start with, they spent more than 430 years in Africa from the time of Jacob/Israel, not counting the sojourns of Abraham and Joseph, who was married to the daughter of the priest of On. Moses was legally the son of Pharaoh's daughter and completely African by upbringing (Acts 7:22) at a time when the Israelites had no worship of YHWH, as witnessed by the incident of the Golden Calf. See further, David Tuesday Adamu, "The Place of Africa and Africans in the Old Testament and its Environment," Ph.D. Dissertation (Baylor University, 1986); idem, "The Table of Nations Reconsidered in African Perspective (Genesis 19)" *Journal of African Religion and Philosophy* 11 (1993) 138–143; idem, *Africa and Africans in the Old Testament* (San Francisco/London/Bethsaida: Christian Universities Press, 1998); T. Okure, "Africans in the Bible: A Study in Hermeneutics" first given at the International Congress on the Bible in Africa, Cairo, 4-20 August, 1987 and represented at the SBL Seminar on the Bible in Africa, Asia and Latin America. New Orleans, 23–26 November 1996.
8. See Matthew 16:14; Mark 6:15; Luke 7:16:39; 24;19; John 7:40, 52.
9. On the Magnificat and its possible significance for African women, see Gertrud Wittenburg, "The Song of a Poor Woman: The Magnificat (Luke 1:46–55)" in ed. Denise Ekermann, Jonathan Draper and Emma Mashini, *Women Hold Up Half the Sky: Women in the Church in South Africa* (Pietermaritzburg: Cluster Publications, 1991) 2–20.
10. A typical example is Timothy whom Paul circumcised to be his traveling companion because his mother was "a Jewish woman" (Acts 16:1-3).
11. I recently made an extensive analysis of this episode in "Jesus in Nazareth (Luke 4:16-30): An Index to the Question of Poverty in Africa", a paper presented at the biennial congress of Panafrican Association of Catholic Exegetes (PACE), Johannesburg, September 2007.
12. This is not the place to go in detail into this matter. For windows into the political and socio-cultural life in Hellenistic and Roman Galilee see, for instance, Morton Smith, *Palestinian Parties and Politics that Shaped the Old*

Testament (London: SCM, 1971); Seán Freyne, *Galilee from Alexander the Great to Hadrian 323 B.C.E. to 135 C.E.: A Study if Second Temple Judaism* (Wilmington: Michael Glazier and Notre Dame: Notre Dame University Press, 1980).

13. See the extensive study on this in *StrB* 1: 540–560, especially on the rules of purity, 540–541; food laws 541–542 and worship 542–544; and my discussion in *The Johannine Approach*, 96.
14. Gail R. O'Day expresses a similar view. "John", in Carol A. Newsom and Sharon Ringe, eds., *The Women's Bible Commentary*, London: SPCK and Louisville, KY: Westminster/John Knox, 1992) 295–296.
15. On the woman's sagacity in the dialogue with Jesus, see Okure, *The Johannine Approach*, 108–131; here I have also argued that the woman's question to her people "Can he be the Christ?" parallels Jesus' own method with her rousing curiosity until they reach their own personal decision about him. Also see T. Okure, "John" in *The International Bible Commentary: A Catholic and Ecumenical Resource for the Twenty-First Century*, ed. William Farmer et alii (Collegeville: The Liturgical Press, 1998); and O'Grady, "John," 296.
16. I made a similar discovery with regard to sacrifice in Hebrews: while human beings offer sacrifice to God to obtain favors or to appease God, in the optic of Hebrews, God is the one who sacrifices himself in the person of his Son in order to bring (or in Pauline terms, to reconcile, 2 Cor 5:18-19) humans to the divine self (T. Okure, "Hebrews: Sacrifice in an African Perspective", in *Global Bible Commentary*; ed. Daniel Patte, Teresa Okure et alii (Nashville: Abingdon, 2004) 535-538).
17. See note 1 above and my "Impoverished by Wealth: Mama Africa and Her Experience of Poverty", Pope Paul VI Annual Lecture, CAFOD London, November 10th, 2007 (A transcript is on the CAFOD website).
18. The Catholic Institute of West Africa (CIWA) devoted its 16th Theology Week to the topic; see my article, "Africa and HIV/AIDS: The Real Issues", *The Church and HIV/AIDS in the West African Context;* ed. Ferdinand Nwaigbo et alii (Port Harcourt: CIWA Publications) 66–94.
19. For my extensive analytical discussion see *The Johannine Approach*, 136–188.
20. On the foundational character of 3:16, see Okure, *The Johannine Approach*, 5–6, esp. n. 10.
21. See my extensive analysis of the dynamics of interaction in *The Johannine Approach*, 91-131; and "John", in *International Bible Commentary: A Catholic and Ecumenical Resource for the Twenty-First Century*; ed. William R. Farmer et alii (Collegeville: The Liturgical Press, 1998) 1438–1502, esp1467–1468; O'Grady, "John," 296; Diarmund McGann, *Journeying within Transcendence: The Gospel of John through a Jungian Perspective* (London: Collins, 1989) 52–60 esp. 53–54.
22. This point is extensively developed in *The Johannine Approach*, 129–131, 174–175, 197–198.
23. The attitude of the hierarchical church which continues to legislate for the exclusion and silencing of women or gives them only token considerations

that are subject to the "sensitivity of the faithful" in any local church, must be revisited and declared to be totally anti-gospel and *anti-Christos*. It is remarkable that in the commentary on "John in an Orthodox perspective" by Petros Vassiliades (*IBC*, 412–418) none of the passages on women seemed to be relevant to this Orthodox perspective. Similarly that of Kyung-mi Park "John", *IBC*, 401–411.

24. T. Okure, "Salvific Option for the Rich: A Gospel Imperative for Mission in the Twenty-First Century," Third Annual Mission Lecture of the Holy Cross Mission Center, Notre Dame, Indiana, February 18th 2007.

25. T. Okure, "Africa, A Martyred Continent: Hope for a New Humanity," in T. Okure, Jon Sobrino and Felix Wilson eds., *Martyrdom Reconsidered*, Concillium 1/3 (London: SCM 2003) 38–46.

The Galilean Jesus

Creating a Borderland at the
Foot Of The Cross (JN 19:23–30)

Sophia Park, S.N.J.M.

Postcolonial theory allows a reading of John 19:23–30 from a perspective that is hopeful and empowering for dislocated persons such as Asian immigrant women. In this reading the dislocated persons are enabled to gain a hybrid identity through the Gospel's invitation to join and participate in a "borderland community" created by Jesus on the cross.

ONE DAY I WENT WITH A FRIEND to the cemetery where her mother is buried. She told me that the name inscribed on the epitaph—Grace Maria Park—was unfamiliar, even to her mother. Grace was the American name given her mother when she immigrated to the United States; Maria was the Christian name she received when she was baptized, just before she died; and Park was the name she took when, adapting to the American custom, she took her husband's surname, a practice not followed in Korea. This story impressed upon me a strong sense of being dislocated—invisible, nameless, and alienated.

As a first-generation Asian immigrant and a member of an American religious community, I also experience dislocation. As a resident of this third space—"neither this place, nor that place"—I have met many Asian immigrants who also struggle with identity. This is not surprising, for in the global context the emergent international division of labor depends heavily upon the mobility of women workers. Consequently, the feminization of migration is quite noticeable.[1] Asian immigrant women workers from various countries, along with the vast majority of women in developing countries, experience severe dislocation in this global market system.[2]

As one such person, I offer this article as a reading of John 19:23–30 from a perspective that is hopeful and empowering for Asian immigrant woman. The focus is on the Galilean Jesus of John's Gospel, who invites the dislocated person into a hybrid identity through the creation of and participation in a borderland community. Galilee in Jesus' time was a place where various Mediterranean cultures intersected. From a Jewish religious perspective, Galileans were seen as impure and suspect. The Galilean Jesus represents the dislocated, who live in liminal space and for whom he envisions new life. I begin by explaining the concept of the hybrid identity and the notion of the borderland in relation to the experience of dislocation. Next, I examine how the narrative of John's Gospel envisions the ideal of the borderland community using the language of exclusivism and inclusivism. I will then examine the narrative of the final moments before Jesus' death, focusing on the setting and literary structure in relation to John's construction of the borderland community. Finally, I offer an interpretation, suggesting how the pericope revolves around John's construction of hybrid identities for its various characters. I emphasize that persons who experience dislocation also experience empowerment through membership in the borderland community. I attempt to show that they achieve a hybrid identity by engaging with "the other" and by becoming members of the borderland community of fragmented and dislocated disciples that the Galilean Jesus of John creates at the foot of the cross.

Hybrid Identity and the Borderland

"Dislocation" is a term used to describe the experience of those who have relocated from a familiar to an unfamiliar place. "Dislocation" refers to the situation of "having or living in more than one culture," and often implies suffering caused by receiving "multiple and opposing messages."[3] "Dislocation" also implies the occupation of marginal status or a liminal space, marginal not only in physical territory but also in emotional and social territories. The situation of dislocation is highly insecure and can include violence. Often in such situations, those dislocated are voiceless, invisible, and powerless.

The Borderland: An Alternative Sense of Space

The concept of the borderland suggests some possible benefits of dislocation. The borderland can be a place within metropolitan centers for the meeting of cultures rooted in class, gender, and ethnicity.[4] A border is an outer part or edge; it sets limits: "It keeps people in and out of an area; it marks the ending of a safe zone and the beginning of an unsafe zone."[5] The notion of borderland extends the geographical understanding of "borders" to include the space between cultures.[6] Thus, borderland signifies the in-between space where more than two cultural or political elements are joined.

The borderland space invites people into the alternate awareness that there is no safe home except the in-between space. This awareness moves away from a notion of home it sees as "an illusion of coherence and safety based on the exclusion of specific histories of oppression and resistance, the repression of differences even within oneself."[7] Those in the borderland community dwell in a different type of home, the in-between space where an uprooted person is re-rooted in herself, others, and God, and finds no security outside the in-between space.

The borderland, according to the postcolonial scholar Homi Bhabha, is "the third space," the in-between space. The identity of an individual in this third space must be "hybridized" as a prerequisite for experiencing transformation. For Bhabha, the transformational liberating value of this hybrid identity "lies in the rearticulation, or translation, of elements that are *neither the One . . . nor the Other . . . but something else besides.*"[8]

John's Gospel as A Narrative Envisioning an Imaginary Borderland Community

I read John's Gospel as a narrative that imagines a borderland community where dislocated people find acceptance and protection. The theory of the Johannine community, which presumes a historical community as the recipient of the Gospel, has been challenged by the notion that "the genre of the Gospel of John does not support the reading strategy that might reveal the existence of the Johannine community behind the text."[9] I do not focus on the historical critical question, i.e., on what John's community was actually like. Rather, I assume that the author attempts to communicate with an implied group or community, and focus on the way the narrative discourse rhetorically constructs the group identity.

First, I explain the usage of the language of inclusivism and exclusivism as a way of creating a space for a borderland community. I then offer a close reading of John 19:23–30, focusing on the pericope's setting and literary structure.

The Language of Inclusivism and Exclusivism

John's Gospel imagines an ideal community, a borderland community that provides the dislocated with safety and a sense of belonging.[10] In this section I examine how the narrative of John's Gospel constructs this borderland community using the language of exclusivism as expressed in the concepts of "other" and "othering," and the language of inclusivism as expressed through friendship and kinship.

Exclusivism

Johannine scholar Wayne Meeks argues that exclusive language in the Gospel of John "vindicates the existence of the community that sees itself as unique, alien from its world . . . but living in unity with Christ and through him with God."[11] John's narrative exemplifies the function of exclusive language, which Bruce Malina and Richard Rohrbaugh argue "arises among persons in groups espousing and held by an alternative perception of reality."[12] Accordingly, I submit that this language provides a protective border for its members. Below, I argue that the language expresses exclusivism through the concept of "the other" and the inverting process of "othering."

Other

The identity of a person or group can be shaped by differentiating the self from others by means of boundaries. The concept of self is also shaped by the perception of others. However, for the sociopolitically oppressed, the position of the self is often inverted; "the other" becomes the self or the subject.

The elaboration of the concept of the other is a way of articulating the identity construction of the dislocated. Postcolonial scholar Gayatri Chakravorty Spivak advances the concept of the other, borrowing from

Jacques Lacan's psychoanalytic theory.[13] For Spivak, "the other" with a lowercase "o" designates the colonized self, marginalized by imperial discourse and identified by his or her distance from the center. "The Other" with a capital "O" designates the exterior realm that impacts one's subjectivity, such as the dominant culture or hegemonic power, language, or religion.[14] This distinction between "the other" and "the Other" helps describe the reality of dislocated persons, who construct their identities by differentiating themselves from the individual or group that has power over them.

The narrative of the Fourth Gospel equates "the Other" with "the world" and "the Jews." The narrative frequently uses the terms "the Jews" (71 times in John, five times each in Matthew and Luke, and six times in Mark) and "the world" (87 times in John, three times in Mark and Luke, and nine times in Matthew). I will briefly examine how John describes each of these terms.

John's Gospel often expresses hostility toward the group called "the Jews." For example, Jesus condemns "the Jews" saying, "You are from your father the devil" (8:44).[15] The narrative of the healing of the blind man (Jn 9) also expresses negativity toward "the Jews." The Johannine Jesus refers to Nathanael as a "true Israelite" (1: 47), a rare occurrence, which nonetheless shows the narrative playing on the distinction the Gospel draws between "the Jews" (in mostly negative references) and "Israel" (positive).

Sometimes, however, the Fourth Gospel uses "the Jews" with neutral or even positive connotations. In these instances the term refers to friends of the disciples. In the Lazarus pericope, the narrator says, "The Jews were with Mary and Martha to console the sisters as they mourned their brother's death" (11:19). In this case, "the Jews" is a neutral term signifying status as friends of the disciples. The narrator also uses "the Jews" to indicate believers (11:45). After witnessing Jesus' resuscitation of Lazarus, many "Jews" believed in Jesus. The meaning of "the Jews" must therefore be determined by context of each occurrence.[16]

Similarly, John uses "the world" (*kosmos*) ambiguously; its meaning too emerges according to context. In the narrative discourse, "the world" runs the full range of meaning from "universe" (17:5) to the world of those estranged from God and imprisoned in darkness.[17] On the one hand, "the world" connotes the object of God's love and redemption:

"For God so loved the world that he gave his only Son" (3:16), whom he "did not send . . . into the world to condemn the world, but in order that the world might be saved through him" (3:17). On the other hand, "the world" also has a negative meaning. In his farewell discourse, Jesus says, "If the world hates you, be aware that it hated me before it hated you. If you belonged to the world, the world would love you as its own. Because you do not belong to the world, but I have chosen you out of the world, therefore the world hates you" (15:18). In this passage Jesus uses spatial terms to explain the relationship between his disciples and the world.[18] As Jesus does not belong to the world, neither do his disciples. They become dislocated, nonmembers of the world. The narrative emphasizes the negative aspects of the world, caused by its refusal to believe in Jesus, the Son of God. Thus, just as the term "the Jews" carried ambiguity, so too does the term "the world" appear ambiguous, varying with its context.

A further question concerns the rhetorical function of these terms. As the narrative emphasizes, "the Jews" and "the world" reference those who do not belong. Craig Koester demonstrates that these words are used negatively only when the narrative describes a situation in which designated groups reject Jesus as the Son of God.[19] Adele Reinhartz argues that the narrative rhetorically develops exclusivity toward particular groups, specifically "the Jews" or "the world" and, through this rhetoric, the discourse differentiates members from nonmembers.[20] Clearly the rhetoric strengthens the identity of the imagined community by establishing a boundary between it and other groups. These boundaries then insulate the community against assimilation into the mainstream religion or culture. The Johannine narrative builds up the imagined community's self-identity by differentiating itself from "Others."[21]

Othering

The Johannine narrative proactively strengthens the identity of its imagined borderland community by creating its own inverted othering process.[22] The term "othering" refers to a rhetorical process that makes the marginalized even more insignificant and invisible. This process leads the colonized subject to feel inferior to the colonizer. The narrative of John's Gospel, however, inverts the othering process by employing the term "Father" for one who stands with the imagined community. "Father" indicates absolute power and authority; it is a synonym for God;[23] it rhetorically negates and inverts the dominance of the "Others."[24]

In John, Jesus often challenges the Others, especially the group called "the Jews," using "Father" language. For example, when "the Jews" criticize Jesus for violating the Sabbath, Jesus replies, "I work because my Father works" (5:17). Similarly, he asserts that Abraham, a representative authority figure in Judaism, cannot be superior to the Father. Furthermore, the narrative focuses on Abraham's fatherhood by having "the Jews" pose the question to Jesus, "Are you greater than our father Abraham?" (8:53) Jesus responds, using his own "Father" language to signify "the Others" as inferior: "It is my Father who glorifies me, he of whom you say, 'He is our God.'" (8:54).

"The Other," as represented by the term "the world," is also challenged by the word, "Father." As closure for the discourse in chapter 14, Jesus concludes that "the prince of this world is on his way. He has no power over me; but I do as the Father has commanded me, so that the world may know that I love the Father" (14: 30b–31). Later Jesus says, "about who was in the right: in that I am going to the Father; about judgment in that the prince of the world is already condemned" (16:10–11). These two passages, quoted from the New Jerusalem Bible, show the parallel between the Son of God and the son of the world, and reveal the superiority of the Son of God. As the Son of "the Father," Jesus receives power from "the Father," who has absolute power, whereas the prince of the world receives power from "the world," which is by comparison powerless. John's clarifies that "the Father" is far more powerful than "the world" and, by using "Father," Jesus and his disciples are depicted as more powerful than "the world." In this logic, "the world" is challenged by "the Father," and the power and authority carried by "the world" as "the Other" is inverted.

Fernando Segovia argues in his study of the dynamics of inclusion and exclusion in John 17 that "the inverted dichotomy revolves around socio-religious beliefs, access to God, and the other-world: on the surface, the center is represented by the world-at-large, while the disciples constitute the margins; in reality, the disciples constitute the center, while the center is in the margins."[25]

The narrative world of the Fourth Gospel not only claims its unique identity by differentiating itself from others but also strategizes the inversion of the power and authority of the Others through the "othering" process.²⁶ In so doing, the Gospel of John envisions an imagined community, the borderland community, where the dislocated experience safety and perhaps can overcome a sense of inferiority.

Inclusivism

The language of inclusivism in the Fourth Gospel functions to reinforce the ideal of the borderland community. The two types of inclusive language used by John are that of friendship and kinship among members. Those who respond to Jesus in faith are called to unity as a family, based on a friendship with Jesus and his disciples. For the dislocated who suffer from alienation, calling each other sister and brother and becoming friends fulfills a hunger in their hearts.

Friendship

The whole Fourth Gospel develops a spirituality of friendship. In this narrative, the title "friend" refers to in-group members who are under the obligation to love one another.²⁷ Jesus calls the disciples friends (15:15) and confers this obligation on them. Friendship is critical for dislocated individuals and communities. The Gospel narrative vividly describes friendship through—as Sharon Ringe puts it—"not only the sayings about friendship in 15:12–17, but also [through] the three-year saga of the daily rhythms of friendship and the stunning examples of solidarity in moments of crisis."²⁸

Sandra Schneiders contends that the Johannine community was one of friendship based on equality and service.²⁹ She argues that the theme of friendship in John's Gospel grew out of the belief, articulated in the Hebrew Scriptures from the first creation account in Genesis through the covenant stories of Abraham and Sarah, as well as Moses, Miriam, and Aaron, "that as humans and believers we are called to community."³⁰

The nature of this friendship is also explored in Greek philosophy, an important element of Mediterranean culture in the late first century. Alan Mitchell asserts that Greek philosophy of friendship is based on equality, justice, and total commitment to friends, and involves a communal dimension.³¹ Aristotle speaks in the *Nicomachean Ethics* of the essence of friendship: "Those who wish good things to their friends for the sake of the latter are friends most of all, because they do so because of their friends themselves, and not coincidentally."[32] Friendships thrive on the basis that one desires the good of the friend for the friend's own sake.

Aristotle explains that there is no friendship without justice between the friends, pointing to equality as an essential value of friendship.[33] But he also considers unequal friendships: a friendship of kinship, which includes parental and fraternal friendships, based on proportionality of equality. Parental friendships are unequal in that the parents love the children more than the children love them, but fraternal friendships are like friendships of comrades in that they share commonalities—the same upbringing and a similarity of age.[34] Thus, kinship relationships can be understood as a type of friendship.

John's Gospel demonstrates the links between friendship and kinship. One disciple's friendship with Jesus leads to a brother/sister friendship with another disciple who has an established friendship with Jesus. John emphasizes that an individual's friendship with Jesus is the fundamental requirement for being a member of the community. The metaphor of the vine in chapter 15 illustrates the principle of friendship in that, to bear fruit, each branch must be attached to the vine.

Brotherhoods and sisterhoods emerge because each disciple has become a child of God. In other words, a new kinship or parental friendship is forged from the communal dynamics of a friendship with Jesus. Friendship and kinship are deeply related and intersected. The narrative discourse idealizes a new kind of "fictive" kinship as an extension of friendship. For the community of the dislocated, serving each other in a friendship grounded in equality and mutuality functions to empower the members.

Kinship

Along with friendship, kinship is a strong indicator of inclusivism among members of the community in the Johannine narrative. Adeline Fehribach argues that kinship, understood as the so-called *Familia Dei*,[35] is a fundamental value of the community portrayed in John. The narrative speaks the language of kinship, which strengthens insiders' sense of belonging.

John's notion of kinship is not grounded in blood relation, but is instead rooted in one's commitment and responsibility as a friend of Jesus. Nonetheless, having blood ties to Jesus does not eliminate the possibility of entering into this new form of kinship with him. Friendship with Jesus guarantees that the disciple will enter into kinship with God, and entering into kinship entails corresponding external actions, including such behaviors as giving life or holding possessions in common.[36]

In summary, I have examined how the Fourth Gospel constructs an image of an ideal community, that is, the ideal of the borderland community. The lexical root of the word community is "relations."[37] According to Homi K. Bhabha, language is deeply concerned with the construction and maintenance of community and/or national boundaries.[38] On the one hand, the Johannine narrative emphasizes the boundary, promoting an exclusive attitude toward two groups, those represented by "the Jews" and "the world." On the other hand, the narrative also emphasizes acceptance, the promotion of intimate friendships, and a kinship system among community members. In the following section, I will read the pericope in question as the birth narrative of the borderland community.

John 19:23–30: Constructing Borderland Community

This section offers a close reading of John 19:23–30 as the dramatic birth of the borderland community brought to life by John's Galilean Jesus at the foot of the cross. The borderland designates the in-between space of anonymity, ambiguity, and violence. But it also designates the space of transformation and new life.

The Setting: Space of Borderland

The pericope is carefully situated in the space of border crossings, located in a borderland setting and including several paradoxical and conflicting characteristics. First, the setting suggests a highly complex reality that transcends the simple violence of the scene. In 19:25 readers see the *quaternion* of soldiers, and the three women—"his mother," "his mother's sister, Mary the wife of Clopas," and "Mary Magdalene"— standing near the place of execution at the foot of the cross. The four soldiers crucifying Jesus and the three women mourning Jesus' dying are standing together.[39] These men and women are present at the same time and place, but for opposing reasons. We can take the four soldiers as representing the harsh, violent environment of borderlands and the women as representing people who face border-crossings at many border towns around the world.

Second, the scene is complicated and paradoxical, a place where death meets life. The place of execution is macabre, described as "Golgotha" or "The Place of the Skull" (19:17). Death, however, is not the whole story, for Golgatha is also the setting for the birth of a new community. This is the borderland where death and life intersect, where the persecutor and the victim stand together, and where transformation happens. This complexity conjures up the image of a borderland that is highly violent, complicated, and destructive, yet simultaneously creative and generative.[40]

Finally, the setting of the pericope suggests a borderland where everyone is more or less equal. Jesus, on the cross, stands at the center of the scene. With this focal point there can be no vying for positions of honor among the disciples, who are merely described as "standing by the cross" (*eistēkeisan de para tō stayrō*), gathered around the one who is "lifted up." This focal point maintains the reader's focus on Jesus on the cross and disciples gathered at its foot, with no position of hierarchy established among them.

Literary Pattern

Turning now to the literary pattern of the pericope, I will show how it emphasizes Jesus' role in the birth of the borderland community. To this end I divide the pericope as follows:

19:23–24, the preparation of the death of Jesus/birth

19:25–27a, the process of the death/birth

19:27b–30, the completion of the death/birth.

John 19:23–24 reports that "the soldiers had crucified Jesus" and, after dividing his garments, they cast lots for his tunic, which "was seamless." The narrative, citing the soldiers' action as fulfillment of Psalm 22:18, emphasizes that these actions were performed not on account of worldly power over Jesus but in accord with the plan of salvation history.

I come then to the birth of the borderland community. Raymond Brown's examination of the literary structure of the passion characterizes John 19:25–27 as the most important scene in the entire narrative.[41]

The section uses an adoption formula to show that the new community is equal to the family.[42] The verses "Woman, here is your son"

(v. 26a) and (to the disciple) "Here is your mother" (v. 26b) constitute this formula. In this moment, the mother of Jesus becomes the mother of the beloved disciple, signifying the initiation of a new familial relationship. However, the narrative transforms the formula by using the words differently and, in so doing, demonstrates a key characteristic of the borderland community. In this formula, Jesus calls his mother "woman." In Jewish and Greco-Roman sources there is no other instance of a son addressing his mother as woman. In the narrative, nevertheless, the appellation is in no way derogatory or unusual as an address for women. Jesus used "woman" to denominate female disciples (4:21; 20:13).[43] This exchange, therefore, serves to show that kinship in the community of disciples is not based on conventional family kinship according to patriarchal societal norms, but is a new kinship based on friendship with Jesus and his followers.

With its description of the action of the beloved disciple, the third part of the pericope (19:27b–30) narrates the final step in the birth of the new community: "And from that hour the disciple took her into his own home" (19:27b). The verb *elaben* means not only to take someone into a place; it also implies entering into a close relationship.[44] The phrase "from that hour" helps clarify the long-term consequences of this action.

Most translations render the phrase, *ap' ekeinēs tēs ōras*, as "from that hour" or "after that hour," but, besides the temporal meaning, the phrase can also mean "because of that hour." Francis Moloney insists that v. 27 connotes both meanings, given the theological and dramatic significance of the word "hour" in the whole of John's Gospel.[45] I agree with Moloney. The hour in question, like the entire scene, is built on the lifting up of Jesus on the cross (see 12:23; 13:1; 17:1). Additionally, the scene is clearly designed to make the claim that the beloved disciple and the mother of Jesus entered into kinship *because of what transpired at that hour*. Thus, the narrative stresses that it is precisely as members of the community of disciples that the mother of Jesus and the beloved disciple entered into a relationship of family and initiated their community life. In sum, the narrative demonstrates that the community, born as a "family" in the midst of and because of the passion of Jesus, transcends norms and values conventional in Jesus' day.

Most scholars agree that this pericope describes the process of the birth of a new community. The narrator describes Jesus' death on the cross as a crossing over "out of this world to the Father" (13:1).[46] In the midst this crossing over, however, the Galilean Jesus gives birth to the new community, the borderland community, as the fulfillment of his mission. To this point, the very next section (John 19:28–30) employs an inclusio to emphasize the birth of the new community as the fruit of accomplishing the mission of Jesus in this world. In v. 28, the narrator says, "Jesus knew that all was finished" (ēdē panta tetelestai). The narrator then concludes: "When Jesus had received the wine, he said, 'It is finished'" (tetelestai, v. 30). The word *tetelestai* means finishing an activity, as well as carrying out an obligation and fulfilling it.[47] Through the *inclusio* or repetition of the word *tetelestai*, the narrator indicates that when Jesus' mission is completed, his birthing of the new family is also completed. Here, new life is generated out of a violent death on the cross. In this borderland, the new community is born and sustained. This community is an exemplary borderland community for all who are dislocated.

An Interpretation of John 19:23–30: Creating a Hybrid Identity

This section offers an interpretation of John 19: 23–30, focusing on how each character achieves a hybrid identity as members of the new borderland community. The silent, relatively undefined, characters in the scene, especially the women disciples, remain fragmented, ambiguous, and passive. The space at the foot of the cross of Jesus serves as the borderland, where the gathered anonymous, silent, and/or marginal characters are empowered by achieving hybrid identities. To demonstrate the process by which characters gain this identity in John's narrative world, I will first explain the hybrid identity of John's Galilean Jesus and the role of that identity in constructing the borderland community. I will then explain the literary device of configuration and its role in the construction of hybrid identities for characters of a narrative world. Finally, I will show how the pericope uses a device to achieve hybrid identities for those gathered at the foot of the cross, the potential members of the new borderland community.

John's Galilean Jesus

Jesus is the central figure of the pericope. Unlike other characters who remain largely silent or undeveloped, the character of Jesus is given a name and a voice that provides him with an identity and self-conscious mission.[48] The passion narrative establishes a solemn mood in which Jesus uses his power and authority as the Word made flesh, the Son of the Father, to initiate border-crossings into the new community he creates at the foot of his cross. In this moment, he resides simultaneously in the borderland between earthly and heavenly realms.[49] Throughout John's Gospel, and specifically this pericope, Jesus transgresses and crosses this border; he is the Son of God with a hybrid identity.[50] As a borderland person, he remains connected with his disciples, who live in the earthly realm, while he is simultaneously united with the Father. On the cross, John's Galilean Jesus invites his disciples into a kinship with each other and with his Father. In this borderland he acts as a mediator, and through him the people gathered around the cross enter into a new borderland community.

Going one step further, we can also say that Jesus assumes the role of a woman in giving birth to the borderland community. This birthing process is accompanied by enormous pain and, in fact, by death. To confirm his death, soldiers stabbed him in the side, and from it "there came out blood and water" (v. 34), an image associated with a woman giving birth. If we follow this image, then, Jesus can be understood as a woman who gives birth to her infant, the community of disciples. Thus, Jesus is a borderland character who crosses boundaries and gives birth to a borderland community.

Configuration

Configuration is a literary device used to develop a hybrid identity for a character through his or her engagement with other characters in a narrative. This is a symbiotic process in which the character does not lose his or her unique identity but, in fact, strengthens it. As part of a reading strategy, configuration may be defined as a constellation or grouping of characters.[51] In any given narrative, certain characters influence each other and complicate each others' lives. Feminist biblical scholars often explore reading strategies that interconnect several fragmented minor (female) characters according to a particular theme, such as violence or murder.[52] Through this configuration, each fragmented character acquires integrity as well as empowers other fragmented characters. This interaction can be a way of constructing hybrid identities. Such configuration requires a mutual relationship: one person is never simply dependent on the other, but each is called into a new and interdependent relationship that configures the borderland community.[53]

I would assert that the female characters gathered near the cross are empowered through configuration. Ingrid Rosa Kitzberger analyzes the female characters of John's Gospel as configured characters, establishing a connection among them. My character analysis relies heavily on her work.

Configuration at the Foot of the Cross

Considering the space at the foot of the cross as the borderland where all elements are mixed, reversed, and finally transformed, the fragmented identities of the various anonymous, silent, and/or marginal characters gathered there gain hybrid identities through configuration. Those in the circle of disciples are configured with each other and empowered through the development of hybrid identities. In John 19:23–30 multiple and simultaneous configurations occur on three different levels.

Three Levels of Configurations

On the first level of configuration, two characters, the mother of Jesus and the beloved disciple, are configured. Jesus becomes the mediator of this configuration by calling them a family. On the one hand, the mother of Jesus, both as his birth mother and as a believing witness to his entire life, represents the continuation of Jesus' earthly ministry. On the other hand, the beloved disciple represents the future of the ministry,[54] symbolizing all who will become disciples. Through Jesus' configuration of his followers into fictive kinship, he fulfills 10:15b–16: "I lay down my life for the sheep. And I have other sheep that do not belong to this fold. . . . So there will be one flock, one shepherd." We should also notice that the configuration happens at the foot of the cross where memory of the past and hope for the future mirror each other. This moment of configuration establishes a family bond, providing a lasting foundation for security and love between the two characters. Through this process, each character is granted a hybrid identity: the mother of another's child and the son of a friend's mother, united in a borderland community of discipleship.

On the second level, each woman present at the birth of the borderland community is interconnected and configured with all the others, including the mother of Jesus and the beloved disciple.[55] Here, despite being named, each woman retains a certain degree of anonymity. According to v. 25, all the women under the cross are named Mary, which seems to work against giving each character a defined identity. Instead, these Marys are configured within a circle of largely anonymous female disciples who are composed of friends and blood relatives. Thus, the partial anonymity of the female characters tends to blur the boundaries between them.[56] The relatively undefined characters function as an open invitation to the reader to come into their space under the cross, where those gathered will continuously transform one another in the borderland.

On the third level, the narrative's invisible and forgotten characters also experience the power of configuration. Any character can be simultaneously configured with the whole circle of disciples. Thus, configuration is open to the invisible, forgotten, and dislocated characters, whom this reading of the Fourth Gospel must recover. They would have followed Jesus with the crowd, mourned at his passion, or even reached an outer circle of those gathered in the space beneath the cross. We could think of them as the ones who had heard Jesus preach, had witnessed his ministry, and had their eyes opened. In this narrative, these characters are not merely fragmented; they are also silenced and ignored.

Asian immigrant women who experience dislocation in the United States resonate with the anonymous characters in John's Gospel. Configuration provides readers who experience their own dislocation with a space where they can configure themselves with not only the Johannine female characters but also, by extension, Jesus himself. Through simultaneous and multiple configurations, attentive readers who often feel uninvited, dislocated, forgotten, and silenced can experience empowerment by standing in this borderland space at the foot of the cross.

Conclusion

I have argued that John's Gospel uses configuration to cross over invisible and visible boundaries, and to bring the fragmented and dislocated characters of his narrative into relationships that enable them to achieve rich and empowering hybrid identities in the new borderland community that Jesus creates at the foot of the cross. I have also argued that the configuration of the disciples gathered at the foot of the cross can be an invitation to all dislocated and discarded people to embrace the hybrid identity of the new borderland community made up of disparate followers of Jesus.

I am convinced that invisible and dislocated individuals have always found a dwelling space in what I have called the borderland community of John's Gospel. Within the circle of the dislocated and fragmented, each disciple experiences acceptance as a member of the family and finds friendship with Jesus and his followers. This is the borderland community to which John's Galilean Jesus gives birth at the foot of the cross, and wherein transformation occurs. I believe it is a community that the historical Jesus of Galilee would have recognized as his own, and where contemporary followers of the risen Jesus will continue to welcome the dislocated borderland rejects of a global world.

SOPHIA PARK, S.N.J.M., received her Ph.D. in Christian spirituality from the Graduate Theological Union, Berkeley, Calif. Currently adjunct lecturer in the Religious Studies Department, Holy Names University, Oakland, Calif., she specializes in biblical spirituality and cultural studies. Her publications include "Doing Theology: Asian Women's Christian Spirituality" and "Inter-generational Interpretation of Numbers 12:1–10: From a Korean Woman's Perspective," *Ewha Journal of Feminist Theology* 3 (2005) and 5 (2006). In progress is a work entitled "Cross-cultural Spiritual Direction: Dancing with a Stranger."

Notes

1. See Avtar Brah, "Diaspora, Border and Transnational Identities," in *Feminist Postcolonial Theory: A Reader*, ed. Reina Lewis and Sara Mills (New York: Routledge, 2003) 614.
2. Youngbok Kim, "Power and Life in the Context of Globalization: A Biblical and Theological Perspective," *Madang* 1.1 (June 2004) 17.
3. Gloria Anzaldúa, *Borderlands/La Frontera: The New Mestiza* (San Francisco: Aunt Lute, 1999) 100.
4. I am aware of the danger of mystifying the image of the border as a way of studying relationships between cultures. I do not intend to ignore the violent

aspects of the border but to appreciate its transformative potential. Also, I adapt this theory from postcolonial discourse, not from sociological discourse. On the danger of mystifying the image of the border see Thomas M. Wilson and Hastings Donnan, "Nation, State, and Identity at International Borders," in *Border Identities: Nation and State at International Frontiers*, ed. Thomas M. Wilson and Hastings Donnan (New York: Cambridge University, 1998) 1–30. See also Akhil Gupta, "Beyond Culture: Space, Identity and the Politics of Difference," *Cultural Anthropology* 7 (1992) 6–23.

5. Wilson and Donnan, "Nation, State, and Identity at International Borders" 3.
6. Ibid.
7. Chandra Talpade Mohanty, *Feminism without Borders: Decolonizing Theory, Practicing Solidarity* (Durham, N.C.: Duke University, 2004) 90.
8. Homi K. Bhabha, *The Location of Culture* (New York: Routledge, 1996) 28, emphasis original.
9. John Ashton, "Second Thoughts on the Fourth Gospel," in *What We Have Heard from the Beginning: The Past, Present, and Future of Johannine Studies*, ed. Tom Thatcher (Waco, Tex.: Baylor University, 2007) 10.
10. By definition, the dislocated are unsafe until they become part of the borderland community. In my analysis of John's narrative, I do not assume the members of the new kinship community were unsafe before they joined the community. In becoming believers they might have voluntarily left their "land" in order to live in the "borderland." In the early decades the Jews who became part of the Jesus movement did not leave anything behind. Rather, they incorporated their faith in Jesus into their ongoing identities as Jews. Historically, the rupture with Judaism came at a later time. In this article, I examine only how the narrative functions to create a space of the borderland where the dislocated, if there are any, can find safety.
11. Wayne A. Meeks, "The Man from Heaven in Johannine Sectarianism," in *The Interpretation of John*, ed. John Ashton (Edinburg: T. & T. Clark, 1997) 193. See also David Rensberger, "Sectarianism and Theological Interpretation in John," in *"What Is John?": Literary and Social Readings of the Fourth Gospel*, ed. Fernando F. Segovia (Atlanta, Ga.: Scholars, 1996) 145–46. I acknowledge that not all scholars agree in their assessment of Johannine language, and other readings of the John's Gospel are certainly possible. For a critique of historical approaches to the Johannine community, see Richard Bauckham, "For Whom Were Gospels Written?" in *The Gospels for All Christians: Rethinking the Gospel Audiences*, ed. Richard Bauckham (Grand Rapids, Mich.: Eerdmans, 1998) 9–48.
12. Bruce J. Malina and Richard L. Rohrbaugh, *Social-Science Commentary on the Gospel of John* (Minneapolis: Fortress, 1998) 10.
13. See Gayatri Chakravorty Spivak, "The Rani of Sirmur: An Essay in Reading the Archives," in *Europe and Its Others: Proceedings of the Essex Conference on the Sociology of Literature, July 1984*, ed. Francis Barker (Colchester, UK: University of Essex, 1985) 128–51. See also Spivak, "Bonding in Difference," in

An Other Tongue: Nation and Ethnicity in the Linguistic Borderlands, ed. Alfred Arteaga (Durham, N.C.: Duke University, 1994) 273–85.
14. Bill Ashcroft, Gareth Griffiths, and Helen Tiffin, *Post-Colonial Studies: The Key Concepts* (New York: Routledge, 1998) 169–70.
15. Biblical citations are from the New Revision Standard Version.
16. Alan Culpepper, "The Gospel of John as a Document of Faith," in *"What Is John?": Readers and Readings of the Fourth Gospel*, ed. Fernando F. Segovia (Atlanta, Ga.: Scholars, 1996) 115.
17. Stanley B. Marrow, "Κόσμος in John," *Catholic Biblical Quarterly* 64 (2002) 97.
18. Scholars argue that the Johannine narrative deconstructs the notion of the importance of the space and land of the Hellenistic Jewish communities of the Diaspora. See Gary M. Burge, "Territorial Religion and the Vineyard of John 15," in *Jesus of Nazareth, Lord and Christ: Essays on the Historical Jesus and New Testament Christology*, ed. Joel B. Green and Max Turner (Grand Rapids, Mich.: Eerdmans, 1994) 384–96.
19. Craig R. Koester, "Κόσμος in John," *Catholic Biblical Quarterly* 64 (2002) 97–102.
20. Adele Reinhartz, "On Travel, Translation, and Ethnography: Johannine Scholarship at the Turn of the Century," in *"What is John?": Readers and Readings of the Fourth Gospel* 255.
21. Reinhartz, "The Johannine Community and its Jewish Neighbors: A Reappraisal," in *"What Is John?" Volume II, Literary and Social Readings of the Fourth Gospel*, ed. Fernando F. Segovia (Atlanta, Ga.: Scholars, 1998) 138.
22. Tat-Siong Benny Liew, "Ambiguous Admittance: Consent and Descent in John's Community of 'Upward' Mobility," in *John and Postcolonialism: Travel, Space, and Power*, ed. Musa W. Dube and Jeffrey L. Staley (New York: Sheffield Academic, 2002) 195.
23. "Father" was used as the root metaphor for God in the Hebrew Scriptures as well as in the New Testament. In particular, the use of "father" influenced trinitarian theology in the early church. Because of the gender-specific nature of the word, feminist theologians have challenged the term "God the Father." This article focuses only on the rhetorical function of the word in the narrative. For a feminist critique see Sallie McFague, *Metaphorical Theology: Models of God in Religious Language* (Philadelphia: Fortress, 1982, and for the influence of "father" in John's Gospel in the development of Trinitarian theology, see Peter Widdicombe, "The Fathers on the Father in the Gospel of John," *Semeia* 85 (2001) 105–25.
24. Ashcroft et al., *Post-Colonial Studies* 171.
25. Fernando F. Segovia, "Inclusion and Exclusion in John 17," in *"What Is John?": Vol. 2* 208.
26. Ibid.
27. Raymond Brown, *The Gospel according to John*, 2 vols. (London: Geoffrey Chapman, 1966) 2:682–83.

28. Sharon H. Ringe, *Wisdom's Friends: Community and Christology in the Fourth Gospel* (Louisville: John Knox, 1999) 82.
29. Sandra Schneiders, *Written That You May Believe* (New York: Crossroad, 1999) 172-73.
30. Sandra Schneiders, *Commitment, Consecrated Celibacy, and Community in Catholic Religious Life* (New York: Paulist, 2001) 294.
31. Alan Mitchell, "'Greet the Friends by Name': New Testament Evidence for the Greco-Roman Topos on Friendship," in *Greco-Roman Perspectives on Friendship*, ed. John Fitzgerald (Atlanta, Ga.: Scholars, 1997) 257.
32. Aristotle, *Ethica Nicomachea*, trans. W. D. Ross (Oxford: Clarendon, 1925) 1156b.
33. Ibid. 1163b.
34. Ibid.
35. Adeline Fehribach, *The Women in the Life of the Bridegroom: A Feminist Historical-Literary Analysis of the Female Characters in the Fourth Gospel* (Collegeville, Minn.: Liturgical, 1998) 20.
36. Malina and Rohrbaugh, *Social-Science Commentary* 228.
37. Raymond Williams, *Keywords: A Vocabulary of Culture and Society* (New York: Oxford University, 1985) 75.
38. Homi K. Bhabha, "DissemiNation: Time, Narrative, and the Margins of the Modern Nation," in *Nation and Narration*, ed. Homi K. Bhabha (New York: Routledge, 1990) 291–322.
39. Mark W. G. Stibbe, *John as Story Teller: Narrative Criticism and the Fourth Gospel* (New York: Cambridge University, 1994) 153.
40. On the violent and destructive nature of the borderland, see Jacques Audinet, *The Human Face of Globalization: From Multicultural to Mestizaje*, trans. Frances Dal Chele (Lanham, Md.: Rowman & Littlefield, 2004) 109–22.
41. Brown, *Gospel according to John* 2:911.
42. Stibbe, *John as Storyteller* 152.
43. Elisabeth Schüssler Fiorenza, *In Memory of Her: A Feminist Theological Reconstruction of Christian Origins* (New York: Crossroad, 1998) 327.
44. Francis J. Moloney, *"A Hard Saying": The Gospel and Culture* (Collegeville, Minn.: Liturgical, 2001) 176.
45. Ibid.
46. L. William Countryman, *The Mystical Way in the Fourth Gospel: Crossing over into God* (Valley Forge, Penn.: Trinity Press International, 1994) 118; Leticia Guardiola-Sáenz, "Border-crossing and its Redemptive Power in John 7:53–8:11: A Cultural Reading of Jesus and the Accused," in *John and Postcolonialism* 144.
47. Frederick William Danker, ed., *A Greek-English Lexicon of the New Testament and Other Early Christian Literature* (Chicago: University of Chicago, 1979) 997.
48. See Mark W. G. Stibbe, *John*, Readings, A New Biblical Commentary (Sheffield, UK: JSOT, 1993) 197.

49. Ingrid Rosa Kitzberger, "Border Crossing," in *The Personal Voice in Biblical Interpretation*, ed. Ingrid Kitzberger (New York: Routledge, 1998) 125.
50. Dorothy A. Lee, "Women as 'Sinners': Three Narratives of Salvation in Luke and John," *Australian Biblical Review* 44 (1996) 13.
51. See Wolfgang G. Muller, "Interfigurality: A Study on the Interdependence of Literary Figures," in *Intertextuality*, ed. Heinrich E. Plett (Berlin: Walter de Gruyter, 1991) 101–21.
52. Feminist biblical scholars chose to break with established notions of literary unity by reading unrelated stories based on themes. As seen in the stories of Jephthah's daughter (Judg 11) and Michal (2 Sam 6, these two women's stories are similar regarding women's treatment within the patriarchal system. See J. Cheryl Exum, *Fragmented Women: Feminist (Sub)Versions of Biblical Narratives* (Valley Forge, Penn.: Trinity Press International, 1994).
53. Martin Scott, *Sophia and the Johannine Jesus*, Journal for the Study of the New Testament Series 71 (Sheffield, UK: JSOT, 1992) 219.
54. Gail R. O'Day, "John" in *The Women's Bible Commentary*, ed. Carol A. Newsom and Sharon H. Ringe (Louisville: Westminster John Knox, 1992) 300.
55. I consider the beloved disciple to be a literary figure, an ideal borderland person who has crossed over the boundaries of gender.
56. Adele Reinhartz, *"Why Ask My Name?": Anonymity and Identity in Biblical Narrative* (New York: Oxford University, 1998) 5.

Jesus of Galilee from the Salvadoran Context
Compassion, Hope, and Following the Light of the Cross

Jon Sobrino, S.J.
Translated by Robert Lassalle-Klein

The article analyzes a threefold isomorphism between the realities of Galilee and El Salvador: (1) the two realities are subjugated by imperial realities; (2) the isomorphism least mentioned by commentators between Jesus and the Salvadoran martyrs; and (3) the isomorphism between Jesus and the crucified people understood as the servant of Yahweh who brings salvation. The article then considers three central realities—mercy, hope, and following—in light of the cross, Jesus, and the people.

THIS ARTICLE RESPONDS to a request for a reflection on Jesus of Galilee from the perspective of El Salvador. The fundamentals of what I have to say have already been set out, for better or worse, in two books: *Jesucristo liberador: Lectura teológica de Jesús de Nazaret* (1991) and *La fe en Jesucrist:. Ensayo desde las víctimas* (1999). In these books I have tried to deal from the perspective of faith with the totality of the life and destiny of Jesus, and with his ultimate reality. Here I will concentrate on certain elements that, while central to the Gospels, I see as especially clarified by the Salvadoran context.

The task of selecting these fundamental elements is not simple. I will take *the cross* into special account, not only because the Gospels are "a passion narrative with an extended introduction" (Martin Kähler, 1896),[1] but because the Salvadoran context is, above all else, the reality of "a crucified people" (Archbishop Oscar Romero, Ignacio Ellacuría). It is not simply metaphorical to say that we live here under a "reign of the cross," while in other places it is possible to live a "reign of *the good life.*"

This is not to devalue the pascal experience as a whole, which is truly central to Christian faith, but it christianizes it. Nonetheless, I will not treat the cross thematically, but rather as a principle, more useful than others, for interpreting the totality of the life of Jesus and its fundamental elements.

Among these elements, I will focus on mercy, which—and this is important—takes the form of justice; and I will focus on hope—which above all takes the form of liberation and of life. Building around these themes, it is possible to analyze many realities. Some are positive: the kingdom of God, the God of the kingdom, the Father and ultimate mystery, the little ones, liberation, resurrection, faith, and grace. Others are negative: the antikingdom, oppression, idols of death, sin, crucifixion. All of this will held implicit in what follows.

Finally, I will also focus on following. While following is not everything, it is the axis around which the Christian life—and Christology—must turn in order to "put on" Jesus. Following is central in the biblical text: "'follow me' are the first and last words of Jesus to Peter," as Bonhoeffer noted.[2] And following is central for the Salvadoran context. "A great cloud of witnesses" (Heb 12:1) has emerged here, martyrs who have been distinguished followers. If the following of Jesus is not central, the edifice of Christianity falls. It is still the *articulus stantis vel cadentis vitae cristianae* (the article of faith by which the Christian life stands or falls) in today's world.

As necessary as it is to use exegetical and historical-critical methods in presenting the reality of Galilee and Jesus, I have nothing to add to the many studies on these topics. I will expand, rather, on the importance of the context, because being consciously and actively immersed in the reality of El Salvador during the 1970s and 1980s has greatly enhanced my understanding of Jesus of Galilee. This methodological consideration may be perhaps the most specific contribution I can offer.

Finally, I will comment on two elements that have been recently and especially influential in these reflections. First, regarding the reality of the context of a world of oppression and repression, I will mention the generosity, love, and martyrdom of many men and women, led by Archbishop Oscar Romero. Second, regarding thought, I will focus on the work of Ignacio Ellacuría to illumine this reality in the light of Jesus of Galilee.

The Contextual Structure of Theology: Location and Sources

It used to be thought that theology was universal, a notion that contributed to the almost exclusive emphasis on the use of sources: Scripture, tradition, and magisterium. *Location* was taken into account only for pastoral reasons. But things are not so simple. In a crucial, much cited text Ellacuría says:

> The difference [between location and source] is neither strict nor, still less, exclusive, since in a way, location is a source, inasmuch as it makes the source give of itself to the other, so that, thanks to its location and by virtue of it, certain determinate contents are actualized and are really made present. Granting this distinction, it would be erroneous to think that direct contact with the sources (even if we believed and prayerfully lived them) is enough to put us in a position to see in them and draw from them the right thing for what must constitute theological reflection.[3]

This means that sources must be read in a *context*, a *location*, the *ubi* of the Aristotelian categories, to which must be added the *epoch*, the *quando*. This spatio-temporal context can make the *text* give something or other of itself, so that the fundamental question will be, What is the best context from which to read the texts about Jesus of Nazareth? I do not have a definitive answer, but I will share Ellacuría's programmatic statement, which is generally true: "the Third World[4] is the place of the gospel."[5] In this article I want to show how the Gospels' *text* about Jesus has been read in the Salvadoran *context*—which stands as a symbol of a much larger Third World—with the conviction that this reading has made the text "give of itself" its Christian content, more than other readings in other contexts have done, at least in some important respects. Before I take up the aspect of *ubi* or location in the context, however, I would like to offer some clarifications.

"Giving of itself" does not mean to quantitatively add content to the text. It means that the context can, in fact, help ensure that the most original and profound meaning of a text is discovered. What does *liberation* mean in Exodus, what is meant by the sin of the world, or a utopia of the reign of God, etc.? When texts have been buried or marginalized for eons, context can help recover their relevance or sometimes even their existence—for example, even progressive European theology did not used to treat the Beatitudes and the woes of Luke, justice and injustice in the prophets, and the liberation of Exodus as central themes.

Since the context as well as the texts has *virtus*, power, and energy, "giving of itself" also means that, by virtue of the context, the texts end up affecting those who study and read them in new, unanticipated, and more profound ways, both intellectually and existentially. This rereading has certainly happened with texts about the kingdom of God, the Jesus of history, and the cross and martyrdom when the texts are read in the Salvadoran context.

Texts therefore end up generating a collective consciousness that is more widespread than the forms of individual or group knowledge that experts study, including, for example, the collective knowledge of rural peasants. This has certainly occurred with texts about the poor and evangelization, about prophetic denunciation and against lies, and about hope for the kingdom of God, etc.

Finally, "giving of itself" means that some texts bring about new formulations-syntheses that show us how to understand the larger whole, and become an *articulus stantis vel cadentis fidei*: "the crucified people is *the* sign of the times" (Ellacuría), "the glory of God is the poor person who lives" (Archbishop Romero).

There is no apodictic answer to the question of how one knows whether "the more" that a *context* can generate really supplies a "better" understanding of the *text*. More *objective* intellectual arguments help us know whether this statement is accurate: texts reread in this way give the faith a better internal coherence. However, in my opinion *subjective* experience—that place where each person must determine the ultimate truth of a text for him- or herself—is more decisive in this matter.

Stated phenomenologically, I think one can verify that the text has given more of itself in a context like that of El Salvador if, for example, an experience occurs like that of the disciples on the road to Emmaus (Lk 24:13–35): "Were not our hearts burning within us?"—which could be translated today as, "with this vision of Jesus, does not everything seem *more* human and *closer* to the man from Nazareth?" That a text has given more of itself is confirmed by an experience like that of Jesus when he says in a moment of exultation: "I give you thanks, Father, because the poor and the humble have understood, not the proud and the powerful,"[6] which could be translated today as "we have finally uncovered something fundamental that was buried: the truth lies with the poor of history, not with their oppressors." It is verified by those who find themselves saying, "rereading Jesus from El Salvador has helped us act more justly, love the poor more tenderly, and walk more humbly with God," the words of Micah 6:8 expressing what God finally requires.

What is important is that we see a text's "giving of itself" as something real, good, and humanizing. For this to happen, it is not sufficient simply to refer to the orthodoxy of the magisterium to verify that a text has given of itself what it has to give (this idea will be important in my upcoming sections). What a text has to give must be able to be felt in reality, as has been the case in El Salvador.

To illustrate this point we should think about the reinterpretation of a foundational scriptural text, the liberation of Egypt, which 40 years ago was a minor inflection in theology in the church. But, "thanks to the Latin American context" and "by virtue of it," this text yielded something substantial that had lain dormant: God listens to the cries of slaves and decides to liberate them. This became clear in contexts like El Salvador, while in others the text remained practically mute or little discussed.

The 1984 Vatican Instruction on Certain Aspects of the "Theology of Liberation," affirms, for example, that God's specific purpose in initiating the liberation of the Hebrew slaves was the creation of a people who would celebrate his cult, which he would seal with the covenant on Mount Sinai.[7] Juan Luis Segundo criticized this interpretation and insisted that in the three great, most ancient sources, the Yahwist, the Elohist, and the Deuteronomist, "there is no trace of this supposed purpose."[8] The text states that the essential purpose of the Exodus is that an oppressed people might have life and live in freedom as a people, which seems to me the most correct exegesis. At this point, however, I am interested in emphasizing the question why there would be such different interpretations of the same text. Fundamentally, I believe that different contexts have made the same text yield different meanings, and this explains why one reading has prevailed over some other in the collective consciousness attached to a particular context.[9]

The Context: Isomorphism, Irruption of Reality, and Epistemological Rupture

I will now look in some detail at the Salvadoran context and focus on three things. First, simply put, there exists a certain *isomorphism* between the reality of Galilee then and our reality in the Third World today. Second, during the 1970s *reality broke in*, and made itself deeply felt. Third, there occurred a powerful *epistemological rupture* in the functioning of intelligence in Salvadoran reality, though this rupture was not exclusive to that context.

Isomorphism between the Reality That Appears in the Text and in the Context[10]

When we read a *text* narrating the reality of Jesus of Galilee, and we do so from within the *context* of the reality of El Salvador, what isomorphism may exist between the two pertains to similarities between their historical and social realities and the realities of followers of Jesus, especially the martyrs.

Isomorphism of the Social Realities of Galilee and El Salvador

In terms of a *location* from which the sources are being read, I understand El Salvador not just as a special reality, an *ubi*, nor simply as a cultural reality (although one must take this into account as an important element, especially in the neighboring indigenous world of Guatemala), but rather above all as a substantial *quid*. The essential elements of this reality are poverty, injustice, structural oppression, and repression, and slow violent death. These elements also include clinging to life (humanly and religiously) and hope for the liberation of the majorities who, though innocent and substantially undefended, have been slowly and violently rewarded with death. This is historically evident, and it is critical to take it into account, if not in the details at least in substance, if one is to understand the Galilee of Jesus. The reality of El Salvador helps one understand Jesus' Galilee The nature of Galilee's historical sin and grace is better understood through the *real* sin and grace of El Salvador, not only our thoughts *about* that sin and grace.

Isomorphism Among the Bearers of Salvation: Jesus and the Salvadoran Martyrs

It is important to emphasize another form of isomorphism, however, one that is almost never taken into account, even though it should be carefully considered. In El Salvador—a Third World country not normally considered a part of the world of abundance, certainly not with regard to martyrdom—many human beings, despite suffering greater or lesser poverty or austerity, live, like Jesus, with unconditional mercy, defending the poor and the victims produced by very real economic, military, political, cultural, media, and imperial gods. They do this in fidelity to God with integrity *to the very end*, and with a love that makes them willing to give their lives. These are the martyrs. And Jesus is well pleased to call them *brothers and sisters*.

These men and women provide a privileged place from which to reread the texts about Jesus of Galilee and to better understand his life, praxis, and destiny. They even shed light on the *pro me* of Jesus, so beloved by Paul and Ignatius of Loyola, though the *pro me* must be historicized from the *pro pauperibus*.

The poor also help us get to know, or at least guess at, Jesus' filial relationship with a God who is a Father in whom one can trust, and with a Father who continues being a God to whom one must always remain available for service. I cannot expand on this point here, but it is important, since Christologies usually squeeze out an inadequate treatment of the relationship of Jesus to God in favor of the relationship of Jesus to the kingdom of God. Nonetheless, the Salvadoran context illuminates the relationship of Jesus to God, certainly in quality if not in quantity. One has only to mention the names of Archbishop Oscar Romero and Rutilio Grande, S.J. They not only resemble Jesus the *evangelizer and prophet*, but also Jesus, the *Son* of God.

We must also remember the theologal dimension of this isomorphism. Jesus "went about doing good, for God was with him" (Acts 10:38b), said Peter in the house of Cornelius. So too, three days after Archbishop Romero's assassination, Ellacuría said in a homily at the University of Central America, "With Archbishop Romero, God passed through El Salvador."[11] Once again, then, given all the required qualifications, we cannot ignore the fundamental isomorphism of these events with the journey of Jesus through history.

Global Isomorphism of Oppression and Repression

Readers who inhabit contexts far from ours may obviously conclude that, as El Salvador is not his or her context, the Christology emerging from here is not straightforwardly transferable. But things are not so simple, for the context I have described is not an esoteric exception or an unimportant anecdote to the story of the planet today. Indeed, the truth is quite the opposite. What is esoteric is the world of prosperity, not the world of El Salvador. As Pedro Casaldáliga recently put it,

> There is great wealth on the earth, but there is more injustice. Africa has been called "the dungeon of the world," a continental *Shoa*. 2.5 million people survive on less then one dollar a day, and 25,000 people die each day of hunger according to the Food and Agriculture Organization of the United Nations. Desertification threatens the lives of 1,200 million people in about a hundred countries. Immigrants are denied human fellowship, and a floor under their feet. The United States is constructing a wall of over 900 miles to shut out Latin America; and Europe is erecting a barrier against Africa in the South of Spain. All of this, besides being evil, is part of a plan.[12]

If one goes to the real foundation of our world—which is a jealously guarded secret—one discovers a fundamental isomorphism between the Galilee of Jesus and the many other galilees of our world, a world of those who are poor and victims. This world structurally reproduces what occurred in the Roman Empire, under which Galilee lived.

Trying to make the language of *empire* disappear is a coverup. And it is self-interested euphemism to substitute the language of *globalization*, which is also deceptive since the term "globe" is close to "sphere," suggesting a "perfection"[13] that is absolutely nonexistent in the terrestrial globe today. And we must not forget the fundamental reality of the *imperium magnum latrocinium* (great thieving empire), as Augustine called it, which yesterday was Rome and today is life under the aegis of the United States. This larceny is the ground of the isomorphism of which I speak. exposing both its existence and its cruelty. The *pax romana* was cruel. Today UN expert Jean Ziegler says that the world of plenty is an assassin: "'Every child who dies from hunger is assassinated' because it could have been prevented."[14]

This is the dominant isomorphism from the perspective of sin. However, this isomorphism can also be seen *sub specie contrarii*, i.e., from the perspective of grace: the hope of the Galilee of Jesus; the many movements in which his hope was expressed; the incipiently liberating praxis; and finally utopia: the life blood of the poor. It is enough for the moment to mention it.

Global Isomorphism of Martyrs like Jesus

The isomorphism of those who bring salvation is also global. There have been movements of life and liberation in many places, and, above all, an immense collection of martyrs on which I will focus now. Limiting myself to El Salvador and Guatemala, two well-known bishops, Romero and Juan José Gerardi (plus a third in El Salvador, Joaquín Ramos, who is less well known,), around 30 priests, and a dozen religious have been assassinated. There is also an interminable list of catechists, delegates of the Word, workers for nongovernmental organizations, and solidarity groups that began their work long before they began to officially exist as such. They did their work without administrative apparatus, with only the light of the gospel and a bit of enlightenment contributed by the theology of liberation, sometimes with rudiments of Marxism, with limitless generosity, and with a *parresía* for speaking the truth and denouncing the horrors of oppression and repression. They are the glory of the people and of many churches, not only in El Salvador and Guatemala but the entire Third World—for example, Archbishop Christophe Munaihirwa of Bukavu, Congo, assassinated in 1996 for defending hundreds of thousands of refugees in Rwanda; today he is called "the Romero of Africa." Jesus-like martyrdom is neither esoteric nor exceptional on the world stage.

*Isomorphism of Faith: The Crucified People,
Suffering Servant of Yahweh*

To the above-named isomorphism I must add another that extends throughout the Third World: *the analogical isomorphism of the poor and victims of today with the Suffering Servant who carries the sin of the world, ransoms, and saves us.* While this isomorphism is more difficult to specify factually because it is perceptible only from a faith-based interpretation of the texts, nevertheless, this is how we have seen the Suffering Servant in El Salvador. Referring to the poor and the vicitms as "the crucified people" and "the pierced divinity," Archbishop Romero and Ignacio Ellacuría have described them as a historical sacrament of the Suffering Servant. At the descriptive level the Servant Songs of Isaiah and Passion Narratives of the Gospels correspond with what is happening in our world today, and vice versa. The originality of this idea, however, lies not in asserting this correspondence but in conceding dignity to the victims of today: there is something sacred about them. The greatest innovation, however, has been to consider them bearers of salvation. In this above all they converge with the Servant who takes away the sin of the world, and, scandalously, brings salvation.

There are hundreds of millions of poor and oppressed in the world, in whom appears what I have called "primordial holiness,"[15] seen in their untiring clinging to life, one to another in repressions, wars, migrations, and refugee centers. Miraculously many times they remain hopeful, offer pardon, and search for reconciliation. Moreover, they have a convening power, which generates solidarity, understood as mutual support, giving to one another and receiving one another with the best that one has. Those who come from the world of plenty to help the poor repeatedly say, with thanks, that they have received more than they have given. Therefore, looking at both the world of abundance and the world of poverty, I have said *extra pauperes nulla salus* (outside the poor there is no salvation).[16] Taking one step further, salvation comes from the poor. They are the servant of Yahweh.[17]

The Servant and the Crucified One help us understand the poor and the victims of our context. This does not imply that I think it is possible to turn to reflection without falling into oversimplifications, because the victims do not make us almost mechanically and entirely understand the figure of Jesus. His everyday life was not like that of the majorities of the poor and oppressed of our world. But they can certainly help us understand the significance of his life and destiny. We accept in faith that Jesus is the Servant who brings salvation. But understanding—with all the required qualifications—that today's victims can bring salvation allows one also to understand, a bit, what it is about Jesus of Nazareth and his destiny that brings salvation.

The conclusion, then, is that El Salvador (the Congo, Haiti, Bangladesh), and not the world of abundance (Washington, Paris, Madrid), offers an isomorphism with the Galilee of Jesus and with Jesus of Galilee. The crucified people bear the sin of the world and redeem it, saving us.

The Irruption of Reality

The isomorphism I have analyzed is finally based in poverty, yesterday and today. It has existed for centuries, but neither the poverty that appears in the Gospel *text*, much less the Salvadoran *context*, has been taken into account in Christology. Since the end of the 1970s, however, theology has in fact taken poverty seriously. The conclusion is that in order to understand the context, one must add the *quando* [when] to the *ubi* [where]. During those years something happened that changed theology. Reality, which occurs in time, has a *quando*, so one could say that this epoch was a *kairos* during which there was a discernment of the *signs of the times*. But I think something more radical occurred: the poverty that had always been there *irrupted*. It made itself noticed in a way that could not be hidden.

It is true that in the lives of believers and in theology, especially in its biblical roots, it has always been important to take reality into account. But reality can simply "be there," or it can "break in." The great events of the Bible are not simply "there" but rather "break in." In the Hebrew Scriptures the cries of slaves "broke in," and the God of the fathers "broke in" with his promise to always be with his people and bring them life. In the New Testament the sufferings of the poor, the sick and widows "broke in" (even though the language is not as strong as in the Exodus), and Jesus of Nazareth is described in the texts as having "broken in." He spoke with authority; no fear kept him from speaking the truth or constricted his liberty. He did not flee from conflicts, dangers, or death threats. His walking through Galilee was not a stroll, nor was his work reduced to doing good things; it involved conflict. Neither was he limited to communicating generic or only ethical truths, for his most central theme was prophecy. After going about doing good he died on a cross with "a loud cry" (Mk 15:38). His was not an agreeable death like that of Socrates or Seneca. In life and in death, Jesus "broke in." Indeed, the resurrection itself was not a prodigious event but rather an "irruption" of God.

This "irruption of reality" is what shapes theology. It is true that the mystery of God manifests itself in everyday life. But when reality "breaks in," the manifestation of God has a special quality. It shakes things up and forces us to think, to do theology.

The radical character of the irruption of reality cannot be required or programmed, and it does not offer reasons for its occurrence, even in intrinsically important circumstances. In my opinion while many things were well stated at Vatican II and, more recently, at Aparecida, I do not think that reality got to the point of "breaking in." It did break in at Medellín, in a way that the participants—and analogously the texts—did not simply amplify on Vatican II, but allowed themselves to be shaped by the reality that was powerfully "breaking in," which explains the impact it made.[18] Also the theology of liberation has been built on this irruption. It was not built on and driven by an already constituted tradition or an already conceptualized doctrine, though some of the best theology Europe had to offer helped. The foundation and the beginning—what got theology going—was the irruption of the poor and of God in the poor, as was well understood at an early stage by Gustavo Gutiérrez.[19]

We could say something similar about the Christologies that were developing among us during this period. Without doubt the reflections from abroad by Karl Rahner, Jürgen Moltmann, Jacques Dupont, and Joachim Jeremias helped. But to bring about a rereading of the texts, it was essential for a reality to break in that reminded us of oppressed Galilee, and for human beings to break in who reminded us of Jesus: his compassion, his honesty about reality, his prophecy, his courage in the face of conflict, his fidelity undeterred even by the cross, his prayer, his trust in and availability to the Father-God. This is the Jesus who broke in as the Son, the one to whom we must conform ourselves, and the older brother we must follow. Both Son and brother became realities in Jesus.

The conclusion is clear. A theology grounded in the irruption of reality has, it is worth repeating, radical roots. Such a theology has problems by definition, since irruption does not occur every day, and it is not easy to maintain the light and the intensity that produced the original irruption. But whatever the difficulties in keeping them going, we have to overcome the temptation to ignore them. Pedro Casaldáliga, Jean Ziegler, and Ignacio Ramonet tell us that realities continue to exist today capable of producing an equally or even more powerful impact than those that broke in to our context during the 1970s. Communication media, governments and political parties, and cultural, political and religious institutions, each in their own way, take charge of trivializing reality and of concealing it. And they try, above all, to keep it from becoming an irruption that generates praxis and theology.

Specifically with regard to theology, a variety of factors, but especially the costs, deter it from maintaining the original power of the inciting irruption: in society these factors include slander, persecution, and death; in the churches they take other forms. This has been evident in El Salvador. But it is also clear that if reality is not allowed to break in, the texts of the past become mute and do not give of themselves to the present.

The Epistemological Rupture

The irruption of reality in Latin America accompanied an *epistemological rupture* in theology. The most novel aspect of this movement was the act of relating theological reason and praxis (historical, ecclesial, and pastoral), on which theologians as diverse as Gustavo Gutiérrez and Hugo Asmann agreed. Here in El Salvador, inspired by Xavier Zubiri, Ellacuría elaborated and amplified a specific understanding of the meaning of intellective knowing. It should be applied to every form of intellective knowing, but in fact he more deeply analyzed the intellection of Latin American theology as a theology of liberation.[20]

Ellacuría's proposal turned out to be a novel one and, in important aspects, practically contrary to the epistemologies currently in use. For this reason I speak of an epistemological *rupture*, the foundation of which consists in the idea that intelligence should throw itself into reality. His proposal was that human intelligence must "apprehend reality and face up to it,"[21] an assertion that he breaks into in three dimensions: "realizing about reality" (the *noetic* dimension) from Zubiri; to this Ellacuría added "picking up reality" (the *ethical* dimension), and "taking charge of reality" (the *praxis* dimension).[22] For my part, more from experience and intuition than from theological reflection, I have added another step: "allowing oneself to be carried by reality" (the dimension of a *graced* intelligence).

Applying this proposal to *theological* intelligence, the notion of *taking charge of reality* led Ellacuría to define "theological intelligence" as "the ideological moment of ecclesial praxis,"[23] whose end was "the fullest realization possible in history of the kingdom of God."[24] For my part, I tried to pick up this intuition from Ellacuría and defined theology as *intellectus amoris (iustitiae, misericordiae)*,[25] going a step beyond the *intellectus fidei* of Augustine and the *intellectus spei* of Moltmann in his *Theology of Hope*.

Emphasizing the praxis dimension of intelligence was not totally novel in Latin American theology, as I have said. I actually think the dimension of "picking up reality" was more novel and demanding. Ellacuría argues that intelligence "has not been given to humanity so that we might evade our real obligations, but rather so that we might pick up and carry on our shoulders what things really are, and what they really demand.[26] It is not possible to adequately grasp reality intellectively without the willingness to pick up what is burdensome in it—which is not usually taken seriously. The assassinated Ellacuría—thinker, philosopher, and theologian—can stand as a symbol for an intelligence that picked up reality. Nor is it by chance that Salvadoran theology has pioneered persecution and martyrdom as central themes for theology in a strict sense—not only pastoral or spiritual theology—because it picked up the reality that produced persecution and martyrdom.

There has also been a rupture in the way of "realizing about reality," which implies "a being in the reality of things, and not merely a being before the idea of things, or a being in their meaning."[27]

Thus understood, an exercise of the intelligence has as its referent the concrete reality that I have called the "context." And being adequately in the context, which is to say, "in the reality of things," the "texts" about Jesus were reread and intellectively known praxically, ethically, and gracefully. Let us see how.

"Taking charge of the reality [of Jesus]" (the *praxis* dimension) principally signified *constructing* the kingdom today, which made one better understand, through a certain affinity, what the kingdom proclaimed by Jesus meant: a kingdom of life, of justice, mercy, and hope. It also brings one to understand better all that Jesus did in service of the kingdom—his proclamation, mercy, prophecy. . . . It also certainly signified recognizing more clearly what constitutes the antikingdom, since dealing with reality in order to change it made one experience it as a negative, destructive, powerful, and opposing force. This in turn, *sub specie contrarii*, helped us Salvadoran theologians understand the kingdom. Further, through taking charge of the kingdom today, this improved understanding of both the kingdom and the anti-kingdom helped us "realize about" the person of Jesus, since the kingdom of God was not just one reality for him, or even the most important reality among others; rather it was that reality to which his life had a constitutive relationship.

"Picking up reality" (the ethical dimension) signified *picking up* what Jesus bore: persecution, slander, and torture by economic, military, cultural, religious powers. And again, through a certain affinity, that made it easier for us to "realize about" the cross of Jesus and its causes, as well as the crucified Jesus and his victimizers. "Picking up reality" helped us understand the crucified Jesus.

"Allowing oneself to be carried by reality" (the dimension of a graced intelligence) signified gracefully accepting a force and a light, as did those who "picked up Jesus." It is not easy—from the texts—to know what it was that historically "picked up Jesus" (another example is his experience of the Father). But at least this makes us ask if Jesus also experienced grace, and in what that might consist, a question not habitually asked in Christology.

In a different context Rahner wrote some lucid words that help illuminate this dialectic of "carrying and being carried"—or in my terms: "picking up and being picked up." In one of his last writings he says that "being a Christian is a heavy-light burden, as the Gospel calls it. When we carry it, it carries us. The longer one lives, the heavier and the lighter it becomes."[28] Something similar, I think, has happened in El Salvador. We have had to pick up reality, but reality has also picked us up. Archbishop Romero had to pick up the repression of his people, but he said that "with this people it is not difficult to be a good pastor." In our context, then, in order to "realize about" Jesus, we must "pick him up." On the other hand, however, "Jesus picks us up."

The conclusion is that it is not enough "to be among concepts," if one wants to grasp intellectively who Jesus is. Instead, it is necessary today "to be among realities," analogous to how Jesus was among the realities of his day. Even a *kniende theologie* (kneeling theology) is not sufficient, as good and desirable as it might be. We must go through the epistemological rupture, throw ourselves into the real, take charge of it, pick it up, and allow ourselves to be carried by it. If we try to do it any other way, the texts give less of themselves.

Sometimes the texts have given of themselves the opposite of what we think was their original message. With no desire to exaggerate, it is paradoxical, on the one hand, that the reality of Jesus of Galilee has been well investigated, and that these investigations have yielded important theoretical results. On the other hand, the reality thus attained has not had as powerful an effect on the reader and on the collective consciousness as it could and should have had, given that these concepts have not only "content" but also "weight."

Without *an irruption of reality* and *a rupture of the way of knowing intellectively*, the concept can be correct, but exceedingly trivial. In that case the reality behind the concept can remain far outside the grasp of theology and the collective consciousness, so that only with great difficulty can they unleash a living and creative thought process. But with the irruption of reality and an epistemological rupture, the concept has weight and can help transform the thinking subject, making demands and pushing the subject in that direction. It can become part of the collective consciousness and trigger an intense and creative process.

This is what I believe has occurred in the Third World with the concepts of *liberation* and the *historical Jesus*. They may of course be limited and always subject to improvement, but they have a special *pondus*.[29] When one is truly in the midst of reality, and the intelligence takes charge of the cause of Jesus, picks it up, and allows oneself to be carried along by it, the concept can become not only precise and scientific but also powerful. It has a *pondus*. And this is usually transmitted, with limitations, of course, to the sayings of Jesus.

A final reflection on the context. I have spoken about its importance for making the text yield more and better of itself. But we must also remember what the New Testament scholar Xavier Alegre Santamaría frequently says: "a text outside its context can be easily turned into a pretext." Although he is referring to the *context* in which the biblical *texts* were written, his warning can also be applied to the context in which those texts are read today. Without taking the context of present reality centrally into account, a text—as distinguished as the Gospel of John, for instance—can be reduced to shaping the personal experience of the believer (a very important thing), to information about the realities of the past, or as a reference to misty realities. And when this happens, the text becomes a pretext, an *excuse* for not having to face up to Jesus today, for not taking charge of what reality demands of us and makes possible in the present, and for not picking up its demands.

Fundamental Elements of Jesus of Galilee

The Cross of Jesus: A Light That Illuminates Everything

The life of Jesus has many dimensions.[30] Now the context can illuminate his life as a whole, but, depending on the exact nature of the context, it will illuminate some dimensions more than others. In what follows I will briefly analyze three dimensions of Jesus' life from the perspective of the Salvadoran context: the mercy of Jesus, the hope that he evokes, and the following he demands. It is possible to analyze many things in relation to these themes, and I will say a few words about each, but I will start from the specific light provided by the cross.

It is not arbitrary to give priority to the cross. I said at the beginning that the cross is central to the *text* of the Gospels. And with regard to the Salvadoran context, I said that we are living under "a reign of the cross," while in other places one can live under a "reign of the good life." The cross has also been central in theology, such as the theologies of Paul, Mark, John, Luther, Bonhoeffer, and Moltmann. Although the cross is not central in many theologies today, it certainly is in those of the most lucid theologians. In his treatment of religious pluralism, José Ignacio González Faus insists on "'the uniqueness of the crucified' as [what is] inescapably Christian."[31] The cross is the nonnegotiable. Even the resurrection of Jesus, and the hope of Christians—without which there would be no Christianity—are better understood from the perspective of the cross of Jesus and the love of the martyrs.

Mercy

Mercy in Jesus and the Salvadoran Context

"Mercy"—or "compassion," the term preferred by Johann Baptist Metz among other theologians—is central for Jesus. To gain his favor, the poor and the sick had only to say, "Sir, have mercy on me." For his part, Jesus speaks and, in his own way, theorizes about it, above all in the parable of the Good Samaritan (Lk 10:29–37). In doing this, he describes himself.

In Jesus, mercy is not just a feeling; it is also an action. More exactly, it is a re-action to the deeds of oppressors and victimizers. It does not consist in complying with a commandment, though Jesus tells the parable of the Good Samaritan to show the meaning of the great commandment, love of neighbor. It does not belong in the ambit of the religious (though it can and should be present there), since neither God nor the synagogue—the churches we would say today—appear, essential for demanding compliance. Nor does it appear that a special predisposition for its exercise exists in the religious sphere, since the priest and Levite do not react with mercy, but with its opposite. In fact, the one who does respond, the Samaritan, is not well situated religiously. .

For Jesus, therefore, mercy refers to ultimacy: it is not possible to go further. The victim lying in the road touches the deepest fiber of the human, *splachnon*, entrails, heart. And mercy restores the ultimate to the victim: life. It also restores dignity. The first is evident, but it is important to emphasize the second. When Jesus acts with mercy, persons in need not only receive help; they also recover their dignity. He says to those who were healed: "Your faith has healed you," which is to say, "You have helped cure yourself." And he says to the woman caught in sin, "Your faith has saved you." Human beings are no longer divided into two groups: some being merciful benefactors, and others being those who receive help. All are human.

The Salvadoran context sheds light on the ultimacy of mercy. When people asked Archbishop Romero what to do in response to the suffering of the people, he said, "do not forget that they are human, and that they are here, dying, fleeing, seeking refuge in the mountains." He suggested concrete ways of helping, but he ended with something more fundamental, which refers to ultimacy: "Do not forget that we are human." In this way mercy reclaims its proper ultimacy.

As with Jesus, the exercise of mercy restores dignity. A teacher for his people, Archbishop Romero used to say, "You are my prophet." Like a lawyer risking everything for his client, he used to say, "With this people is it easy to be a good pastor." The people recovered their dignity.

Mercy takes different forms depending on context, which is important to take into account. The mercy expressed by Fr. Maximilian Kolbe who took the place of another man condemned to death in a concentration camp, for example, was different from that of Mother Theresa, who would do anything for the most abandoned. Mercy has taken diverse forms in El Salvador: assisting the fleeing, helping popular organizations, defending human rights, even burying the dead, which Archbishop Romero used to mention. Also, working for negotiations to bring a cruel war to an end, as Ellacuría did, and during which he lost his life, was also an outstanding example of mercy.

Liberation has been the horizon of mercy in the Salvadoran context, and its fundamental instrument has been *justice*. Mercy and justice can be conceptually distinguished, but really and existentially they are interrelated. Mercy-justice is essentially a dialectic, and therefore conflictual: it involves defending some against others who victimize them. It draws one into the struggle against the oppresser.

The Light of the Cross

The cross of Jesus specifies the nature of his mercy. He entered into conflict by being *dialectically* merciful, by struggling against injustice. It also helps us see that he was *consistently* merciful, since he remained in that struggle to its end on the cross.

The cross of Jesus also sheds light on Salvadoran reality. As Archbishop Romero memorably stated on the occasion of the assassination of one of the six priests who preceded him, "the one who gets in the way gets killed." The archbishop consistently got in the way by exposing and denouncing the oppressors, but not to take advantage for himself, or to defend the Church, or even to advance a cause in itself (liberty, justice, democracy). His interference stemmed from the desire "to defend the poor who are defenseless, threatened, oppressed, tortured, disappeared, and assassinated." The cross is, then, the clear consequence of a specific mercy: the mercy that arises from defending victims against their victimizers. It is from the perspective of this mercy, which does not merely assist but defends victims, that the new and massive phenomenon of martyrs must be understood.[32]

"Martyrdom" is a historical concept, and we could argue about its *analogatum princeps* and what standard is most relevant today. But in the Salvadoran context a martyr is one who gives his or her life to defend the poor, which is to say, for the cause of justice—and by this means testifies that Jesus is the Christ. The martyrs, then, are those who are distinguished in mercy, who love and defend victims, who transform that love into a struggle for justice, and who for that reason are assassinated. They are the consistently merciful. They resemble Jesus in life, and they die like Jesus. I call them martyrs like Jesus.

This mercy-justice, illuminated by the fact that it ends in a cross, sheds even more light than do the beautiful words of the psalms on what it means to say that God is a God of mercy. In speaking of the option for the poor, Puebla adds two essential clarifications in making this solemn *theologal* affirmation. One is that God's option for the poor is gratuitous: "whatever the moral situation in which it is found." The other is that the option defends the poor against their oppressors: "God comes to their defense and loves them."[33] The love of God is an active mercy, but it is also a risky mercy, since it defends the poor against their victimizers. That risk—mysterious, scandalous—which God himself assumes, is what seems to be historicized in the cross of his Son.

Hope

Hope in the Gospel and Hope in the Salvadoran Context

Hope is central in the text of the Gospels. Jesus says programmatically: "The kingdom of God is at hand." Leonardo Boff comments: "Jesus articulates a radical fact about human existence, about its principle of hope and its utopian dimension. He promises that *utopia* will no longer be an object of anxious expectation (Lk 3:4), but rather a *topía*, an object of hope for the entire people (Lk 2:10)."[34] In the time of Jesus the kingdom of God gave historical expression to the hope of a people in great material difficulties and immersed in a political and cultural identity crisis. For this reason Jesus provoked an exuberant response among the common people.

One can also inquire about Jesus' own hope. At the last supper Jesus expresses the hope of returning to "drink wine in the kingdom." However, I think his various words about the poor and the humble should be interpreted as experiences not only of trust and joy but also of hope—as in his amazement at the generosity of the widow in the Temple and the audacity of the woman with the hemorrhage. His joy over the fact that the little ones understand, whereas the great and the wise do not, must have given him hope. And his hope is certainly present in his trust in his *Abba*.

Experiences like these are also real in El Salvador, and I believe that such contexts have opened the eyes of many to understand the hope of the poor and of Jesus himself. When looked at from the perspective of historical liberation with its difficulties, failures, and disappointments, the good news that the kingdom of God "is coming" has regained its value.

The Light of the Cross

The Christian paradox also breaks in here. Hope, as found in El Salvador and in the New Testament, is intimately related to the cross in two ways. First, the resurrection of Jesus is a symbol of qualified hope, by virtue of the cross. Peter formulates it exactly in five discourses in Acts: "You killed him, but God raised him from the dead" (Acts 3:15). God's resurrecting action is not, then, simply omnipotence before a cadaver, which would generate an expectation of "more life," but rather it is justice before an innocent victim, and so it generates a specific hope: that, as Horkheimer so often put it, the executioner should not triumph over the victim. Especially in this sense, the resurrection is a symbol of hope in El Salvador.

But there is something even more audacious here: the cross itself has been a source of hope. This conclusion comes not from being oblivious or insensitive. In Scripture the suffering servant and Christ on the cross create hope, just as do the innumerable Salvadoran martyrs. The facts are clear, as difficult as it is in other places to comprehend and accept. The key is knowing and explaining why. In Moltmann's words: "Not every life is an occasion for hope, but the life of Jesus, who took up the cross for love, certainly is."[35] In our context this is true. Beyond calculations, optimism, and expectations, where there is love, there hope arises. Love is what moves one to believe and to hope, mysteriously, that good has more substance and more power than evil. In the presence of love it is possible to go on living. The cross that is a cross of love also produces hope.

Earlier we remembered the martyrs in the context of mercy: they are the consistently merciful. Now we remember them in the context of hope: they have given their lives for love, and so they are producers of hope. This fact cannot be denied. It happens with Archbishop Romero and with thousands of martyrs. They awaken graces, and they are given graces. Their anniversaries with tears are moments of joy, and of remembering a great love. It supports hope.

Following Jesus and Easter

In the Gospel Jesus calls us to follow, to imitate the praxis and the evangelizing of his life. One must "go about doing good" as he did. He demands the same of his disciples. In regards to El Salvador, there is no lack of talk about the cloud of witnesses in recent Salvadoran history, many of them martyrs: they have gone about doing good.

And Jesus adds with clairvoyance that in history doing good implies meddling in conflict and picking up what is burdensome: "if any want to become my followers, let them deny themselves and take up their cross and follow me" (Mk 8:34; Mt16:24; Lk 9:23). We just saw this in the martyrs. However, responding to the call to follow is the Jesus-like way of fulfilling what God asks in Micah 6:8: "to do justice, and to love kindness, and to walk humbly with your God." In both cases the text speaks of walking.

Following bring us face to face with the way Jesus walked, and the cross grants it absolute ultimacy. This is how it appears in the text of the Gospel and in the Salvadoran context. What I want to emphasize in bringing these reflections on Jesus and Galilee to a close is that following him conforms us to Jesus; it conforms us, some more and some less, to his reality. And this has decisive consequences: in following, we can, by affinity, take a step of faith—and yet following is logically also the place where one could abandon the path of faith.

It is in following rather than in not following that questions about faith can emerge most acutely: like Jesus, we can be faced with ultimate questions: whether everything makes sense or is absurd, whether hope makes more sense than hopelessness, resignation than *carpe diem*. The same holds true of the question of theodicy: if the Son of God, and God in him, has passed through this world, why does the world continue doing so much evil rather than good? Why does the world not change? Why does God not change it? Are not Mark and Matthew correct in having Jesus die, representing all of us, with the heartrending cry: "My God, my God, why have you forsaken me" (Mk 15:34, Mt 27:46)? To this unanswerable question one can only reply, babbling, that God is an unfathomable mystery, silent and inactive in the face of evil. But one must pass through the questions. And the passing is more insightful, I think, in following rather than in just contemplating.

But following also enables meaning and joy to appear. Being like Jesus gives meaning to life itself, and one sees, or glimpses, that "the gentleness of God has appeared among us." This kindness, with many ups and downs, continues driving history forward toward the good and the new. By following Jesus, our older brother and the first-born Son, we can keep walking until "God becomes all in all" (1 Cor 15:28). For many people following has meant rediscovering a good news.

Passing through history *in this way* is an anticipation of Easter: we go through death and pass into life. The dialectic is only resolved at the end. We are saved in the present *in spe* (in hope). But the reality of the present looks like a modest sacrament of the final paschal event.

Perhaps what is most extraordinary about the context of El Salvador and similar locations is that there are believers who follow Jesus, and who continue walking humbly with God. They are people of faith and commitment. And many others are carried in their own faith by the faith of these martyrs.

For me there is no doubt that these martyrs are the most crucial reality of our *context* for understanding the reality and the *texts* about Jesus of Galilee. Simply stated, without them it would be difficult to understand texts like the Gospel of Jesus, much less with any depth.

For that reason, personally, the lack of interest in the martyrs of not a few theologies makes me uneasy.

Conclusion

In conclusion I draw attention to three more or less obvious considerations. The first is that this article could have analyzed many other aspects about Jesus of Galilee. In the two volumes mentioned earlier, I treated some aspects that are absolutely central, such as the relation of Jesus with the Father and Jesus' final reality—his "metaphysical" reality. . Other aspects are au courant and need to be addressed: Jesus and the religions, women and their position in creation and in the Church, an understanding of salvation that integrates the achievements of reason into the task of liberation, the real posture of Jesus toward service and power, freedom and subjugation. Nonetheless, I hope what I have said is enough to demonstrate the importance of the Salvadoran context and the martyrs for Christological reflection.

The second consideration is whether and how to historicize today what we learned in an epoch-shaping context of irruption and martyrdoms that is difficult to repeat, though not totally unique. I hope my words help in some way to advance understanding of the "original irruption," and to discern new "irruptions" that are, finally, the truest signs of the times. And I hope my thought helps support the martyrs. If this task seems almost impossible for theology to fulfill, consider whether this, and no other, is the fundamental job of a Christian theology: to keep alive the "irruption of the martyr Jesus."

The third consideration is the most obvious. I have given my personal opinion about Jesus and some aspects of who he was and is as a person. And I have focused here more than in other writings on what is usually called *method*. In my other texts I have not followed a method in an a priori way, both because I do feel qualified to do so, and because, frankly, I do not have much confidence in such an approach. In this article I have simply rethought the path that I have tread in El Salvador. Undoubtedly Ellacuría would have said it differently, as would other theologians, male and female, from Latin America and the whole Third World. But perhaps there is something common to us all: taking seriously the context of the world of poverty, passing through an epistemological rupture, and thinking placed in the service of liberation.

And from the perspective of El Salvador, to the list I would add: taking the martyrs seriously.

JON SOBRINO, S.J., received his Th.D. from Hochschule Sanckt Georgen, Frankfurt, and is now professor of theology at the University of Central American, San Salvador. His areas of special interest are Christology and martyrdom for faith and justice. Having recently published *Fuera de los pobres no hay salvación* (2007), he is preparing a work on Christian identity in the light of the following of Jesus.

Notes

1. Martin Kähler, *The So-called Historical Jesus and the Historic, Biblical Christ*, trans. and ed. Carl E. Braaten (Philadelphia: Fortress, 1964) 80 n. 11.
2. Dietrich Bonhoeffer, *El precio de la gracia* (Salamanca: Sígueme 1968) 20–21.
3. Ignacio Ellacuría, *Conversión de la Iglesia al reino de Dios* (San Salvador: UCA, 1984) 168.
4. The "Third World" is not just a geographical concept; it is fundamentally historical. It can be described as a world of poverty and insults in which life and dignity are not taken for granted, and as an impoverished world, since its prostration has, as an important if not determinate cause, the oppression by other worlds. It can also be described as a world that both hopes for salvation and can generate it.
5. Ellacuría uses "the Third World" to introduce the Christian paradox: it is the place to announce the good news; there the good news is accepted connaturally, and, like the Suffering Servant, the Third World brings salvation.
6. This is a paraphrase of the quotation by Archbishop Romero's reading of Matthew 11:25, "I give you thanks, Father, because you have hidden these things from the wise, and have revealed them to the humble and the simple" ("Salvation, Initiative of God," homily of Archbishop Oscar Romero, July 9, 1978, on Zacharias 9:9–10, Romans 8:9, 11–13, and Matthew 11:25–30, http://servicioskoinonia.org/romero/homilias/A/780709.htm [accessed March 9, 2009]).
7. See Congregation for the Doctrine of the Faith, Instruction on Certain Aspects of the "Theology of Liberation" IV no. 3, http://www.vatican.va/roman_curia/congregations/cfaith/documents/rc_con_cfaith_doc_1984 0806_theology-liberation_en.html (accessed March 11, 2009).
8. Juan Luis Segundo, S.J., *Theology and the Church: A Response to Cardinal Ratzinger and a Warning to the Whole Church*, trans. John W. Diercksmeierm,

rev. ed. (San Francisco: Harper & Row) 45: "We have to arrive at the last source of the Pentateuch—the Priestly, written during the Exile—to be able to speak of 'the Covenant cult celebrated on Mt. Sinai'" (cf. Ex 25–31 and 35–40), although we could not speak of this as the *purpose* of he Exodus."

9. Various First World scholars of the Hebrew Scriptures had already found in the text what was reread in the Third World. That rereading was even facilitated by those scholars. But the new reading of the Exodus became the interpretation most often taken into account in systematic and pastoral theology, much more in the Third World where it generated a "collective consciousness" and became a paradigm for praxis, hope, and faith. This was due to the context.

10. In addition to being a fundamental geographical reality in the life of Jesus, Galilee is also a symbolic reality that gives expression to the world of the poor. The faithfulness of Jesus to the reality Galilee and its people creates conflicts, which become geographically explicit in Jerusalem.

11. Ignacio Ellacuría, "Monseñor Romero, un enviado de Dios para salvar a su pueblo," *Sal Terrae* 811 (1980) 825–32; republished in *Diakonía* 17 (1981) 2–8; *Estudios centroamericanos* 65 (1990) 141–46; *Revista latinoamericano de teología*, 19 (1990) 5–10; and Ignacio Ellacuría, *Escritos teológicos*, 4 vols. (San Salvador: UCA, 2002–2002) 3:93–100.

12. Pedro Casaldáliga, "Utopía necesaria como el pan de cada día," a circular letter of January 2006, http://urc.confer.es/urc/publica/recursos/art/utopia_necesaria_como_el_pan_de_cada_dia.pdf (accessed March 10, 2009).

13. Plato, *El banquete* (*Symposium*) 189c–192d. The sphere is a geometrical location in which all the points on the surface are equidistant from the center. The *equidistance* functions to subliminally suggest that there exists an *equity* in the globalized world, which is a notorious falsehood.

14. "Press Conference by United Nations Special Rapporteur on Right to Food," October 26, 2007, http://www.un.org/News/briefings/docs/2007/071026_Ziegler.doc.htm (assessed March 16, 2009).

15. See Jon Sobrino, *Terremoto, terrorismo, barbarie, y utopía* (San Salvador: UCA, 2003) 129–40.

16. See Jon Sobrino, *Fuera de los pobres no hay salvación: Pequeño ensayo utópico-profético* (Madrid: Trotta, 2007).

17. The poor have also tried to organize themselves and to struggle against an enemy that is a thousand times stronger.

18. In my view the 32nd General Congregation of the Society of Jesus, called by Pedro Arrupe, caused a fundamental irruption of reality when it defined "the struggle for faith and the struggle for justice" as the crucial mission of our time ("Jesuits Today," Decree 2, of *Documents of the Thirty-second General Congregation of the Society of Jesus*, [Washington: Jesuit Conference, 1975] 12). I do not believe this irruption emerged as a conclusion of reflection, or even as a result of discernment. It came from outside, sovereignly,

powerfully. The reality of injustice and idolatrous unbelief had irrupted along with the need to return to the essence of Christianity. From that point on 49 Jesuits have been assassinated in the Third World for struggling against injustice. I think this is proof that reality had irrupted and that reality was moving toward this crucial struggle.

19. See Jon Sobrino, "La raíz de la *teo*-logía de la liberación," in *Teologías del tercer mundo,* Cátedra Chaminade 15 (Madrid: PPC-Fundación Santa María, 2008) 163–77.
20. See Ignacio Ellacuría's programmatic article,: "Hacia una fundamentación filosófica del método teológico latinoamericano," *Estudos centroamericanos* 50 (1975) 409–25. For my reflection on the epistemological rupture, see Jon Sobrino, "El conocimiento teológico en la teología europea y latinoamericana," *Estudios centroamericanos* 50 (1975) 426–45. The context can make the text not only give more of itself, but it can also help intelligence function in a specific manner, in this case, better.
21. Ellacuría, "Hacia una fundamentacion" 419.
22. Ellacuría's original text reads: "'hacerse cargo de la realidad' (dimensión *noética*), de origen zubiriano, a lo cual Ellacuría añadió el 'cargar con la realidad' (dimensión *ética*) y el 'encargarse de la realidad' (dimensión *práxica*)" (Ignacio Ellacuría, "Hacia una fundamentacíon filosófica del método teológico latinoamericano," *Estudios centroamericanos* 322-323 [1975] 419; also in *Liberación y cautiverio: Debates en torno al metodo de la teología en América Latina, las comunicaciones y los debates del Encuentro Latinoamericano de Teología,* Mexico City, August 11–15, 1975, ed. E. Ruiz Maldonado and Enrique D. Dussel [Mexico City: Comité Organizador, 1975] 609–35; Ellacuría, *Escritos teológicos* [San Salvador: UCA, 2000] 2:208).
23. Ignacio Ellacuría, "La teología como momento ideológico de la praxis eclesial," *Estudios eclesiásticos* 53 (1978) 457–76.
24. Ignacio Ellacuría, "Aporte de la teología de la liberación a las religiones abrahámicas en la superación del individualismo y del positivismo," *Revista latinoamericana de teología* 10 (1987) 3–28, at 9.
25. Jon Sobrino, "Teología en un mundo sufriente: La teología de la liberación como 'intellectus amoris,'" *Revista latinoamericana de teología* 15 (1988) 243–66.
26. Ellacuría, "Hacia una fudamentación" 419.
27. Ibid.
28. Karl Rahner and Karl-Heinz Weger, *Our Christian Faith: Answers for the Future,* trans. Francis McDonagh (New York: Crossroad, 1981) 178–79.
29. The *pondus* of *liberation* finds verification in many places in the theology that bears its name, and also in the naturalness with which its content has continued to be amplified: liberation from oppression connected with race, ethnicity, gender, religion—including, analogically, even the suffering of mother earth. Christians and theologians have captured in "liberation" a concept of enormous depth and utility for putting hidden oppressions

into words and for fomenting hopes of liberation. It has not been a case of *marketing* a hidden agenda far removed from the concept of liberation, but rather the *pondus* of the concept itself. The credit for having presented the concept in this way must be given to Gustavo Gutiérrez, the pioneer of this work.

30. As is demonstrated in the recent book by José Antonio Pagola, *Jesús: Aproximación histórica* (Madrid: PPC-Fundación Santa María, 2007).
31. José Ignacio González Faus, *El rostro humano de Dios: De la revolución de Jesús a la divinidad de Jesús* (Santander: Sal Terrae, 2007) 203.
32. It is well known, but it is good to recall (to illustrate the "added" significance that martyrdom grants to mercy) that Archbishop Romero and Mother Theresa were distinguished in mercy—both were nominated for the Nobel Peace Prize in 1979. Archbishop Romero died a martyr. Mother Theresa did not. The process of beatification of Archbishop Romero is stalled because his mercy was conflictive, and his memory continues to be so. Mother Theresa has already been beatified.
33. Bishops of Latin America, Evangelization in Latin America's Present and Future, no. 1142 (Puebla, Mexico, February 1979), in *Puebla and Beyond: Documentation and Commentary*, ed. John Eagleson and Philip Scharper, trans. John Drury (Maryknoll, N.Y.: Orbis) 264–67.
34. Leonardo Boff, "Salvación en Jesucristo y proceso de liberación," *Concilium* 96 (1974) 375–88, at 378.
35. Jürgen Moltmann, *Umkehr zur Zukunft* (Hamburg: Siebenstern-Taschenbuch, 1970) 76.

www.ingramcontent.com/pod-product-compliance
Lightning Source LLC
Chambersburg PA
CBHW030109010526
44116CB00005B/174